Parallelism and Programming in Classifier Systems

Stephanie Forrest
Center for Nonlinear Studies and Computing Division
Los Alamos National Laboratory

Parallelism and Programming in Classifier Systems

Pitman, London

Morgan Kaufmann Publishers, Inc., San Mateo, California

PITMAN PUBLISHING
128 Long Acre, London WC2E 9AN

A Division of Longman Group UK Limited

First published 1991

Available in the Western Hemisphere from
MORGAN KAUFMAN PUBLISHERS, INC.
2929 Campus Drive, San Mateo, California 94403

ISSN 0268-7526

British Library Cataloguing in Publication Data

Forrest, Stephanie
Parallelism and programming in classifier systems. –
(Research notes in artificial intelligence; 0268-7526).
1. Computer systems. Parallel programming
I. Title II. Series
004.35

ISBN 0-273-08825-4

Library of Congress Cataloging-in-Publication Data

Forrest, Stephanie
Parallelism and programming in classifier systems/Stephanie Forrest.
p. cm. – (Research notes in artificial intelligence (London, England), ISSN 0268-7526)
Includes bibliographical references and index.
ISBN 1-55860-107-4
1. Parallel processing (Electronic computers) 2. Parallel programming (Computer science) I. Title II. Series.
QA76.58.F66 1990
005.2—dc20 90-41616
CIP

Reproduced and printed by photolithography in Great Britain
by Biddles Ltd, Guildford and King's Lynn

Contents

List of Figures

List of Appendices

Preface

This work originally appeared in 1985 as my Ph.D. thesis at the University of Michigan in Ann Arbor. In updating it for this volume, I have tried to place it in a broader context of research on parallelism, intelligent systems, and emergent computation. Many people have contributed constructive criticism, new insights, and moral support over the years, and it is a pleasure to acknowledge their contributions.

At the University of Michigan, my fellow students had a strong influence on the work. They helped me refine vague and imprecise ideas, discouraged me from pursuing dead-ends, and faithfully read and criticized every word of the original dissertation. Large sections of Chapter 4 in particular are the result of their efforts as well as mine. Specifically, I would like to thank Rik Belew, Lashon Booker, Laurette Bradley, Paul Grosso, Dan Kaiser, Chris Langton, Melanie Mitchell, and Rick Riolo for all of the hours they have spent helping me think about parallelism, classifier systems, and KL-ONE.

I am also grateful to John Holland and the Logic of Computers Group for convincing me to join the Computer and Communication Sciences Department, and for the intellectual and financial support that they provided through graduate school. The other members of my doctoral committee, Arthur Burks, Michael Cohen, and Paul Scott, each helped me in their own way and the work profitted tremendously from their suggestions. Although not an official committee member, Quentin Stout read the original thesis carefully and provided a number of important suggestions.

Tom Lipkis and Bill Mark, who were at USC/Information Sciences Institute during my graduate years, answered endless questions about KL-ONE and got me started on the problem of classification.

N.S. Sridharan first encouraged me to consider the *Research Notes in Artificial Intelligence* series, and I would like to thank him and the other editors at Pitman Publishing for their support and patience. In preparing the revisions, Ron Brachman, Michael Fehling, Stevan Harnad, and Robert MacGregor made helpful suggestions for updating the references. Erica Jen and Pat McGee read the revised manuscript in several versions. Ronda Villa-Butler and Della Ulibarri of the Santa Fe Institute typeset and copyedited the manuscript. Jane Self designed the original figures, which appear largely unchanged in the revised version. The anonymous reviewers read the manuscript very carefully and made many helpful suggestions. Finally, I would like to thank my husband Fred Carey for putting up with me and the thesis for all of these years.

This research was supported by National Science Foundation Grant DCR-8305830.

For my mother,
Who gave me the opportunities she never had.

1 Introduction

A classifier system is a computational model of cognition based on the principles of learning, intermittent feedback from the environment, and construction of internal models [73]. Classifier systems are relevant to the study of intelligence both as a theory of cognition and as a parallel architecture for implementing artificial intelligence (AI) models efficiently. These two aspects of classifier systems are interrelated, and it is their interplay that is the subject of this book. The possibility that parallel architectures such as classifier systems could implement AI models directly has focused attention on models that might have both efficient hardware implementations and plausibility as intelligent systems. The interplay between cognitive modeling considerations and the requirement for reasonable performance is captured by the following questions: What kinds of architectures can most effectively implement computational models of intelligence? What computational systems are most appropriate for modeling intelligent behavior? How does intelligent behavior emerge from the interactions of many components?

A classifier system consists of three layers: a parallel rule-based message-passing system, the bucket-brigade learning algorithm, and the genetic algorithm. The message-passing system is the fundamental computational engine of the system. It consists of a database of condition/action rules, called classifiers, that read and write messages on a short-term message list. At the second level is the bucket-brigade learning algorithm which manages credit assignment among competing classifiers, distributing external reward to the rules that contribute to successful behavior. The bucket brigade plays a role similar to that of back propagation in neural networks. Finally, at the highest level are genetic operators that create new classifiers. A more detailed description of classifier systems appears in Chapter 2.

The message-passing part of a classifier system can be viewed as an abstract parallel machine, and the learning algorithms as mechanisms for adjusting the configuration of the machine over time. Under this view, each classifier is a separate processor, reading in messages as input and writing out others as output. The system exhibits parallelism at several levels, including: matching all of the bits in a message simultaneously, matching all conditions against one (or all) message(s) in the system simultaneously, and allowing more than one classifier to be active simultaneously. In the expected case of many classifiers and a small message list, massive parallelism is obtained through the parallel matching process and implicit parallelism arises when many classifiers share the same message.

The classifier system model can also be viewed as a parallel programming language in which correct programs are either pre-specified ("programmed") or learned dynamically. Any particular configuration of a classifier system is interpreted as a program, or set of instructions. There have been many attempts to apply machine learning algorithms to the problem of generating and debugging computer programs. These efforts have been largely unsuccessful due to the brittle nature of conventional programming languages, in which a program's behavior can be changed dramatically by one misplaced character. In a classifier system, however, the restricted syntax of each instruction allows almost any combination of instructions to form a legal program. Additionally, the relative position of a single instruction does not determine its effect on the program. These two properties of classifier systems support the notion of a program as an "ecology" of individual instructions, each instruction filling some useful niche in the overall program and evolving in the context of the other instructions. This aspect of classifier systems emphasizes their potential for complex high-level behavior, called "emergent computation," in that local interactions among primitive elements can result in a global computation.

Unlike many AI systems, low-level mechanistic models of intelligence, such as classifier systems and connectionist networks, are based on analogies with biological, physical, or psychological phenomena. Their representations and learning algorithms operate at the "sub-symbolic" level in task environments where performance is measured in terms of input/output pairs. Classifier systems are one of the few alternative models to connectionism that have the same basic assumptions of massive parallelism, low-level domain-independent learning algorithms, and an emphasis on dynamic processes over static representations.

A common criticism of such systems is that they do not explicitly manipulate high-level symbolic structures such as those that are the basis of many current knowledge representation systems [18], programs that model human expertise [21], and systems that perform goal-directed planning [40]. By describing a classifier system implementation that represents and processes high-level symbolic knowledge structures, this book addresses the symbolic/subsymbolic issue. Here, the term "knowledge representation" includes both the data structures which store information and the algorithms that manipulate those structures.

The learning properties of classifier systems have been explored in much greater detail than the message-passing system. Holland described both the mechanics and underlying theory of genetic algorithms [67], and more recently Riolo investigated the bucket brigade's ability to maintain hierarchies and sequences of rules [101]. Several other researchers have recently explored the mathematics of bucket brigades [2, 51, 110]. This book is concerned with the computational properties of the underlying parallel machine, including computational completeness, programming and representation techniques, and efficiency of algorithms. In particular, efficient classifier system implementations of symbolic data structures and reasoning procedures are presented and analyzed in detail.

1.1 Parallelism and Classifier Systems

In Chapter 2, research on parallelism is described in terms of two categories: "coarse-grained" and "fine-grained." Coarse-grained architectures are composed of a small number of computationally complete heterogeneous processing units; they have a relatively low rate of communication between processors and often execute asynchronously. Fine-grained structures are composed of a large number of simple processors that also have a high rate of communication. Complex behavior can emerge from fine-grained systems as a higher-level phenomenon built up from the interactions among very simple units—an example of emergent computation [47, 48]. In these systems, the patterns of activity produced by the lower-level processors are only meaningful when interpreted at the higher level. This is in contrast to coarse-grained organizations in which each processor works on a part of a larger problem, but each part has meaning independently of the remainder of the system. As an ecology of instructions, classifier systems illustrate many of the features of emergent computation [49].

Classifier systems provide an excellent example of fine-grained parallelism. The underlying action of the system is extremely simple, yet its global behavior can be highly complex. Each processor is limited computationally and there are many of them in a typical classifier system. Each unit (classifier) is locally controlled because its local properties (the condition and action parts of the classifier) determine which messages it will match and which messages it will produce.

The organization of information into fine-grained units is important for systems that learn. As Holland [67] and Lenat [83] have both pointed out, it is desirable to build up representations out of small units, or building blocks, so that simple learning rules can be applied to the parts rather than to their aggregates. Thus, it is reasonable to expect that the fundamental units of such systems will be "fine-grained." From the architectural point of view, fine-grained parallel models are promising implementation vehicles because they allow the large amounts of parallelism that are required to make experimental systems useful in real-time settings. Fine-grained organizations are appropriate for knowledge representation systems in which small amounts of information are added incrementally to existing systems. Additional processing power can be added as the system grows and high-level behavior, such as that exhibited by semantic networks, can be introduced through local interactions among small units.

Knowledge representation is an appropriate problem domain for studying the parallelism of classifier systems. Knowledge-based systems have traditionally been applied to static off-line domains where the facts of a case remain constant throughout the problem-solving process. For example, there are many knowledge-based systems that diagnose mechanical failures. These applications can be carried out with dedicated machines in environments where real-time response is not required. These systems also enjoy the advantage of a relatively stable knowledge base in which the system's knowledge about a given domain changes very slowly after the initial expertise has been "acquired." Once the description of a particular problem (e.g., symptoms of the mechanical failure) has been entered, there is little additional information to be absorbed in the course of its use. This approach is appropriate for problems that have a high payoff and can be solved "off-line," such as diagnosis, location of drilling sites, and configuring computers.

There is, however, increasing interest in applying knowledge-based systems technology in domains that require real-time interactions with ongoing processes [1, 27, 41, 56]. Examples include: natural language processing, autonomous vehicles and other robots, process control, aircraft control, medical applications (e.g., monitoring inhalation therapy), and intelligent computing environments. Current technology for building knowledge-based systems does not lend itself to continuous, real-time operation in dynamic environments. A system that is connected to its environment must produce output on a time scale that is appropriate for that environment. For example, it would not be appropriate to spend two hours processing an alarm condition that needs to be handled within seconds. Reliable real-time behavior is difficult to achieve because the performance of AI systems can vary dramatically with different problem configurations.

For these systems to succeed, fast and frequent access to and on-line augmentation of large, dynamic knowledge bases are required. This implies a need for knowlege bases that have two properties: (1) predictable retrieval times and (2) the ability to add information dynamically. The KL-ONE family of languages addresses both of these issues.

1.2 Classification and KL-ONE

At the heart of any knowledge representation system is the problem of classification. In its most general formulation, classification relates incoming information to an existing knowledge base. In network-based systems, this is the problem of deciding which links to add between new and old nodes when incorporating new structures into the network. In expert systems, the classification problem arises when, for example, the system is asked to associate a set of symptoms with a particular disease [24]. In analogical reasoning systems [23] the problem of classification is implicit in deciding how to organize the growing data base of solved problems from which analogies can be drawn.

Classification is also central to retrieval operations in knowledge-based systems. The way in which information is organized determines how difficult various retrievals will be. For example, a representation system that organizes cities according to size rather than location will make it difficult to discover the name of all cities within a hundred mile radius of Spokane. Thus, any system that organizes or modifies information on an ongoing basis must address the issue of classification of new facts with respect to an existing information structure and with respect to the ways in which it may later be retrieved. In addition, access and storage patterns may change over time, creating a need for databases that can adaptively reorganize themselves.

Of the various knowledge representation paradigms in use today, one family of semantic network formalisms has focused directly on the problem of classification. This is the KL-ONE family [14], including KL-ONETalk [40], Krypton [16], KL-TWO [120], NIKL [103, 77], KANDOR [93], BACK [90], LOOM [86, 87] and CLASSIC [13, 20]. In all of these systems there is a well-defined notion of classification that allows the system to incorporate new concepts into existing network structures automatically. This is important because manual classification is only feasible in small systems that are relatively static, where the efficiencies of automation are not required. For large systems that change over time, some sort of automatic classification procedure is required. The classification issues in KL-ONE have been studied extensively and are reasonably well understood. This feature makes the KL-ONE family a particularly good place to begin considering the advantages or disadvantages of parallelism for knowledge representation systems.

In the KL-ONE formalisms, a distinction is drawn between definitional and assertional knowledge. This divides each system into two components: the definitional part, where descriptions are stored, and the assertional part, where extensions (the actual objects being described) and facts about those extensions are represented. The definitional part of the system is represented as a structured semantic network. Thus, a collection of definitions can be thought of as a graph, and individual descriptions within the network can be regarded as subgraphs of the larger structure. In the assertional part of the system, propositions about the world (or some possible world) are represented as sentences in a formal logic.

An instance of the general classification problem arises in KL-ONE systems when a new description is added to the network. A new description must be attached to the existing network someplace and classification is the process of deciding where that place is [85]. The new description is a subgraph built out of other subgraphs whose relationship to the existing network is already known. The classification procedure is reducible to the problem of deciding subsumption relations between concepts (see Section 2.3will refer to the technical decision question in KL-ONE, while in other contexts "classification" will refer to the more general form of the problem described above.

Subsumption in KL-ONE is provably time-consuming. Brachman and Levesque showed that complete subsumption is NP-Complete even for restricted languages of the KL-ONE family [17]. More recently, Patel-Schneider showed that it is undecidable [94]. As a result, existing subsumption algorithms are designed to be sound but not complete. These results suggest that the more general problem of classification is inherently difficult. However, formal complexity analyses are rarely available for corresponding operations in most other systems (in other representation languages, classification is usually not isolated as a separate well-defined operation). If the subsumption problem can be made tractable through the use of parallelism, and if simple retrieval operations can be made more efficient, then parallelism will be a demonstrably useful technique for increasing the efficiency of current knowledge representation formalisms.

1.3 Subsymbolic Models of Intelligence

Classifier systems and connectionist models are both subsymbolic models of intelligence in the sense that their primitive components have meaning only in the context of the rest of the system. That is, an individual synapse in a connectionist model or a single classifier in a classifier system is uninterpretable without the context of the rest of the system. Intelligent behavior arises in subsymbolic systems through complex interactions among many low-level components and is a collective property of the units. The global behavior of the system is therefore intimately connected with functioning of the underlying components. In contrast, the Physcial Symbol System Hypothesis asserts that the essence of intelligence lies in the logic of symbol processing systems and that the details of how such systems are implemented are not important [92].

There has been a great deal of debate over which of these two approaches is preferable for modeling intelligent behavior (see for example [95, 114]). There is a growing consensus, however, that each view makes important contributions and that a full account of intelligent processes must take both into account [7]. The work reported here contributes to the growing body of research that studies how the two approaches fit together. Generally, these studies are existence proofs that show how connectionist architectures can implement a given symbolic procedure. Examples include Shastri's work on evidential reasoning in semantic networks [109], Touretzky and Hinton's connectionist implementation of a production system interpreter [115], and other connectionist implementations of AI systems [32, 116]. This work focuses on how symbolic structures can be implemented efficiently in a subsymbolic massively parallel system. The criterion of efficiency is important since virtually all intelligent systems operate in resource-constrained environments of some form and cannot afford computationally unreasonable solutions.

1.4 Overview

This book focuses on the following specific questions:

(1) What are the basic computational properties of classifier systems?
(2) How does one represent symbolic structures with classifier systems?
(3) Can the parallelism of the classifier system be exploited to implement symbolic reasoning efficiently?
(4) Which operations are efficient and natural in classifier systems and which are not?

In the following chapters, I show how classifier systems can be used to implement a set of useful operations for the classification of knowledge in semantic networks. A subset of the KL-ONE language was chosen to demonstrate these operations. Specifically, the system performs the following tasks: (1) given the KL-ONE description of a particular semantic network, the system produces a set of production rules (classifiers) that represent the network, and (2) given the description of a new term, the system determines the proper location of the new term in the existing network. Chapter 5 describes these two parts of the system in detail.

The implementation reveals certain computational properties of classifier systems, including completeness, operations that are particularly natural and efficient, and those that are quite awkward. The work shows how high-level symbolic structures can be built up from classifier systems, and it demonstrates that the parallelism of classifier systems can be exploited to implement them efficiently. This is significant since classifier systems must construct large sophisticated models and reason about them if they are to be truly "intelligent."

The remaining chapters are organized as follows: (2) Background (3) Approach, (4) Classifier Systems, (5) Classifier System Implementation of KL-ONE, (6) Analysis of Results, and (7) Conclusions. The chapter on Background reviews previous results and develops a framework for organizing various classes of parallelism. In addition, it provides a general introduction to classifier systems and to the subset of KL-ONE that was implemented. Chapter 3, Approach, describes how the implementation is organized and the tools and methods that were used. Chapter 4 presents theoretical results and practical algorithms for classifier systems that are independent of the KL-ONE part of the project. Chapter 5 presents the implementation of KL-ONE using classifier systems. Chapter 6 analyses the material of Chapters 4 and 5, and the final chapter contains the conclusions.

The KL-ONE algorithms were implemented on top of the generic operations developed in Chapter 4 (Boolean operations, simple numerical processing, transitive closure, and synchronization). As a result, the parallel algorithms for KL-ONE could be implemented on any machine that supports efficient computation of these intermediate operations. These intermediate operations are similar to those that Fahlman [38] has argued are necessary for "intelligent systems." The ability to perform these computations efficiently in classifier systems demonstrates the appropriateness of classifier systems as an architecture for artificial intelligence.

Parallel organizations are of interest to many areas of computer science, such as hardware specification, programming language design, configuration of networks of separate machines, and artificial intelligence. These applications are widely varied and raise many issues related to their own domains. Yet, they also share many of the same organizational concerns, such as communication, modularity, synchronization, control, and the overhead of dividing up a task into its parallel components. This book concentrates on a particular type of parallel organization and a particular problem in the area of AI, but the principles that are elucidated are applicable in the wider setting of computer science.

Since any well-defined algorithm can in principle be implemented as a serial computation on a Turing machine (Turing's Thesis), the contribution of parallel architectures and languages is not one of absolute computational power. Rather, the potential advantages lie in the areas of efficiency, ease of representation, and flexibility. It is therefore necessary to discover what the advantages or disadvantages are with respect to other architectures. One weakness with many research projects in this area is that they only show the possibility for solving certain classes of problems on particular architectures. Rigorous complexity analysis and consideration of fundamental computational tradeoffs are rarely provided. These tradeoffs include: space versus time, global versus local communication, centralized control versus local autonomy, and the cost of dividing up a task into its parallel components and managing the parallel processes versus the speedups that are obtained.

Since there is no unifying formal framework within which to examine these questions generally, analysis of results and comparison with other systems are difficult. However, classifier systems are powerful and flexible enough to support examination of these tradeoffs in the context of the particular problem, classification in KL-ONE. Chapter 6 presents a detailed analysis of the results of this project, discussing the complexity of the algorithms and the computational tradeoffs within the formalism.

2 Background

Background material is organized into three sections: (1) parallelism, (2) introduction to classifier systems, and (3) description of the subset of KL-ONE that was implemented.

2.1 Parallelism

It is difficult to categorize research on parallelism. Projects have often focused on the solution of one particular class of problems with a specific architecture rather than on the organizational principles underlying that architecture. In addition, it is not always obvious which types of architectures can be implemented reasonably or which ones can best support diverse algorithms. The result of this confusion has been a wide variety of proposed architectures, some of which fall into easily identifiable categories and many others that are hybrids of simpler designs.

This section first discusses previous classifications of research on parallelism, why they are inadequate, and how they can be refined. I then discuss two classes of parallelism, "coarse-grained" and "fine-grained," paying particular attention to their appropriateness as implementations of knowledge representation systems. The emphasis is on structures that best reveal the inherent parallelism of intelligent processes rather than on particular hardware implementations.

The literature on parallel machines has traditionally divided them into two classes: Single Instruction Stream Multiple Data Stream (SIMD) and Multiple Instruction Stream Multiple Data Stream (MIMD) (see for example [98]). In SIMD organizations, each processor (optionally) performs the same operation on each clock cycle, but every processor operates on its own data. In MIMD organizations, every processor executes its own instructions on its own data. While this distinction points out some general differences between proposed architectures, it is not sufficient. For example, it does not capture the difference between architectures whose individual processors are computationally complete and those whose units have limited processing power. In addition, usage of the term "single instruction" varies widely (see, for example, [5] and [97]).

The distinction between "fine-grained" and "coarse-grained" systems has now become widespread [38, 76, 121]. Fine-grained, or massively parallel, systems are those with a large number of processors (on the order of 10^3 or greater), while coarse-grained systems have relatively few processors (usually less than 200). Intermediate-sized systems are often referred to as "medium-grained." Each processor in a fine-grained organization typically has limited computational power and a relatively high rate of communication with other processors; coarse-grained systems are composed of more complex processors that have limited communications requirements. The coarse-grained/fine-grained distinction is also useful, but it is incomplete in that it does not account for different communications topologies, asynchronous versus synchronous execution, or single versus multiple instruction streams.

A third view concentrates on how data are passed through the system [117]. This is particularly useful for distinguishing between the data-flow languages [3, 31], and data-reduction machines [9]. In [117] two broader classes of architectures are described: data-driven and demand-driven. Data-flow machines are the primary example of data-driven architectures. In data-flow systems, an operation is executed as soon as its operands become available. Algorithms are expressed as graphs of the data dependencies between operations. Since it is possible that the operands for more than one operation might become available simultaneously, these systems are potentially parallel. Likewise, data-reduction machines provide an example of demand-driven architectures. Demand-driven architectures are organized so that an operation is only executed when its result is needed (for example, the arguments in a function call). In side-effect-free applicative languages, such as some dialects of Lisp, the order in which sub-expressions are evaluated is not fixed, and they may be reduced in parallel. The data-flow and data-reduction machines exploit parallelism in a very different way from the other systems described here. The flow of control is associated with the data being processed rather than with the operations on that data. For this reason, the distinction between demand-driven and data-driven organizations is not particularly helpful in organizing more traditional approaches to parallelism that enforce the flow of control from one instruction to the next.

None of the three categorizations discussed above is sufficient to capture the wide range of parallel organizations being investigated today. These descriptions fail to account for all of the relevant distinctions, and they ignore many of the most important features of the articulated classes. However, it is possible to identify a set of properties that are useful in describing any particular parallel machine. These include: the ratio of inter-processor to intra-processor communication, the topology of communication among processors, the complexity of each processor, how uniformly the processors behave, control (form of instructions, role of the supervisor, etc.), the distribution of memory across processors, and synchronous versus asynchronous communication. While in principle there are a very large number of classes that can be formed by combining these properties in different ways, in practice there are a small number of distinct groups within which most proposed designs can be placed. For example, most systems that are composed of simple processors also have high communication rates. In the following paragraphs, two principle classes of parallelism are discussed: "coarse-grained" and "fine-grained." This choice of terminology follows current usage, but the description of these classes is in terms of the properties mentioned above; the classes that they describe are characterized by a richer set of properties than those indicated by the labels.

2.1.1 Coarse-Grained Parallelism

A large number of parallel systems fall into the group that has been referred to as "coarse-grained" [76], MIMD [76], and microcomputer arrays [108]. While there are many distinctions within the group, these systems share the following properties: complex processors, low ratio of inter-process to intra-process communication, heterogeneous processes, and asynchronous behavior. Formalisms that are capable of expressing this kind of parallelism include Ada (with tasking) [75], some simulation languages (for example, GPSS) [107], and Communicating Sequential Processes (CSP) [65]. Hardware implementations of coarse-grained parallelism include the Butterfly, Encore Multi-Max,

Sequent, and Ethernet-connected networks of workstations [89]. Divisions within the group include local (Ada, CSP) vs. global (Ethernet) communications schemes, and shared memory (CSP) vs. private memory (Ethernet). Granting the existence of subclasses within the class, I will refer to this collection of systems as "coarse-grained."

Coarse-grained systems are not the most appropriate way to implement efficient knowledge representation systems. There are three reasons for this: (1) they exhibit a relatively small amount of parallelism, (2) there is a poor match between the natural units of the problem (computing inheritance relations) and the complexity of each processor in a coarse-grained system, and (3) efficient implementation of property inheritance, a central part of many current knowledge representation systems, requires high rates of communication between processors. The first two reasons are related, they are examined together, and then the third issue, property inheritance, is discussed.

In the area of knowledge representation, huge amounts of parallelism are required to attain desired speedups, but the amount of processing required of each parallel unit is quite small. For this class of problems, it is important that the number of processors can be increased with the size of the knowledge base. A coarse-grained structure, which offers a relatively small speedup factor, does not seem promising in this context. Gupta's research on parallelism in production systems reached a similar conclusion [57]. He conducted experiments using coarse-grained models of parallelism to implement production systems. The results suggest that for production systems such as OPS5 the maximum speedups to be gained through the use of coarse-grained parallelism are on the order of five to ten. While these gains may be significant for some existing applications, they will not provide real-time access to large complex knowledge bases. These results provide evidence that coarse-grained systems are not a promising way to implement knowledge representation systems. They could also be interpreted as an argument against the potential for any parallelism in AI. However, it is unclear that the empirical results obtained for coarse-grained systems apply directly to fine-grained systems. Further, the results were obtained by observing what kind of knowledge bases people actually construct using production systems. Thus, they combine two factors: (1) inherent parallelism in production systems, and (2) the programming practices of people using production systems. Finally, the results were obtained for one particular family of production systems architectures. The production systems approach is only one of many different techniques used for representing facts in a knowledge base.

Forgy et al. pointed out a fundamental problem in attaining time efficiencies through the use of parallelism: the tradeoff between distributed processing and shared data [42]. For problems that can be completely decomposed into independent subparts, the advantages of parallelism are obvious. However, for problems with complex data dependencies, there will always be a tension between the advantage of distributing a computation over many processors and the disadvantage of having to communicate shared data. In the case of production systems, this translates into the desire to have all production rules matched in parallel and to share a common working memory. This tradeoff exists for both coarse-grained and fine-grained organizations. However, it is especially acute for AI systems, which have data structures that are both irregular and dynamic.

Property inheritance is a central feature of many knowledge representation systems. Efficient property inheritance requires some form of global communication, either through the use of shared memory or through globally connected processors. The need for a large amount of global information was pointed out by Fahlman's notion of a virtual copy [36]:

> What we really want is to create virtual copies of entire descriptions. These descriptions can be arbitrarily large and complex pieces of semantic network. When we learn that Clyde is an elephant, we want to create a single VC link from CLYDE to TYPICAL-ELEPHANT and let it go at that, but we want the effect of this action to be identical to the effect of actually copying the entire elephant description, with the CLYDE node taking the place of TYPICAL-ELEPHANT. ...It must be possible to climb around on the imaginary copy-structure and to access any part of it in about the same amount of time (speaking in orders of magnitude) that would be required if the copy had actually been made. ...A description may also contain other descriptions—the parts of an object, for example—that are themselves expressed as virtual copies. We want all of this structure to be virtually, but not physically, present. (pp. 25–26)

In KL-ONE, the classification problem is intimately connected to inheritance of properties because concepts are classified on the basis of their defining properties. Property inheritance in KL-ONE has the same global requirements as Fahlman's virtual copy. Many coarse-grained systems limit the degree of communication between processors, which makes it difficult to implement property inheritance efficiently.

For these three reasons (the requirement for a high degree of parallelism, grain-size considerations, and the need for global communication), fine-grained approaches have been a natural choice for a wide variety of problems in AI.

2.1.2 Fine-Grained Parallelism and Emergent Computation

The "fine-grained" class of parallelism has also been referred to as "massively parallel" [38], "highly parallel" [59], and "logic enhanced memories" [108]. These titles do not capture the most interesting feature of this class of systems: the emergence of complex behavior from the interactions among very simple elements. The individual units of these systems are so simple that no one of them alone is powerful enough to carry out the operations required of the entire system. The kind of parallelism exhibited by fine-grained systems is radically different from that of coarse-grained systems because the global behavior of the system arises from the collective behavior of the components. The components only have meaning in the context of the entire system and that meaning is naturally interpreted at a higher level than the concrete behavior of the parts. This contrasts with coarse-grained parallelism in which the units are complex, and the efficiencies of parallelism are obtained by identifying independent parts of a fundamentally sequential computation and executing those concurrently. Fine-grained systems that have the following properties will be referred to as "emergent-computations": they are constructed from many simple components (fine-grained), they have local interactions among the components (decentralized), and they have interesting collective properties such as self-organization or the capacity for cooperative behavior. The premise of emergent computation is that interesting and useful computational systems can be constructed by exploiting local interactions among primitive components, and further, that for some kinds of problems (e.g., modeling intelligent behavior) it may be the only feasible method.

The remainder of this section explores three themes: (1) why fine-grained parallelism is most appropriate for implementing AI systems, in particular knowledge representation problems, (2) why fine-grained parallelism is most appropriate for modeling intelligent behavior, and (3) how emergent properties of fine-grained parallel systems are relevant to (1) and (2). These three themes are closely related, and this is reflected in the discussion.

From the intelligent systems perspective, learning considerations provide another reason for favoring fine-grained over coarse-grained parallelism. Any truly intelligent system will have to incorporate some form of learning or adaptation, and systems constructed out of small units, or building blocks, are more amenable to learning than monolithic stuctures that do not have natural decompositions [67, 83]. A fine-grained representation allows simple domain-independent learning rules to be applied to the units rather than their aggregates. In these fine-grained representations, variations of small building blocks, such as those tried by learning algorithms, are more likely to be meaningful than random variations in larger units with complex internal structure.

Within the fine-grained class of parallelism, the SIMD/MIMD distinction holds. Fine-grained SIMD architectures are characterized by a large number of simple processors which are globally connected to a supervisor that sends instructions to each processing element. Each element typically contains data, some local state information, and limited processing capability. The data stored at every element are usually independent of the other data in the system or only dependent on a small local neighborhood. Most communication is with the supervisor that emits instructions synchronized by a global clock. This is in contrast with decentralized (MIMD) models, such as the Actor formalisms [60], in which each processing element is autonomous and executes its own set of instructions asynchronously. Examples of SIMD architectures include: Illiac IV [5], MPP [6], the systolic arrays [80], and more recently the Connection Machine [61, 62]. The Actor formalisms are one of the most decentralized systems under investigation. At the lowest level, the system passes messages asynchronously between individual objects, called actors. Higher-level actors are built up hierarchically through composition of lower-level actors.

Because "real-world" knowledge rarely exhibits uniform mathematical structure, a system with flexible connections like the Actor model is more likely to be able to support knowlege representation efficiently. In problems whose data interactions have a regular topology, fine-grained SIMD organizations are ideal, while for those that cannot be decomposed at all, parallelism is probably not appropriate. However, for problems that are "nearly decomposable" [111], parallel solutions that can optimize the distributed-processing/shared-data tradeoff are needed. A high degree of connectivity is required to support some global communication and flexible augmentation of knowledge bases. However, it is impossible to have a large-scale totally connected parallel ("cross-bar") system due to the combinatorial number of links in a cross-bar.

Fine-grained parallel systems address this need for flexible interconnectivity in different ways. The Connection Machine alternates between SIMD mode and message-passing mode. In message-passing mode, the interconnection network allows any element to communicate with any other element through a routing network. Classifier systems (see

Section 2.2) use a large but finite global message list under the assumption that it is necessary for any processor to have the ability to communicate with any other processor, but that at any one time a relatively small number of communications will be active. The Actor model assumes that messages to any given actor are received non-deterministically. Thus, the system is never dependent on a message arriving within a fixed time period.

Fahlman's work on NETL [36] was the first serious attempt to design a knowledge representation language that would lend itself to implementation on a parallel machine. It emphasized inheritance of properties (virtual copy) and fast computation of certain second-order relations, such as intersections between virtual copies. Communication through the network was accomplished by the propagation of single-bit markers (marker passing) that could have one of two values (true or false). Intersections were computed by looking for nodes that, for example, had two marker bits set to true. Later work on the Thistle and Boltzmann machines [38, 63, 64] concentrated on more sophisticated communication (value passing instead of marker passing) and search strategies based on statistical mechanics. The NETL language is somewhat limited in that it provides no formal apparatus for organizing queries, specifying what sequences of queries will answer which questions, or deciding which part of a virtual copy to access. It specifies how information may be organized into a network, but does not provide precise algorithms for information retrieval or for entering new nodes into the network. In addition, the existing formalism has proved to have semantic difficulties [37]. Despite these drawbacks, the NETL project pointed out an important direction for research in knowledge representation.

As mentioned earlier, one of the most intriguing aspects of fine-grained parallelism is its potential for supporting emergent computation. Researchers in several fields have begun to explore computational models in which the behavior of the entire system is in some sense more than the sum of its parts. These include the connectionist models [104], classifier systems [73], cellular automata [22, 25, 123], biological models [26], artificial-life models [82], and the study of cooperation in social systems with no central authority [4]. In these systems interesting global behavior *emerges* from many local interactions. When the emergent behavior is also a computation, we refer to the system as an *emergent computation.*

As yet, there are relatively few examples of algorithms or architectures that are designed to exploit emergent properties directly. The examples mentioned above were primarily designed as models of specific phenomena; either the phenomena are known to have interesting emergent properties or it is believed that a model with emergent properties can best account for the phenomena of interest. However, the genetic algorithm, the pebble-pond algorithm, and the proposed cyto-architecture each exploit emergent phenomena to perform a computation. From an emergent-computation standpoint, each of these systems illustrates the principles of simple components, local interactions, and emergent properties. The genetic algorithm uses emergent computation principles to sample large search spaces efficiently. At the concrete level, the algorithm evolves a population of bitstrings using selection against a fitness function and recombination operators such as mutation and cross-over. At the emergent, or virtual, level the algorithm can be interpreted as searching a higher-order space of patterns, the space of hyperplanes in $\{0,1\}^n$. For more details on the genetic algorithm, the reader is referred to

[52, 67]. The pebble-pond algorithm uses cellular automata to compute spatial structures for image processing [112]. The algorithm computes all-order Gabriel graphs, Voronoi tesselations and nearest-neighbor graphs. The algorithm directly measures the geometry of evolving wave-front configurations through local cell-site transformations. There are no arithmetic computations of interpoint distances in Pebble-Pond. Rather, they emerge directly from the cellular automaton computation. Dickinson has proposed an architecture called "cyto-architecture" which is based on the principles of self-organization and adaptation [33]. The machine consists of a set of cell sites, each site providing a location for a finite state machine to be defined and executed. Cell sites are connected in a stream that supports symbols flowing past the cell sites. The finite state machines treat symbols in the stream as input, transform them if they can, and replace the input with the output; that is, each cell site contains a transducer. The transducers are designed and assigned cell sites according to principles of adaptation. The principles of the machine have been demonstrated on the problem of combinator reduction.

An increasing number of cognitive models are based on the idea of subcognition, parallel processing, local interactions, and emergent behavior. Hofstadter has argued that subcognitive approaches are necessary to understanding intelligent behavior [66]. Kannerva memories are an excellent example of how distributed representations can support the storage and retrieval of linked concepts, content-addressible memories, and sequences of events with noise [78]. The revival of connectionism [104] is also predicated on the idea that subcognitive models with local interaction are the most appropriate way to model intelligence. Finally, classifier systems are an example of this kind of model. Classifier systems are discussed in detail in Section 2.2.

Fine-grained parallel systems of sufficient complexity can exhibit interesting properties such as self-organization (spontaneous emergence of order, even in the absence of selective pressure) and cooperation. Self-organizing effects can complement (or interfere with) the adaptive processes that respond to direct evolutionary pressure. The role of self-organization in adaptive systems is not yet well understood. However, two types of cooperation have been studied in a computational setting: (1) program correctness and (2) resource allocation.

Classifier systems are a good example of the first kind of cooperation; a collection of independent instructions evolves over time such that their interactions result in the desired global behavior. That is, the adaptative operations take place at the instruction level, but the behavior of interest occurs at the collective level. If the collective instructions (a program) learn the correct behavior, we say that they are cooperating. Huberman's work on computational ecologies is an example of the second meaning of cooperation in which some shared resource on a local area network (e.g., CPU time, printers, network access, etc.) is allocated efficiently among a set of distributed processes [74, 79]. Huberman's work shows how robust resource-allocation strategies can emerge in distributed systems.

In conclusion, fine-grained parallel models are promising for the study of intelligence in two ways: as architectures for AI and as models for cognitive science. Fine-grained systems are more appropriate than coarse-grained systems because they allow the large amounts of parallelism that are required to make experimental systems useful in "real world" settings. They are appropriate for knowledge representation systems where small amounts of information are added incrementally to an existing system. Additional processing power can be added as the system grows, and interesting high-level behavior such as that exhibited by semantic networks can be produced by local interactions between small units. Global communication, which is a property of some fine-grained structures, facilitates property inheritance. There are additional reasons for preferring decentralized over centralized organizations: their suitability for learning algorithms, and the flexibility that is required for the irregular and dynamic structures and algorithms demanded by problems in AI. Current research projects on connectionist models, classifier systems, and Kannerva memories provide evidence that there is a natural mapping between many problems in AI and decentralized fine-grained parallelism. These models have the properties of local interaction at the subcognitive level that produce intelligent behavior as an emergent activity.

2.2 Classifier Systems

Classifier systems, developed by John Holland, provide an excellent example of decentralized fine-grained parallelism [68, 69, 70]. They are also capable of exhibiting emergent computation [49]. Each processor is computationally simple, every processor can communicate with every other processor, and as will be shown, the extent of this communication can be controlled. Each processing element is highly standard, which makes classifier systems a promising candidate for implementation in hardware. Another attractive feature of classifier systems is that all input and output operations are conducted via a global message list. This localization of input and output results in a simpler architecture than those in which the state of the system is distributed over all of the elements. Classifier systems are well suited for problems in AI because they have a high degree of parallelism, provide the flexible connections needed for messy problems, and simple learning mechanisms can be applied within the system.

Classifier systems were originally proposed by Holland in [68, 69, 70]. Since that time, the basic classifier system architecture has changed very little, but the learning algorithms and their integration with classifier systems have evolved steadily. The best generally available descriptions of classifier systems include Holland's chapter in *Machine Learning*, Vol. 2 [72], the book *Induction* [73], the chapter on classifier systems in Goldberg's book on genetic algorithms [52], and a review article in *Artificial Intelligence* [11]. Several papers on classifier systems appear in *Genetic Algorithms and Simulated Annealing* [28] and in each of the *Genetic Algorithms Conference Proceedings* [53, 54, 55]. There are now many implementations of classifier systems, including those described in [10, 50, 101, 113, 122].

Previous implementations have been designed for a specific purpose and they rely on adaptive algorithms to control system behavior. Consequently, the emphasis in classifier system research has been on using adaptation to explore the behavior of classifier systems empirically rather than on understanding the underlying properties of the computational engine. Increasing interest in classifier systems has prompted concern about what sorts of representations are possible, and what sorts of representations work well for different classes of problems [12]. Specifically, the interface between a classifier system and a particular domain commits the system to a *representation*. Chapters 4 and 5 explore some of these representation questions and establish some of the necessary conditions for successful representations. The remainder of this section first describes the classifier system formalism, then compares it with other systems, and motivates the design.

As mentioned in Chapter 1, a classifier system consists of three layers, with the computational engine forming the lowest level. This engine is the fundamental computational component of the system and is a parallel rule-based message-passing system. The remaining layers are algorithms for modifying its structures. At the second level is the bucket-brigade learning algorithm which manages credit assignment among competing classifiers. It plays a role similar to that of back-propagation in neural networks. Finally, at the highest level are genetic operators that create new classifiers.

The lowest level of the classifier system is a kind of production system [29, 91]. It contains a data base of IF/THEN rules, called classifiers. Like production systems, there is a match cycle in which each classifier is matched against the state of the short-term memory. Unlike production systems, each classifier can perform only one action, that of adding messages (represented as binary bit strings) to a global short-term memory called the "message list." The message list corresponds to the working memory of other production systems. In the normal case, it is expected that the number of classifiers will be large with respect to the size of the message list. For example, a classifier system with 500–1000 rules might have a message list of two dozen messages. At each step, the state of the message list determines which classifiers are eligible to write information to the message list at the following time step. As mentioned earlier, the message list is completely rewritten once per time step so that each message has a duration of exactly one time step. Thus, the primary action of the system is a loop in which all of the classifiers access the current message list, each determining if its pre-conditions (a pattern of messages) have been met, and if so, posting its own output message(s) at the next time step. All external communication (input and output) takes place via the message list. As a result, internal control information and external communication reside in one data structure.

The following description of classifier systems emphasizes how they can be used to represent high-level symbolic structures and does not rely on a particular hardware implementation. Thus, it is appropriate to describe the language of possible programs for a classifier system as a formal grammar. The input to a classifier program is the set of external messages (often called detector messages) that are added to the message list during the program's execution. The output is the set of messages (called effector messages) read from the message list by an external agent. Just as many traditional programs can be run interactively, a classifier program can be thought of as receiving intermittent input from the external environment and occasionally emitting output messages. The classifier system syntax used in this book is as follows:

```
<classifier system> ::= <classifier>*

<classifier> ::= <condition>+ => <action>

<condition> ::= <alphabet>n | ~<alphabet>n

<action> ::= <alphabet>n

<alphabet> ::= 1 | 0 | #
```

Each classifier, or production rule, consists of a condition part and an action part; conditions and actions are all the same length (n). The action part specifies exactly one action, while the condition part may contain many conditions (pre-conditions of activation). Rules with more than one condition are referred to as "multiple-condition classifiers." A multiple-condition classifier must have each of its pre-conditions fulfilled in a single time step for it to be activated. The conditions and actions are fixed-length strings over the alphabet (1,0,#) where 1 and 0 are literals, and # denotes "don't care" for a condition and pass-through for an action. The determination of whether or not a specific message matches a condition is a logical bit comparison on the defined (1 or 0) bits. If a "negated" condition (~) is used, the condition is fulfilled iff no message on the message list matches it. The #s in the condition part designate "don't care" positions in the sense that they match either 1 or 0. The action part of the classifier determines the message to be posted. All defined bits appear directly in the output message. Any # symbols in the action part indicate that the corresponding bit value in the activating message should be substituted for the # symbol in the output message.[1] Actual messages never contain "don't care" symbols (since they are bit strings). Separate conditions are placed on separate lines, and the first condition (the distinguished condition) of a classifier is used to pass through messages to the action part.

Each classifier can be regarded as a separate instruction that takes messages as input and produces messages as output. Thus, the basic match/execute cycle of classifier systems can be viewed as an abstract parallel machine. The configuration of the individual classifier determines which messages are accepted as input and how accepted messages are transformed into output messages. A classifier is activated at a given time step if its pre-conditions are satisfied by at least one message which appeared on the message list at the previous time step. The message list is completely rewritten once per time step so that each message has a duration of exactly one time step. Thus, the basic system consists of a cycle in which all of the classifiers access the current message list, each determining if its pre-conditions have been met, and if so, posting its own output message(s) at the next time step. This process continues until the system has iterated a fixed number of times or, in some systems, until the message list remains unchanged (quiescent) for two successive time steps. All external communication (input and output) is via the message list. As a result, all internal control information and external communication reside in the same data structure.

As a simple example, consider the following four-bit (n = 4) classifier system:

```
  #00# => 1101

  #101
  ###1 => ##1#

~ 1111 => 1111.
```

[1]For multiple-condition classifiers, pass-through is ambiguous since it is not clear what it means to simultaneously perform "pass through" on more than one condition. The ambiguity is resolved by selecting one condition to be used for pass-through. By convention, this will always be the first condition. Another ambiguity arises if more than one message matches the distinguished condition in one time step. Again by convention, this system processes all the messages that match this condition. The example illustrates this procedure.

Time Step	Message List	Activating Classifier
T0:	0000	external
T1:	1101	first
	1111	third
T2:	1111	second
T3:		
T4:	1111	third

FIGURE 2.1 Example Classifier System Behavior

This classifier system has three classifiers. The second classifier illustrates multiple conditions, and the third contains a negative condition. If an initial message, "0000" is placed on the message list at time T0, the pattern of activity shown in Figure 2.1 will be observed on the message list. The final two message lists (<empty> and "1111") would continue alternating until the system was turned off. In T1, one message (1101) matches the first (distinguished) condition and both messages match the second condition. Pass-through is performed on the first condition, producing one output message for time T2. If the conditions had been reversed (###1 distinguished), the message list at time T2 would have contained two identical messages (1111).

The global message list is equivalent in connectivity to an n x n network in which every element is potentially connected to every other element (if the message list is large enough to accommodate all messages that are posted). Not all of the connections need to be explicit at any one time, however. The message list organization provides a way for any element to be connected to any other element based on the assumption that at any time, only a fraction of all possible connections will be active.

In large-scale parallel systems such as classifier systems, the issue of control is central. Control issues arise in two ways for classifier systems: in deciding which external classifiers are to be generated, and in deciding which external messages are to be placed on the message list and when. For systems of any complexity it is infeasible to do this by hand. There are two ways of automating the process: learning and compiling. The process of compiling can be viewed as mapping high-level structures onto lower level operations ("top-down"). Likewise, some kinds of learning (for example, genetic algorithms) can be viewed as the gradual emergence of higher-level structures from a random assortment of low-level processes; systems using these kinds of learning organize themselves from the "bottom up." The bottom-up approach has been studied previously for classifier systems. The top-down approach is explored in Chapters 4 and 5 and does not require the additional two layers of classifier systems.

Since similar control problems must be solved by both approaches, it is worthwhile describing briefly how classifier systems learn. There are two ways in which learning algorithms control classifier systems: (1) by controlling write access to the message list and (2) by controlling which classifiers are in the data base of rules.

Access to the message list is limited by choosing an upper bound for the number of active messages at any one time. In current systems this is typically a small number (for example, thirty-two). The classifiers that are potentially active then bid to put their messages on the list, and those with the highest bids are allowed to do so. To facilitate bidding, the basic classifier system is augmented so that each classifier has a quantity called "strength" associated with it. A classifier's strength over time reflects its overall utility, or fitness, to the system. The size of a classifier's bid depends on at least two components: (1) the specificity of the classifier's conditions (how many of its bit positions are set to 0 or 1) and (2) its strength. Sometimes a third component, called "support," is also used. Support corresponds roughly to the number of previously active classifiers that think the bidding classifier should be active now. A learning algorithm adjusts the strengths of the classifiers over time, rewarding those classifiers that have contributed to good solutions and punishing those that do not prove useful. Classifier strength is increased when the system produces a "good" external response. Thus, reward is ultimately dependent on the system's performance in its external environment. That reward is passed "back" to the classifiers that contributed to the correct answer. One important feature of the bucket brigade is that it distributes the reward (credit assignment) using purely local methods.

The genetic algorithm [52, 67] controls the choice of which classifiers are in the data base. The algorithm is used periodically throughout the operation of the classifier system to evaluate which classifiers are doing well (contributing to useful solutions) and which ones are not doing well. The evaluation is based on the current strength of each classifier. Based on this evaluation, weak classifiers are eliminated from the data base, strong classifiers are retained, and new classifiers are generated by applying the "genetic operators" to previously successful classifiers in the hopes of generating even more successful recombinations.

The distinction between the top-down compiled approach and the bottom-up learning approach is not black and white. Treating the message-passing system as an abstract parallel machine makes it possible to consider a classifier system as both a programmable and a learning system [7]. Learning and programming could be combined in a classifier system by compiling initial representations into a set of classifiers, running the classifier set in some environment, and allowing the system to modify its program (either strengths or the classifiers themselves) over time. This vision requires, of course, that the compiled representations be appropriate for the learning algorithms. As one negative possibility, the learning algorithms might dismantle the compiled representation and then build up new solutions from scratch.

In another scenario, either the bucket-brigade or the genetic algorithm could be eliminated from the classifier system cycle. In the case where the bucket brigade is employed without the genetic algorithm, the classifier system program might represent a partial specification in which classifier rules are assigned deterministically (programmed) and the bucket-brigade algorithm is used to adjust individual strengths to a particular environment. Alternatively, the classifiers could be entered with fixed point strengths so no further learning occurred. There are no large programmed classifier systems that use the bucket brigade in either of these ways, but Riolo has used these techniques to study various properties of the bucket brigade algorithm [99, 100]. He constructed individual classifiers by hand, assigned them initial strengths, and then ran the classifier system in various environments to observe how the strengths changed over time. An alternative to using the bucket brigade is to make the message list large enough to process all eligible messages and completely eliminate the bidding process. This approach is illustrated in Chapters 4 and 5.

One apparent drawback of classifier systems is that each classifier reads (examines in its entirety) a potentially large message list of which most of the messages may not be relevant. Having each classifier read the entire message list introduces a time-consuming search. However, it is easy to imagine messages being routed directly to the classifiers that they will activate. Because the format for expressing the condition parts of a classifier is so restricted, it would be possible to sort the conditions of any given list of classifiers so that messages could be routed efficiently. In this case, each classifier would have to read only the relevant messages. Messages that were relevant to many classifiers would still be effectively global, but messages that were relevant to only one classifier would be read only by that classifier. This "data-flow" approach would not change the overall behavior of the system (although it would certainly affect the system's time complexity), and is therefore considered to be at the level of hardware. We will assume that only relevant messages reach each classifier.

Classifier systems differ from traditional production-system architectures in several respects: parallel activation of rules, no permanent memory, and simple syntactic match of rule conditions. Most production system architectures assume that all of the rules are matched against the working memory in parallel. Classifier systems make an additional assumption: in one time step, more than one activated classifier may add its messages to the message list simultaneously. Thus, many classifiers may be active at the same time. Large sets of classifiers and a reasonably sized initial message list may yield highly parallel behavior. The parallelism of the message list allows competing hypotheses to be maintained. The problem of conflict resolution among potentially competing production rules (classifiers) is ameliorated in this scheme because multiple classifiers can be activated at one time (providing that the message list is large enough). In learning classifier systems a form of conflict resolution does arise, however, because the message list is restricted and messages compete to become active. Even here there is a domain-independent way to decide which messages are posted through the bidding mechanism. Conflict resolution plays a major role in production systems that allow arbitrarily complex pattern matching of the left-hand part of a rule against the state of the working memory.

Another way in which classifier systems differ from standard production systems is that they have no permanent memory beyond the information encoded in the rules (classifiers). That is, messages on the message list disappear after one time step unless they are "refreshed" by an active classifier. The absence of a permanent could be a disadvantage in situations where static information needs to be maintained on the message list for large numbers of iterations. Since most information can be quickly regenerated when needed (that is, the classifiers are themeselves a form of long-term memory), this situation should not arise very often. However, in cases where it is a problem, some form of secondary memory could be implemented by partitioning the message list into regions in which messages persist for more than one time step.

Because the syntax of each individual classifier is so simple, the inner loop of the system (the matching algorithm) is fast by comparison with the complex pattern-matching algorithms used in OPS-like languages. Although the classifier system does not have the ability to specify arbitrary patterns with pattern variables (as in the OPS family of languages), it does have the # syntax, which allows some patterns to be represented. This design decision trades off representational power for efficiency and learning capacity, and was based on cognitive modeling considerations (see [73]). As a result, each classifier typically represents a much smaller fragment of knowledge than a standard production rule. Thus, clusters of rule sets must be developed to represent complex patterns in the environment. This leads to finer-grained representations and decreases the amount of computation (the size of the reasoning step) achieved on each cycle of the system.

Since connectionism has become such a dominant approach to modeling subsymbolic cognitive processes, a brief comparison of classifier systems and connectionism is appropriate. The two models are similar in the following respects: (1) they are both massively parallel, (2) the elementary units are limited computationally and denote "subsymbolic" activities, (3) learning is an essential component, and (4) knowledge is active rather than static. In fact, as the following chapters show, it is possible to view classifier systems as a kind of connectionist model by interpreting each classifier (rule) as a link and each message as a node. However, this analogy, which has been investigated recently by several authors (see [8, 39] for example), also reveals some of the key ways in which they differ: (1) specification of patterns of connectivity, (2) synthesis and evolution of connections, (3) computing with recursive connections, and (4) intermittent vs. continuous reward.

Classifier systems use a pattern language in which one rule can represent a multitude of connections. In this sense, each rule is on a somewhat higher level than each synaptic connection in a connectionist network. Both models have learning algorithms that adjust the "strengths" of individual connections (bucket brigade in classifier systems and back propagation in connectionism). However, classifier systems use an additional mechanism, the genetic algorithm, to synthesize connections dynamically. In the typical connectionist model, the initial set of links is complete (that is, all possible links between input and output nodes are represented). The learning algorithms then adjust the weights, and links whose weights fall below some threshold are removed from the graph. In contrast, classifier systems are initialized with a random set of rules that represent a tiny fraction of the space of all possible rules, and the learning algorithms evolve the rule set as well as adjusting the relative strengths of the different rules. Taken together, these two features of classifier systems, a pattern language and the ability to evolve the rule set, result in the ability to manipulate only those connections that are most relevant. For large-scale systems this will be very small fraction of the total number of possible connections. Another distinction between classifier sytems and connectionist networks is the way in which they handle recurrent connections. While both models can represent recurrent (looping) structures, the vast majority of connectionist applications uses feed-forward networks, and there are major difficulties with using the common error-propagation algorithms on recurrent networks. Classifier systems, however, were designed to be recurrent. The learning algorithms work well on recurrent structures, and the constructions in Chapters

4 and 5 show how recurrent connections can be used effectively. Finally, classifier systems can function with intermittent rewards unlike connectionist models which provide error correction on every iteration of the system. This feature of classifier systems can be an advantage in domains where instantaneous feedback is not available.

Belew and Forrest outlined four kinds of representations that are important for intelligent systems and discussed how they relate to classifier systems [7]. These included production rules, reasoning with uncertainty, structured descriptions, and control knowledge. Their discussion is summarized in the following paragraphs.

Rule-based reasoning using simple condition/action rules is the basic structural component of the classifier system architecture. Rule-based systems have the advantages of modularity (each rule or instruction is more or less independent of its location in the rule set), and rules can specify transitions in the environment (to make predictions or to specify actions) [73]. In addition, they can naturally represent competing hypotheses or ordered sequences using tags.

Techniques for manipulating facts and conclusions that are not positively known to be true or false are called "reasoning about uncertainty." Since many observations and conclusions about the world are not based on binary logic, the ability to manipulate uncertain values is an important capability for an intelligent system. Many techniques have been proposed, including different Bayesian calculi, certainty factors, fuzzy logic, and various bidding systems. Learning classifier systems support reasoning with uncertainty in several ways. First, the strength of each classifier reflects the previous utility of its inference in the past performance of the system. In this respect it functions similarly to the certainty factors in other rule-based systems. Second, all classifiers are forced to compete with one another and the winners are those that best balance the evidential support they derive from the input stimulus, their appropriateness to the current situation, and their past success. Third, the fact that the bidding system allows multiple winners means that few choices are critical; a classifier system can maintain multiple alternative hypotheses and defer the selection of a single interpretation until a definitive external action is taken. Finally, in some classifier systems, an "intensity" is associated with each classifier. The intensity indicates the relative importance of the message. All of these mechanisms make the system's treatment of uncertainty an integral part of its operation. However, this robustness is obtained at the expense of complete predictability. The deterministic classifier system used in Chapters 4 and 5 does not use any of these techniques. This is because KL-ONE definitions are completely consistent logically and their implementation does not require reasoning with uncertainty.

Structured descriptions, variously referred to as structured objects, frames, or concepts, are a central part of many formal knowledge representation systems and are the focus of the rest of the book. Structured descriptions are a common data structure for symbolic information. Typically, these data structures are highly interconnected by links called slots, roles, properties, or instance variables. Inheritance relations and object-attribute links are common features of structured descriptions. Most knowledge-based systems provide some way of organizing information into multi-level graph structures (either explicitly or implicitly) such that information associated with nodes at one level pertains to all lower nodes in the network. This technique appears in a wide variety of systems, including semantic networks (e.g., KL-ONE, NETL), object-oriented programming languages (e.g., Flavors, Smalltalk), expert system shells (e.g., KEE), and in some hierarchical databases. Chapter 5 shows how such structures can be represented as a classifier system.

Domain-specific knowledge that controls general inference mechanisms can greatly improve the efficiency and effectiveness of knowledge-based systems. People have strategies about how to solve a problem that are not captured explicitly by context-free rule-based representations. This can be viewed as a kind of meta-knowledge but does not need to be represented that way. Davis's work on meta-rules [30], agenda-based mechanisms in blackboard architectures [34], and the control block construct in S.1 [35] are all examples of mechanisms for implementing problem-solving strategies. Classifier systems do not address this issue architecturally. However, Chapter 5 (pp. 95) provides an example of how such knowledge could be encoded in the classifier system representation. In this example, two parallel computations are synchronized by building synchronization control structures from interacting sets of classifiers. This is a form of control knowledge in that groups and fields of classifiers are controlling (synchronizing) other groups of classifiers.

2.3 KL-ONE

The discussion of KL-ONE is divided into three parts. The first part provides a general introduction to the KL-ONE philosophy; the second part describes in detail the subset of KL-ONE that I have implemented; and the third part discusses the existing literature on the KL-ONE family of languages.

2.3.1 Overview of KL-ONE

KL-ONE organizes descriptive terms into a structured hierarchy that allows properties of a general concept, such as "mammal," to be inherited by more specific concepts, such as "zebra." This allows the system to store properties that pertain to all mammals (such as "warm-blooded") in one place but to have the capability of associating those properties with all concepts that are more specific than mammal (such as zebra). A structured hierarchy such as KL-ONE is easily represented as a graph where the nodes of the graph correspond to concepts and the links correspond to relations between concepts. Such graphs, with or without property inheritance, are often referred to as semantic networks.

KL-ONE resembles NETL [36] and other systems with default hierarchies in its exploitation of the idea of structured inheritance of properties. It differs by taking the definitional component of the network much more seriously than these other systems. In KL-ONE, properties associated with a concept in the network are what constitute its definition. This is a stronger notion than the one that views properties as predicates of a "typical" element, any one of which may be cancelled for an "atypical" case. KL-ONE does not allow cancellation of properties. Rather, the space of definitions is seen as an infinite lattice of all possible definitions: there are concepts to cover each "atypical" case. All concepts in a KL-ONE network are partially ordered by the "SUBSUMES" relation. This relation, often referred to as "IS-A" in other systems, defines how properties are inherited through the network. That is, if a concept A is subsumed by another concept B, A inherits all of B's properties. Included in the lattice of all possible definitions are contradictory concepts which can never have an extension (instance) in any useful domain, such as "a person with two legs and four legs." Out of this potentially infinite lattice, any particular KL-ONE network will choose to name a finite number of points (because they are of interest in that application), always including the top element, often referred to as "THING."

KL-ONE also provides a mechanism for using concepts whose definitions either cannot be completely articulated or for which it is inconvenient to elaborate a complete definition. As an example of the first case, consider Meno's attempt to define virtue for Socrates. In "The Meno" [58] Meno discovers that he is incapable of enumerating a set of defining properties for the concept "virtue." Yet he wishes to explore with Socrates the question of whether or not virtue is teachable. In KL-ONE terminology, the concept "virtue" could be defined as "PRIMITIVE," indicating that its definition in KL-ONE was incomplete. A similar example from the literature of semantic networks is the notion of "natural kind." One might wish to define elephants as "grey mammals." While these two properties might be all that is known about elephants, it is not true that any grey mammal is an elephant; "Grey" and "mammal" are necessary, but not sufficient, conditions for "elephantness."

The problem of definition is a deep issue with a long history, as indicated by the example from "The Meno." KL-ONE does not solve this problem, but it does provide a mechanism to get around it—the PRIMITIVE construct. In other cases, it may be convenient to use a concept that has not been completely specified. For example, if one were representing abstract data types and the operations that can be performed on them, it might be necessary to mention the concept of "Addition." However, it would be extremely tedious and not very helpful in this context to specify the complete set-theoretic definition of addition. In a case such as this, it would be useful to define addition as a primitive concept.

KL-ONE treats all of the above cases identically. The PRIMITIVE construct allows a concept to be defined as having something special about it beyond its explicit properties. Concepts defined using the PRIMITIVE construct are often indicated with "*" when a KL-ONE network is represented as a graph.

While NETL stores assertional information (e.g., "Clyde is a particular elephant") in the same knowledge structure as that containing definitional information (for example, "typical elephant"), KL-ONE separates these two kinds of knowledge. A sharp distinction is drawn between the definitional component, where terms are represented, and the assertional component, where extensions (instances) described by these terms are represented. It is possible to make more than one assertion about the same object in any world. For example, it may be possible to assert that a certain object is both a "Building" and a "Fire Hazard." In KL-ONE, the definitional component together with its attendant reasoning processes of the system is called the "terminological" space, and a collection of instances, and the different reasoning processes that operate on it, is referred to as the "assertional" space. The features of KL-ONE that have been described (structured inheritance, no cancellation of properties, and primitive concepts) reside in the terminological component. Statements in the assertional component are represented as sentences in some defined logic. Reasoning in this part of the system is generally viewed as theorem proving. Two early implementations of the assertional component were the Stickel theorem prover used in Krypton and RUP. These systems are described in [16] and [119] respectively.

Chapter One discussed the importance of classification for knowledge acquisition and retrieval. In the context of KL-ONE, classification is the process of deciding subsumption relationships between terms. A term may be a single concept, or more likely, it may be a complex description built out of many concepts.

Because KL-ONE maintains a strict notion of definition, it is possible to formulate precise rules about subsumption relationships. It is also possible to formulate precise rules about which descriptions in the terminological space apply to a given instance in the assertional space. The former process is called "classification" [85] while the latter is referred to as "realization" [88]. Here, we restrict our attention to the problem of classification in the terminological space.

As an example of this classification process, if one wants to elaborate a new concept XXXX that has the following characteristics:

(1) XXXX is a kind of vacation,
(2) XXXX takes place in Africa, and
(3) XXXX involves hunting zebras,

there exists a precise way to determine which point in the lattice of possible definitions should be elaborated as XXXX.[2] Finding the proper location for XXXX would involve finding all subsumption relationships between XXXX and terms that share characteristics with it.

When the terminological space is implemented as a multi-level network, this process can be described as that of finding those nodes that should be immediately above and immediately below XXXX in the network. The notions of "above" and "below" are expressed more precisely by the relation "SUBSUMES." Deciding whether one concept SUBSUMES another is the central issue of classification in KL-ONE. The subsumption rules for a particular language are a property of the language definition (see [94, 106]) and are discussed in the following section.

An important set of concepts defined for any classified concept are those that satisfy the Most Specific Subsumer (MSS) relation. A concept A is said to be a Most Specific Subsumer of B just in the case that the MSS relation holds between A and B. More precisely, within a given network N

```
A MSS B iff
    A SUBSUMES B, and
    there does not exist a C, such that
    A SUBSUMES C and C SUBSUMES B.
```

In the example above, the most specific subsumer might be a node named Safari, and XXXX would be classified as a particular kind of Safari (one that only hunts zebras).

The classification of new terms is accomplished by locating the set of concepts to which the incoming description should be directly linked. This set is called the set of Most Specific Subsumers (MSS). Actually, the MSS set only contains those concepts that are more general than the incoming concept. However, the set of more specific concepts

[2]More precisely, XXXX has a location role which is value restricted to the concept Africa, an activity role which is value restricted to concept HuntingZebras, and a SuperC link connecting it to the concept Vacation.

to which the incoming description should be linked can be generated from the MSS set by taking the immediate descendants of the MSS set and finding the most general covering of that set (the Most General Specializers). The Most General Specializers can also be found using subsumption tests. The algorithms described in Chapter 5 compute MSS sets.

To summarize, the classification problem in KL-ONE can be reduced to the problem of locating the set of Most Specific Subsumers, and likewise, the set of Most General Specializers, for the concept that is to be classified. While other views of the classification problem are possible, this is the approach used here and in [124].

2.3.2 Description of Implemented KL-ONE Subset

The implemented subset of KL-ONE includes the following constructs (described below): concept specialization, role differentiation, primitive concepts, primitive roles, value restrictions on roles, number restrictions on roles, and role value maps. It does not include "inverses" of roles, "structural descriptions," or "vrdiffs." A Backus Normal Form (BNF) description of the language accepted by the program appears in Appendix A.

The implemented language most closely resembles NIKL [77] in expressive power although the syntactic details are somewhat different.

INVERSEs were not implemented because their status had not been resolved among the different language dialects. "INVERSE" allows one "role" (a two-place relation) to be defined in terms of another role by specifying that the domain of the new role is the same as the range of the old role, and, likewise, that the range of the new role is the same as the domain of the old role. In its simplest interpretation, INVERSE is simply a grammatical convenience; the addition of this construct does not add to the expressive power of the language. However, it is possible that certain kinds of inferences could be based on the knowledge that one role was the INVERSE of another. In this case, the use of INVERSE would be a meaningful addition to the language.

Structural Descriptions (SD's) were omitted for similar reasons. NIKL does not provide any special mechanism for them. There is general agreement that some additional construct is needed to express the relationship between a concept and its "structural predicates." For example, the definition for "arch" should express the relation (supports) that exists between the uprights and the lintel.

The "VRDIFF" construct is used to define roles. It adds expressive power to the KL-ONE language and increases the complexity of the subsumption algorithms substantially. Since this addition has such dramatic effects on the subsumption algorithms, it was not implemented. For a detailed discussion of the relation between KL-ONE language constructs and complexity, see [17, 94].

The remainder of this section contains a short introduction to the language that was implemented. Each major construct is described and examples are given.

All concepts in KL-ONE are partially ordered by the "SUBSUMES" relation. One concept, for example Surfing, is said to SPECIALIZE another concept, say WaterSport, if Surfing is subsumed by WaterSport. This means that Surfing inherits all of WaterSport's properties. The "SUBSUMES" relation can be inferred by inspecting the respective

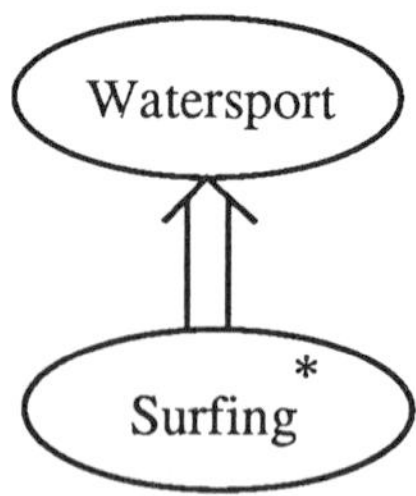

FIGURE 2.2 Concept Specialization with Primitives

properties of the two concepts, or Surfing can be explicitly defined as a specialization of WaterSport using the construct "CONCEPTSPEC":

```
(CONCEPTSPEC Surfing (SPECIALIZES WaterSport)).
```
[3]

Graphically, the specialization is represented by a double arrow (often called a SUPERC link) from the subsumed concept to the subsuming concept (see Figure 2.2). Since the SUBSUMES relation is transitive, SUPERC links could be drawn to all of WaterSport's subsumers as well. Traditionally, only the local links are represented explicitly. It should be noted that this is not a legal definition, even though it is correct syntactically. This is because the definition does not specify how Surfing is different from WaterSport. In a real system, these two concepts would be merged unless some additional property or restriction were introduced in its definition. Determining whether or not two concepts have identical definitions is, in general, as difficult as determining subsumption and can be easily incorporated into the subsumption test. For simplicity, I have not included this check.

One way to change this into a legal definition would be to assert that Surfing is primitively different from WaterSport. That is, the two can be defined as two distinct concepts without specifying how they differ. A legal definition to accomplish this is:

```
(CONCEPTSPEC Surfing PRIMITIVE (SPECIALIZES WaterSport)).
```

Figure 2.2 shows how this would be represented pictorially. In the figure, the "*" indicates that Surfing is a primitive concept.

A role defines an ordered relation between two concepts. Roles in KL-ONE are similar to slots in frame-based representations. The domain of a role is analogous to the frame that contains the slot; the range of a role is analogous to the class of allowable slot-fillers. In KL-ONE, the domain and range of a role are always concepts. Just as there is a partial ordering of concepts in KL-ONE, so is there a partial ordering of roles. The relation that determines this ordering is "differentiation." Pictorially, the DIFFERENTIATES relation between two roles is drawn as a single arrow. Roles are indicated by a circle surrounding a square (see Figure 2.2). This allows roles to be defined in terms of other roles similarly to the way that concepts are defined from other concepts. This version

[3]The period is used here and in all other examples for punctuation. It is not part of the KL-ONE syntax.

of KL-ONE does not include explicit DOMAIN and RANGE constructs (some other implementations do). Here, the domain of a role is taken to be the most general concept at which it is defined, and, likewise, the range is taken to be the most general concept to which the role is restricted (using VRCONCEPT). If no value restriction is mentioned for some role, its range is assumed to be the top element, Thing.

Roles can be defined in terms of other roles using the DIFFERENTIATES construct. This can happen in one of two ways: either the new role can "primitively" differentiate some previously defined role, or the new role can be defined as the conjunction of two previously defined roles. The VRDIFF (not implemented) construct allows for a third possibility: defining a new role as the differentiater of a previous role based on the value restriction that is enforced for the new role.

Role definitions are handled similarly to concept definitions. The role Sibling can be defined as a differentiater of "Relatives" as follows:

```
(ROLESPEC Sibling PRIMITIVE (DIFFERENTIATES Relative)).
```

Building on this definition, the conjunction WealthySibling is defined as follows:

```
(ROLESPEC Wealthy PRIMITIVE)
(ROLESPEC WealthySibling
   (DIFFERENTIATES Sibling)
   (DIFFERENTIATES Wealthy)).
```

Figure 2.3 shows how these would be drawn.

Value restrictions limit the range of a role in the context of a particular concept. To return to the sibling example, we might wish to define the concept of a person all of whose siblings are sisters as

```
(CONCEPTSPEC PersonWithOnlySisters
   (SPECIALIZES Person)
   (ROLE Sibling (VRCONCEPT Female))).
```

In this case the role, Sibling, is a defining property of PersonWithOnlySisters. This is indicated in a graph representation by a line segment connecting the concept with the role. Value restrictions are indicated with a single arrow from the role to the value restriction (a concept). Figure 2.4 illustrates these conventions.

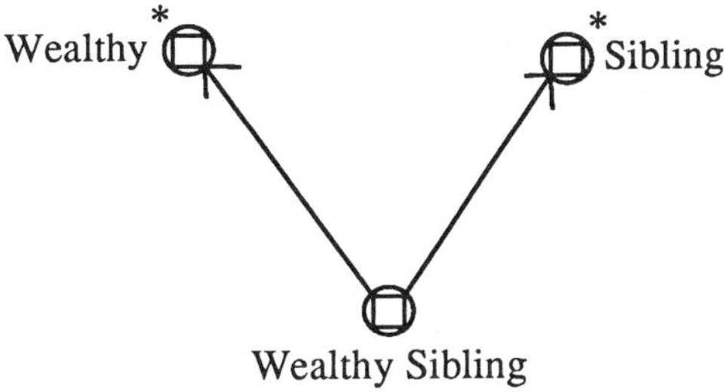

FIGURE 2.3 Role Differentiation

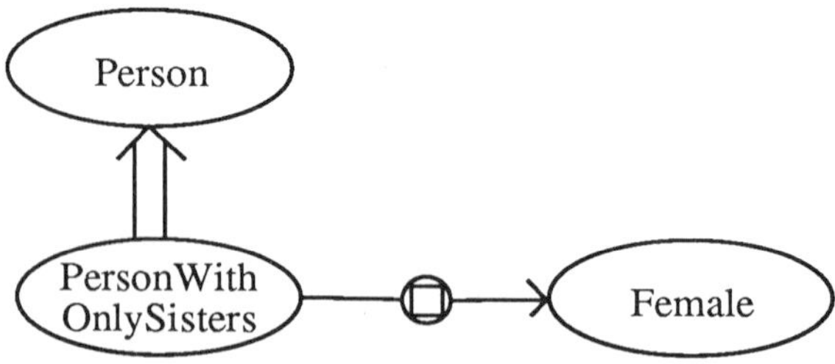

FIGURE 2.4 Value Restrictions

It should be noted that this definition does not require a PersonWithOnlySisters to actually have any siblings. It just says that if there are any, they must be female. The definition can be completed to require this person to have at least one sister by placing a number restriction on the role:

```
(CONCEPTSPEC PersonWithOnlySisters
   (SPECIALIZES Person)
   (ROLE Sibling (VRCONCEPT Female) (MIN 1))).
```

Number restrictions on roles come in three forms: MAX, MIN, and NUMBER. Not surprisingly, these constructs place limitations on the minimum and maximum number of role fillers that an instance can have. "(NUMBER x)" is simply a grammatical shorthand for "(MAX x) (MIN x)." In KL-ONE, number restrictions are limited to the natural numbers. The default MIN restriction for a concept is zero, and the default MAX restriction is infinity. Thus, in the above example, the concept PersonWithOnlySisters has no upper bound on the number of siblings. Pictorially, number restrictions are indicated at the role with (x,y), where x is the lower bound and y is the upper bound. As a further example, consider the concept of an only child, shown in Figure 2.5:

```
(CONCEPTSPEC OnlyChild (SPECIALIZES Child)
   (ROLE Siblings (NUMBER 0))).
```

This expresses the definition of OnlyChild as any child with no siblings and is equivalent to

```
(CONCEPTSPEC OnlyChild (SPECIALIZES Child)
   (ROLE Siblings (MAX 0) (MIN 0))).
```

Role Value Maps enforce a relation (currently only subset or identity) between the fillers of two roles of a concept's description. These relations are expressed in the syntax by the symbols <, >, and =. A Role Value Map can also enforce relations between compositions of roles (analogous to function composition). Role Chain is the syntactic construct that is used to represent role composition. For example, the fact that my mother's sister is the same person as my godmother could be expressed by "(= (Mother Sister) Godmother)." There is a distinction between saying that every mother's sister (aunt) is also a godmother and asserting that some particular mother's sister is some particular person's godmother. Thus, some of the meaning of a RVM is derived from

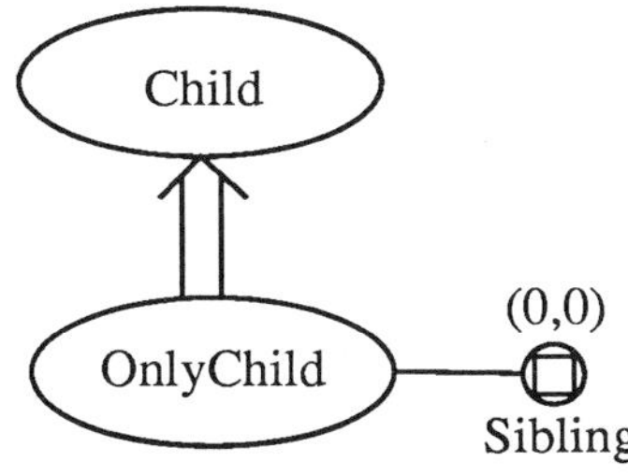

FIGURE 2.5 Number Restrictions

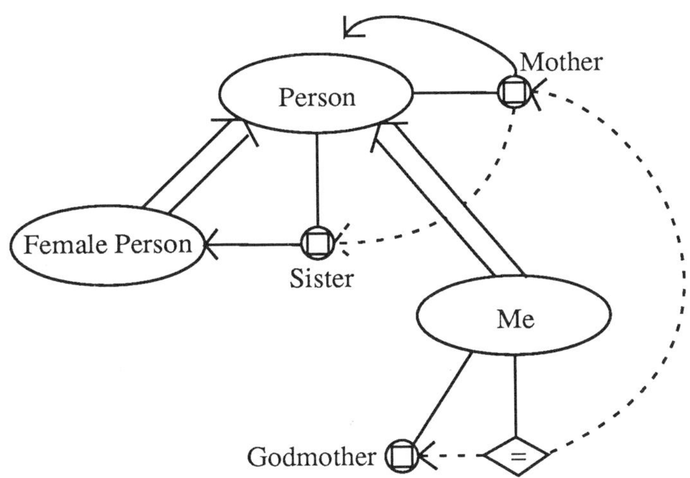

FIGURE 2.6 Role Value Maps

the concepts to which the RVM and the roles of the role chain are attached. The correct way of expressing that my mother's sister is my godmother is by attaching it to the definition of me:

```
(CONCEPTSPEC Person
    (ROLE Mother (VRCONCEPT Person))
    (ROLE Sister (VRCONCEPT FemalePerson)))
(CONCEPTSPEC Me
    (SPECIALIZES Person)
    (ROLE Godmother)
    (= (Mother Sister) Godmother)).
```

In this example, the concept "Me" inherits the role "Mother" from the concept "Person." Figure 2.6 shows how this is depicted using a diamond to indicate the RVM and dashed lines to indicate the respective role chains.

When two or more roles are linked together (as in Mother's Sister), they are referred to as "role chains." The relation "Mother's Sister" is only meaningful if the value restriction of Mother, which is Person in this example, has a "Sister" role. In general, role chains must be "traversable." That is, for each role, a_i, in the role chain, the value restriction of a_i must have as part of its definition (possibly inherited) the role a_{i+1}. Some implementations of KL-ONE (for example, NIKL) allow null role chains. In this implementation, the grammar requires that each role chain have at least one role. However, at the present time, the system does not confirm that each role chain is traversable.

2.3.3 Literature Review for KL-ONE

There are several good descriptions of the KL-ONE system available: [14, 15, 16, 19, 105, 106]. These provide descriptions of KL-ONE at various stages of its development. None of these assumes a prior knowledge of KL-ONE. In addition, there is a large body of technical reports and internal documents that discusses specific issues and various implementations of KL-ONE. These are not very illuminating to the uninitiated reader because they assume some previous knowledge of KL-ONE. When these reports are relevant to a particular section in the following chapters, they are referenced explicitly.

Brachman's Ph.D. Thesis [14] describes the initial ideas and design of KL-ONE. Since that time, these ideas have been refined into several different systems that constitute the "KL-ONE family." The original paper remains useful as an introduction to the philosophy behind KL-ONE and the problems it was intended to address.

The October 1983 issue of *Computer Magazine* was devoted to the subject of knowledge representation. In this issue are two articles that discuss central ideas in KL-ONE: "What IS-A Is and Isn't: An Analysis of Taxonomic Links in Semantic Networks" [15] and "Krypton: A Functional Approach to Knowledge Representation" [16]. The first article explores in detail what the inheritance relation (IS-A links) means in a KL-ONE-like system. The second article provides one of the earliest published accounts of the assertional part of the system.

"KL-ONE: Semantics and Classification" defines a syntax and formal semantics for KL-ONE [106]. This work revealed KL-ONE's mathematical foundations. The paper also describe a formal classification procedure that is provably sound (but not complete). While the results of this paper are of general interest, this is not the best introduction to KL-ONE. The 1985 review article in *Cognitive Science*, however, does provide a good description of KL-ONE and is intended for the general reader [19]. It explains how the various implementation projects have fit into the overall KL-ONE philosophy.

More recently, research on KL-ONE-like languages has followed two major themes: investigating the relation between expressive power and complexity of subsumption operations [17, 84, 94], and building implementations. The most notable result arising from the work on complexity is that complete classification is undecidable. Recent implementations include KANDOR [93], LOOM [86], BACK [90], and CLASSIC [13, 20]. These implementations take different positions with respect to the tradeoff between expressiveness and complexity.

The possibility of parallel classification in KL-ONE was first explored by Woods [124]. He outlined a procedure based on a generalized version of non-deterministic Augmented Transition Networks (ATNs). The parallel algorithms described here were first implemented in 1985 [43, 44, 45, 46], and have since been incorporated into work on the Penman natural language generation system [118].

2.4 Summary

This chapter has provided background information on three topics: parallelism, classifier systems, and KL-ONE. Three kinds of parallelism were described: coarse-grained, SIMD fine-grained, and emergent computation. It was argued that fine-grained organizations are the most promising way to organize parallel computations for knowledge representation. Several examples of of emergent computation were discussed, including classifier systems. Separate sections on classifier systems and KL-ONE provide general overviews, details on the systems as implemented for this dissertation, and a review of the relevant literature.

3 Approach

The issues of classification and parallelism have a broad scope and could be studied in many ways. This chapter outlines the approach taken in Chapters 5, 6, and 7 and addresses the following questions: What role does implementation play in the investigation? How should an implementation be evaluated? How can the results obtained from this specific project be generalized to address the larger issues of parallelism? The answers to these questions raise some additional organizational considerations, which are also addressed.

3.1 Implementation

The emphasis of this research is on demonstrating that a parallel classification algorithm for KL-ONE is possible using classifier systems. Such "proofs of principle" are most easily demonstrated with a working implementation, and this method has been used here.

Specifically, the implemented system performs the following tasks: (1) given a KL-ONE definition (see Appendix A), the system produces a set of production rules (classifiers) that represents the network, (2) given the names of two terms in the network, the system uses the Classifier System representation to determine whether or not one term subsumes the other, and (3) given the description of a new term, the system can determine the set of Most Specific Subsumers (MSS) for that term (again, using the Classifier System representation). Figure 3.1 illustrates how the implementation is organized.

System development was divided into several phases: (1) implementing the Classifier System in software, (2) designing and implementing a program that translates KL-ONE networks into production rules for the Classifier System, (3) developing the parallel algorithms to determine subsumption and control the search for MSS concepts, (4) validating the algorithms, and (5) analyzing the complexity of the system.

Classifier systems have been used with the assumption that they can be reasonably implemented in hardware, although no such machine currently exists. However, the algorithms were developed in two stages: generic operations (e.g., Boolean operations, parallel graph search, etc.) and the special-purpose algorithms for KL-ONE. Chapter 4 describes the former and Chapter 5 the latter. Since the KL-ONE algorithms are expressed in terms of the basic operations, any parallel machine that implements the basic operations could run the KL-ONE algorithms with only minor modifications. The classifier system machine was simulated in software using Lisp running under the UNIX Operating System.

The implemented system (excluding the Classifier System simulation) is divided into four major parts: parser, classifier generator, symbol table manager, and external command processor. The parser takes KL-ONE definitions (as specified in Appendix A) as

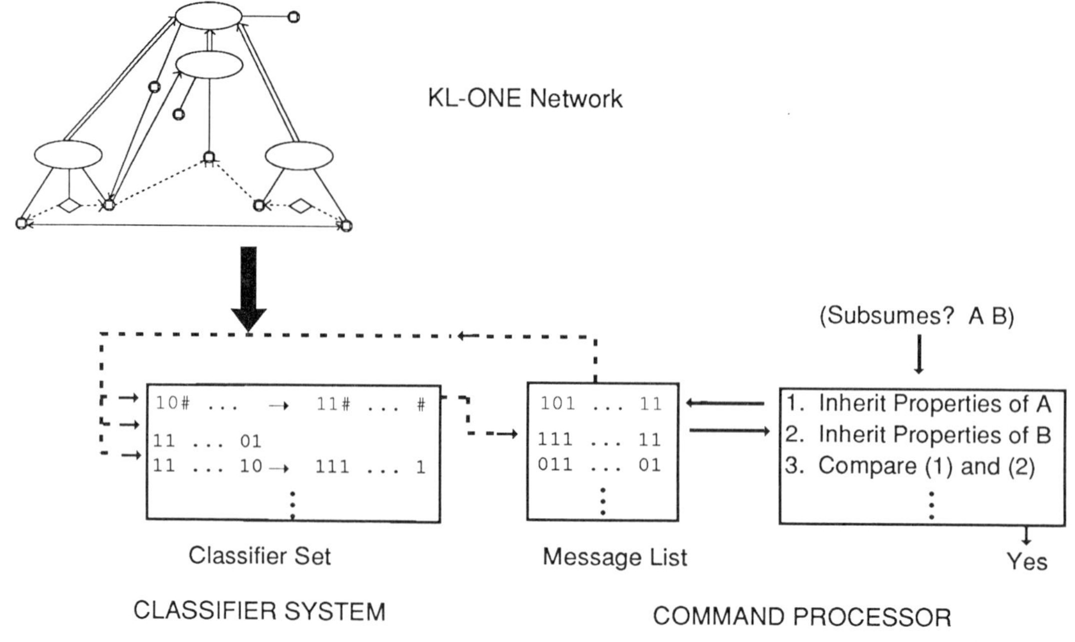

FIGURE 3.1 Classifier System Implementation of KL-ONE

input, checks their syntax, and enters all new terms (concepts or roles) into the symbol table. The classifier generator takes syntactically correct KL-ONE definitions as input and uses the symbol table to construct the corresponding classifier representation of the KL-ONE expression. The parser and classifier generator together may be thought of as a two-pass compiler that takes as input KL-ONE network definitions and produces "code" (a set of classifiers) for the classifier system machine. Additional classifiers that are independent of any given KL-ONE network (for example, many of the classifiers described in Chapter 4) are loaded into the list of network classifiers automatically. This corresponds to the predefined parts of other languages, such as standard IO packages in C, standard data types in Pascal, etc. For this system, the "standard package" includes classifiers to perform Boolean set operations, sorting, arithmetic operations, etc. The symbol table contains the specific bit patterns used to represent each term in a KL-ONE definition. One symbol table is needed for each KL-ONE network. Thus, if new concepts are to be added to a network without recompilation, the symbol table must be preserved after compilation. The external command processor runs the Classifier System, providing input (and reading output) from the classifier program.

The system should be viewed as a combination compiler and interpreter. This can be seen in two ways: (1) after an original network is compiled more information can be added dynamically—thus, the behavior of the program is modified over time, and (2) the symbol table is not thrown away after compilation. Since the classification problem is one of adding new information to an existing structure, the ability to modify the network over time is crucial if the system is to behave correctly. The symbol table is retained so that the system can add new nodes to the network at a later time without recompiling and so that queries can be coded and decoded. Both of these functions result from the decision to assign every term in a KL-ONE network a unique internal bit pattern. For example, the concept "Wave" might be represented internally as "1001001001."[1] Thus, the use of a symbol table increases the efficiency of the system by packing the representation of terms.

The parallel algorithms are formulated as a sequence of queries to the classifier system representation of a KL-ONE network. The queries are initiated by placing a set of messages on the message list, allowing the system to iterate for a fixed number of cycles, and then reading the new set of messages from the final message list. In the current implementation, the algorithms rely to some extent on the host language (Lisp). That is, some of the algorithms take advantage of the control structures and data management facilities of Lisp beyond using it to formulate the queries to the Classifier System. This is an important issue as it would be easy to hide a great deal of complexity in the processing of the host language and make it appear that the parallelism was accomplishing more than it really was. On the other hand, it seems unreasonable to force intrinsically sequential operations into the parallel formulation when there is an adequate sequential language immediately available. In the extreme it would be possible to generate a set of classifiers that could answer the subsumption question with one query, but the number (and length) of classifiers and the time to translate a KL-ONE network into the classifier representation would be unreasonably large (see Theorem 1). The parts of the algorithm that have been implemented in Lisp are either natural components of the host language (such as invoking the classifier system) or they are operations that could be made parallel by using additional tagging (see Chapter 4 for a discussion of tagging). While in principle many of the operations in the latter category could be performed by the classifier system, they are not the subject of this investigation and, if included, would cause the simulation to be much more inefficient. Therefore, only those operations which most benefit from parallelism or illustrate interesting principles have been implemented.

The embedding language (Lisp) is used in four ways: (1) to translate symbolic queries into binary messages and translate them back after the query, (2) to invoke the classifier system, (3) to store the results of queries (for example, a list of messages) that will be needed again later, and (4) to control the sequence of queries through the use of conditional and iterative constructs. The first two of these are appropriate for the command processing role that is played by the embedding programs. The second two are a matter of convenience for the current simulation and could be implemented in the Classifier System. Chapter 4 outlines how a simple stack memory can be implemented using classifiers, and it would certainly be possible to store lists of intermediate results using this method. Since all of the intermediate results would be stored as messages on the message list, this would increase the number of messages being processed at each time step and make the system less efficient. Likewise, the outer loops (that are currently under control of the host language) could be processed in parallel by using additional

[1]Clearly, the string "Wave" itself specifies a unique bit pattern. However, on most systems the representation uses thirty-two bits. To use the bit pattern defined by the characters "W," "a," "v," and "e" directly in the classifier representation would mean that each classifier would have to be extremely long (or similarly, that the allowable KL-ONE names be very short).

tag fields. There are two drawbacks to this method: the coding (translation into tag fields) would be very complicated and would not reveal any new principles, and the total number of messages being processed by the system would be approximately the same as in the current implementation. The use of tagging to accomplish additional layers of parallelism is already illustrated by the Role Value Map (RVM) construction (see Chapter 5).

3.2 Evaluation

Evaluation of the implemented system consists of two tasks: (1) verifying that the implementation is correct, and (2) analyzing the benefits (and costs) of taking advantage of the parallelism of classifier systems. These issues are discussed below.

There are two common approaches to demonstrating that an implementation is correct: (1) proofs of program correctness and (2) validation. Proofs of compiler correctness for reasonably complex languages are generally acknowledged to be infeasible, for two reasons. First, the structure of the compiler is often too complex and irregular, or the underlying semantics of the source and target languages are informally specified. Even in the best of circumstances, proving compiler correctness is an onerous task. The situation is even worse here because the translation programs (the compiler part) and the accessing algorithms would both have to be shown to be correct. The second approach (validation) involves choosing small paradigm examples and demonstrating that the compiler translates them correctly. This approach is often used to validate implementations of standard programming languages, such as Ada. Since there is no official set of validating examples for KL-ONE, one was constructed specifically for this implementation. The smaller examples of annotated program output are shown in Chapter 5 and one large example is shown in Appendix I. A third possibility would have been to obtain examples of large networks that are already in existence and assume that they test the system adequately. Since the dialects are not standard, this would involve writing another program to translate from the dialect of the original network to the dialect of Appendix A. Also, the size of the network that would be required to ensure that every part of the language was adequately tested would be huge. The examples have been designed to test what I consider to be difficult cases and reflect the discussions of KL-ONE classification in Chapter 5.

The standard tools for evaluation of algorithms are empirical testing and complexity analysis. Since I am less interested in the behavior of this particular program than in what programs of this class have to say about the more general problems of classification and parallelism, complexity analysis is the more appropriate method. Because the algorithms to be evaluated are parallel, the analysis is complicated by several factors, such as the number of processors, the number of connections between processors, and the amount of information passed between processors. Analysis of the system includes four measures of complexity: the number of production rules (classifiers), the size of each classifier, the number of times that the system must iterate to complete a computation, and the size of the message list. The time for each iteration is a function of the size of the message list and the size of the largest classifier. Comparison of the parallel results with existing sequential algorithms is complicated because the complexity of existing algorithms is not well documented and the existing classifier program makes many ad hoc assumptions and special purpose modifications to increase efficiency. Even though the complexity of complete classification has been studied extensively, these results are not directly applicable to the incomplete algorithms that are used in practice. In addition, small differences in the language can have an enormous effect on the complexity of the algorithms (see [17]). The details of this analysis appear in Chapter 6.

3.3 Summary

In summary, this research demonstrates the feasibility of a parallel classification algorithm for KL-ONE by constructing an implementation of one. This implementation is structured as a compiler that translates KL-ONE definitions into production rules (classifiers) that are executed by the "Classifier Machine." The correctness of the implementation is demonstrated by a set of validating examples. Analysis of the performance of the system is in the form of complexity analysis rather than testing. This provides more general results than could be obtained with tests. The complexity results provide a framework for discussing the larger issues of parallelism, parallel classification algorithms for KL-ONE, and the appropriateness of classifier systems as an AI architecture.

4 Classifier Systems

This chapter discusses computational properties of classifier systems and presents examples of how classifier systems can be programmed. The first part of the chapter discusses the computational completeness of classifier systems, various assumptions of parallelism, and raises the theme of flexibility. Flexibility in this context means the ability to compute both in parallel and sequentially under different conditions. The distinction between parallel and sequential behavior in classifier systems is difficult to draw because classifier systems exhibit many different kinds of parallelism. These are discussed in detail, a framework is established for making the distinction, and classifier systems are shown to be flexible within this framework. The flexibiliy of classifier systems makes them an ideal formalism for studying the inherent computational tradeoffs among the number of processors, the length of computation, and the degree of inter-processor communication.

The second section of the chapter presents detailed descriptions of general-purpose classifier system algorithms that were developed for the KL-ONE implementation. One of the purposes of this research is to investigate the computational power and efficiency of the classifier system. Thus, some common computations were chosen and implemented in classifier systems. By studying their complexity and the nature of their implementations we can learn a great deal about how classifier systems are organized. In the context of learning, it is also important to understand what kinds of structures and operations can be implemented and therefore possibly learned. For these reasons the algorithms presented in the second section of the chapter are for well-understood computations that can be efficiently implemented in other ways. Although the algorithms were developed in connection with the KL-ONE project, they are solutions to general problems that may be useful in designing classifier systems for other domains.

An underlying theme in this chapter is the tension between the properties of programmed classifier systems and learning classifier systems. Stochastic learning algorithms, such as those used for classifier systems, require representations that have a certain amount of redundancy so that the overall system will be stable to minor perturbations. This redundancy comes at the expense of computational efficiency, and for this reason the algorithms presented here are for a programmed and deterministic classifier system which does not require redundancy to behave correctly. The remarks at the end of the chapter address the question of learnability for some of the techniques.

4.1 Computational Properties of Classifier Systems

Classifier systems are defined in such a way that they can exhibit parallelism at many different levels: (1) all bits in a condition are matched against all bits in a message simultaneously, (2) one condition is matched against all messages on the message list simultaneously, (3) all conditions of one classifier are matched against one (or all) message(s) on the message list simultaneously, (4) all classifiers in a classifier system are matched against one (or all) message(s) on the message list simultaneously, (5) all active classifiers are allowed to post their output messages to the message list simultaneously, and (6) all matching classifiers become active simultaneously. Since not all levels of parallelism would necessarily be implemented in hardware, all performance analysis needs to be clear about which behaviors are assumed. Clearly, some assumptions are stronger than others. For example, it is possible using current technology to match all bits in a condition in parallel while it may not be feasible to match all messages against all classifiers simultaneously. Unless stated otherwise, Items 1 through 5 of the above list are assumed. However, the implications of relaxing some of these assumptions are explored in Chapter 6.

A parallel classifier system, *CFS, has been implemented on the Connection Machine [102] which addresses the feasibility of some of the assumptions. The implementation has the following features:

(1) All classifiers have exactly two conditions. Since any n-condition classifier system can be emulated by a 2-condition classifier system, this is not a significant restriction.
(2) One classifier is assigned to each CM processor. The message list is stored on the front-end machine. The algorithm cycles through the message list sequentially, matching each message against all classifiers simultaneously.
(3) "Matched" classifiers are selected in parallel.
(4) The reported performance figures are: 3.5 milliseconds per match cycle plus 0.5 milliseconds for each message on the message list, regardless of the number of classifiers (up to the number of processors on the machine; usually 65,000).

This demonstrates that Assumptions 3, 4, and 5 are reasonable. Assumption 1 is not easily supported on the Connection Machine but could be implemented with special-purpose hardware. The major assumption not yet addressed is that all of the messages are matched in parallel. Chapter 6 discusses the effect of relaxing this assumption. Considering that the Connection Machine is a general-purpose data parallel machine that was designed without any consideration of classifier systems, the Robertson implementation provides strong evidence that the assumptions are reasonable.

Even if the machine that processes a classifier system were parallel in all of the ways described above, it would be unreasonable to assert that the computation was parallel if any of the following conditions were met: (1) there were only one classifier in the system, (2) the message list were of length one, (3) only one classifier were active per time step, or (4) a classifier system computation were to take as many time steps as a sequential version.

Item 6 requires some explanation, since learning classifier systems violate it by restricting the size of the message list and having classifiers compete to become active. Production systems such as the classifier system are designed to have a large collection of rules of which only some are applicable at any one time. However, the property that distinguishes classifier systems from other production systems is that more than one rule at a time can be active. It is hard to imagine a situation in which all of the classifier system's rules (or even a large fraction of them) would be active simultaneously.

As the second section of this chapter and the next chapter will demonstrate, there are many ways to organize a classifier system program so that one sort of parallelism is emphasized and another deemphasized. For example, it is straightforward to design two sets of classifiers with the same functionality, one with classifiers that have (relatively) many conditions of short length and the other with fewer conditions of greater length. The goal of this section is to show that the property of flexibility holds generally for the functions that the classifier system can compute: the finite functions. This is shown by picking two extremes: the capability of computing any finite function (functions with finite domains and ranges) in one time step, and the behavior of classifier systems that most closely resembles the standard model of sequential processing on a Von Neumann machine executing one instruction (classifier) at a time.

First, it is shown that any finite function can be computed by some classifier system in one time step. This demonstrates one form of computational completeness for the classifier system, and it shows that any classifier system computation can be carried out with an arbitrary amount of parallelism. That is, the representation of a function can be distributed over enough processors to allow it to be computed in one time step. Second, it is shown that a classifier system can be made to behave completely sequentially (only one classifier is active at a time). These results taken together define two extreme behaviors of the classifier system, from maximally parallel to completely sequential. One of the reasons that classifier systems are a good formalism for studying the inherent tradeoffs in parallel computation is their flexibility. The theorems in this section support that claim by showing that the two extremes of computation (completely parallel versus completely serial) can be supported by the same formalism. The advantage of a flexible formalism like classifier systems is that these decisions are not "hardwired." That is, the machine's design leaves the programmer or learning procedure the flexibility to design algorithms that optimize over either the number of processors (classifiers), the length of the computation, or the amount of inter-processor communication.

The syntax for classifier systems was defined in Chapter 2. Here, the functional behavior of classifier systems is specified:

a message (m) is an element of the set $M = \{0,1\}^n$;

a message list (ml) is an element of the set $ML = \mathcal{P}\{0,1\}^n$;

a classifier (cl) is a function: ML -> ML;

a classifier set (cs) is a subset of the set of all classifiers (CS),
and is also a function: ML -> ML;

an iteration is a function: (CS × ML) -> ML such that
$cs(ml) = \sqcup \{ cl(ml) : (ml \in \text{Dom } cl) \text{ AND } (cl \in cs) \}$.

In this context, we can prove one form of computational completeness by showing that the classifier system can realize any function from message lists to message lists.

THEOREM 1 For every function F: ML → ML, there exists a classifier Set CS that computes F in one time step.

PROOF See Appendix B.

This result is important because it shows that within the classifier system formalism the computation of any finite function can be "flattened." That is, the function F is computed in one time step but at the expense of adding huge numbers of classifiers.

Conversely, a classifier system can be forced to behave sequentially (only one classifier active at a time) by modifying the construction of Theorem 4.1 so that only one classifier is active per time step. That is, the order of activation within a group (one CS_{ij}) will be controlled by a "clocking" mechanism or program counter. This is accomplished by assigning each classifier a unique tag (or address). The output message from any classifier always includes the unique tag (in the proper field) for the next classifier that is to become active. The basic counting technique is illustrated by some of the arithmetic algorithms shown in the next section, although they are not entirely sequential.

To show that classifier systems can compute any finite function using this method, the construction of Theorem 4.1 is extended in Theorem 4.2:

THEOREM 2 For every function F: ML → ML, there exists a classifier Set CS′ that computes F and in which only one classifier is active at any one time step.

PROOF See Appendix B.

While one would rarely want to force a classifier system to either of these extremes, this capability demonstrates the classifier system's flexibility as a computational device, ranging from one that can compute very quickly with lots of classifiers or more slowly with a more reasonable number of classifiers. In traditional programming, these considerations are reflected in the tradeoff between table-driven algorithms that store large tables of "pre-computed" answers and more compact procedural representations that take longer to calculate. In designing parallel algorithms, this tradeoff must also be considered, but the tradeoff is among the number of processors, the degree of inter-processor communication, and the length of the computation. For classifier systems several factors must be included in a careful treatment of this tradeoff: the size of each classifier (length and number of conditions), the number of classifiers, the number of time steps the classifier system iterates, and the size of the message list. The fundamental tradeoff between numbers of classifiers and length of computation is illustrated by the next two examples.

A classifier system can be designed that performs binary addition with processing time and number of classifiers that is proportional to the number of bits in the operands (a detailed description appears in the following section). Since the operands of any addition operation can be thought of as a message list of length two and the result (the answer) can be viewed as a message list of length one, the addition operation can be viewed as a function from message lists of length two to message lists of length one. Hence, it is also possible to compute the addition function using the construction of Theorem 4.1. In this case, the number of classifiers would be proportional to the square of the number of elements in the domain (two classifiers for every possible pair of operands). Furthermore, the number of conditions for each classifier would be equal to the number of elements in the domain. In the first case, it takes longer to compute the result (the number of time steps is the same as the number of bits in the numbers), but the number of classifiers and their size is reasonable; in the second case, the result is computed in one time step, but the number of classifiers is huge. In this example, the first method is more reasonable.

The tradeoff between number of processors and length of computation also applies to searching problems such as those discussed for KL-ONE. Here, it would be possible to have a totally connected structure that allowed all relevant information to be gathered in one time step. However, the number and length of classifiers would increase with the number of possible searches rather than with the size of the structure. Also, the length of time to encode the classifiers (translate from KL-ONE to classifiers) would probably increase dramatically. In the more moderate version that was implemented, the number of classifiers increases with the network's size and the searching time increases linearly with the structure's (this is the logarithm of the number of nodes in the structure if it is a completely balanced tree). This seems to be a reasonable tradeoff as it uses parallelism to capture the branching factor at every node, but does not require an unreasonable number of classifiers. Chapter 6 addresses these issues in detail.

4.2 Classifier System Algorithms

The algorithms presented here were developed in connection with the KL-ONE project. The ability to perform Boolean operations on sets, build default hierarchies, and conduct limited numerical processing is potentially useful in many applications, and for this reason, these algorithms have been grouped into one chapter.

Several general techniques for controlling classifiers are illustrated by these algorithms: (1) tagging, (2) negated conditions, and (3) computations that proceed one bit at a time. A fourth technique, synchronization, is illustrated by the Role Value Map algorithms in Chapter 5. Tagging is used to maintain groups of messages on the message list that are in distinct states. The states are defined by specific bit patterns in one selector field (often called the tag field) of the classifier. Thus, messages that have their tag fields set to the same value are said to be in the same state. This technique allows the use of more specific operators that are only defined for particular states (this is similar to the use of exceptions in a default hierarchy). The specificity of operators allows additional parallelism to be added to the system by processing more than one operation simultaneously. Negated conditions are used to terminate computations and to explicitly change the state of a group of messages when the "trigger" message is added to the list. A classifier using negated conditions in this way would have at least two conditions, one of which was "negated." Once the classifier becomes active, it continues producing messages (using a non-negated condition for pass-through) that reactivate itself. Without the negated condition the classifier would remain active for the remainder of the computation. However, when the "trigger" message appears on the message list, the classifier is turned off because the negated condition has been violated. Numerical processing is conducted one bit per time step using control messages to sequence the processing (for example, from high-order to low-order bits). Synchronization techniques allow one operation to be delayed until another has finished. This is also accomplished through the use of negated conditions.

The classifiers that have been designed for these algorithms are presented using Pascal-like type definitions. In the implementation, the types are assigned particular bit patterns that are stored in a symbol table. So, for example, the first three bits of the thirty-two bit classifiers are reserved for the tag field. For reasons of clarity, the higher-level type definitions are used here. The type definitions for Boolean operations and arithmetic operations are:

```
type
    tag = (NORM,ON,HOLD,MEM,NUM,PRE);
    boolcontrol = NORM .. MEM;
    compare = (AFIELD,BFIELD,CFIELD);
    name = string;
    message = string;
    numeric = 0 .. 63;

    classifier_record = record

    case tag : tagfield

        boolcontrol : /* Structural Variant */
            (tagfield name);

        NUM         : /* Numeric Variant */
            (tagfield compare numeric);

        PRE         : /* PreDefined Message Variant */
            (tagfield message);
    end;
```

The symbol nil is used to indicate "don't care" for an entire field (#s in every bit position for that field). The type "name" specifies the universe over which the Boolean operations are defined. In the KL-ONE implementation (Chapter 5), the classifier_record type will be modified to include additional fields.

In the implementation, the various fields are assigned the following bit positions:

```
tag: 0 - 2,
name: 3 - 31,
compare: 21 - 25,
numeric: 26 - 31,
message: 3 - 31.
```

The remainder of the chapter describes classifier system implementations of Boolean queries, arithmetic operations, and default hierarchies.

4.2.1 Boolean Queries

Classifier systems can perform Boolean operations on finite sets of messages. The following operators have been implemented: intersection, union, complementation, and set difference. The operators are defined over a finite universe of elements (instances of type "name"). If one wants the ability to use all of the operators, four classifiers must be constructed for each element in the universe; the universe (U) is composed of just those elements for which the classifiers have been constructed. Formally, only intersection and complementation are needed to provide a complete set of operators. However, set difference and set union are used so often in querying the KL-ONE knowledge base that it was useful to develop the classifiers to perform those operations directly.

One Boolean operation is referred to as an "atomic" query. It is so-called because the classifier system is being "queried" for the result of applying the operator. Sequences of atomic queries are referred to as compound queries. With a memory that can store one message list (this can be thought of as a stack of depth one), any compound query can be processed if the formula is rearranged to an equivalent canonical form. A lemma demonstrating this appears in Appendix C.[1] The memory has been implemented by designing classifiers that can maintain an isolated set of messages on the message list for an indefinite period of time. The messages "in memory" are isolated in the sense that they do not activate any classifiers (except those involved with maintaining the memory) and, therefore, do not interfere with any other computations of the system. This is accomplished through the use of tagging. Classifiers have also been designed to add and remove sets from the memory. These operations are referred to as "push" and "pop," following the stack analogy. There are actually two "pop" commands: POPAND and POPOR. POPAND computes the intersection of the set in memory and the current active set (in the "on" state) on the message list. Likewise, POPOR computes the union of these two sets. Multiple sets are represented simultaneously on the message list by using tags to distinguish elements of one set from another.

Boolean queries to the system begin with a message list that contains a set of messages in the "on" state. A message is in the "on" state if its tag bits have the pattern associated with "on." Tags on messages are indicated by capital letters (as in ON). This set is the first operand of the query and may be empty. A query is invoked by adding a Boolean control message (one of PRE-AND, PRE-OR, PRE-NOT, PRE-SETDIFF, PRE-PUSH, PRE-POPAND, PRE-POPOR) and the second operand (a set of messages in the NORM state) if the operator is AND, OR, or SETDIFF. An initial set A can be placed on the message list by adding the OR message and the set (in the NORM state) to an empty message list. This computes $(\emptyset \cup A)$. A "quiescent" (PRE-Quiescent) message is used to turn off active processing of the query and leave the result on the message list in the "on" state.

4.2.2 Overhead Classifiers

There are several overhead classifiers that are used in more than one of the query types. They are used to keep messages on the message list in a particular state for more than one time step or to change the state of a set of messages.[2] They are:

```
  ON-NIL
~ PRE-ResetMessage => ON-NIL (1)

  HOLD-NIL
~ PRE-SaveMessage
~ PRE-SetDiffMessage => HOLD-NIL (2)

  MEM-NIL
~ PRE-ClearMemMessage => MEM-NIL (3)

  HOLD-NIL
  PRE-SaveMessage => ON-NIL (4)

  ON-NIL
  PRE-SetHoldMessage => HOLD-NIL (5).
```

The first three classifiers illustrate the use of negated conditions as triggers for terminating a computation. All three classifiers keep messages active on the message list until

[1]Originally proved by P. Grosso.

[2]As discussed in Chapter 2, separate conditions are placed on separate lines, and the first condition (the distinguished condition) of a classifier is used for pass-through. "~" denotes a negated condition. The numbers in parentheses are a unique classifier tag used only for this exposition.

a trigger message is added that explicitly deactivates the classifier. Since this classifier system refreshes the message list at every time step, this technique provides a way to maintain information on the message list for an indefinite period of time. The second two classifiers illustrate how trigger conditions can be used to transform information (messages) from one state to another. Thus, the first three classifiers provide the ability to keep a set of messages in one state, and the second two provide the ability to change the state of a set of messages.

4.2.3 Set Union

A typical query to compute the union of two sets A and B begins with the messages which represent A on the message list in the ON state, adding the Or message and the messages of B in the NORM state, iterating the system for one time step, adding the Quiescent message to the list, and iterating the system for two additional time steps.

Two additional classifiers are required for set unions. They are:

```
  NORM-NIL
  PRE-OrMessage => ON-NIL (6)

  PRE-OrMessage
~ PRE-QuiescentMessage => PRE-OrMessage (7).
```

The first of these classifiers places all members of the second operand (B) in the ON state and keeps them on the message list. This produces the union since all the members of the first operand (A) are already in the ON state. The second classifier keeps the Or message active (which in turn keeps the first classifier active) until the Quiescent message is placed on the message list. This is another example of using negated conditions to control the termination of a computation.

An example of two union operations is shown in Figure 4.1 for the set A = {Guava, Pineapple, Papaya} and the set B = {Mango}. First, the union of A and the empty set is computed, and then the union of A and B.[3]

A more complicated query is one in which the set B needs to be computed, for example, when B is the set of nodes visited in the traversal of a network structure. The union operation is conducted simultaneously with the computation that produces the set B. Every time an element appears in the NORM state it is taken to be a member of B and is added to the set union (messages in the ON state) at the next time step. When the computation of B is finished, the Quiescent message is added to the list and the union set is left in the ON state.

The space complexity for set union is constant (2 classifiers) with respect to the set's size. The time complexity is also constant (3 time steps) with respect to the set's size.

4.2.4 Set Intersection

Set intersections are computed similarly to set unions. A typical query to compute the intersection of the sets A and B entails the same basic step as those for union. However, the processing is handled somewhat differently since the resulting set ($A \cap B$) cannot be accumulated directly by adding members of B to A. Rather, members of the resulting

[3]Messages that are prefixed with "→" are added to the message list by the external command processor. All other messages are generated by classifiers that were activated in the previous time step.

Time Step		Message List	Activating Classifier
T0:	→	NORM–Guava	
	→	NORM–Pineapple	
	→	NORM–Papaya	
	→	PRE–OrMessage	
T1:		PRE–OrMessage	(7)
		ON–Guava	(6)
		ON–Pineapple	(6)
		ON–Papaya	(6)
	→	PRE–QuiescentMessage	
T2:		ON–Guava	(1)
		ON–Pineapple	(1)
		ON–Papaya	(1)
T3:		ON–Guava	(1)
		ON–Pineapple	(1)
		ON–Papaya	(1)
	→	PRE–OrMessage	
	→	NORM–Mango	
T4:		ON–Guava	(6)
		ON–Pineapple	(6)
		ON–Papaya	(6)
		ON–Mango	(6)
		PRE–OrMessage	(7)
T5:		ON–Guava	(1)
		ON–Pineapple	(1)
		ON–Papaya	(1)
		ON–Mango	(1)
		PRE–OrMessage	(6)
	→	PRE–QuiescentMessage	
T6:		ON–Guava	(1)
		ON–Pineapple	(1)
		ON–Papaya	(1)
		ON–Mango	(1)

FIGURE 4.1 Example Union Operation

set are "held" in a distinguished state, HOLD, until the end of the computation. When the Quiescent message is added to the message list, all NORM, ON, and PRE messages are removed and all HOLD messages are transformed into ON messages. The additional classifiers that are needed to accomplish this operation are shown below:

```
  PRE-AndMessage
~ PRE-QuiescentMessage => PRE-AndMessage (8)

  PRE-AndMessage
  PRE-QuiescentMessage => PRE-ResetMessage (9)

  PRE-AndMessage
  PRE-QuiescentMessage => PRE-SaveMessage (10)

  for all name_i in the finite universe,

      NORM-Name_i
      ON-Name_i
      PRE-AndMessage => HOLD-Name_i (11_i).
```

The last classifier is a schema for generating classifiers for each element in U. An example of how this schema is translated into classifiers is shown below for the universe U = {Guava, Papaya, Mango, Pineapple}. For this four element universe, the following classifiers would be generated:

```
NORM-Guava
ON-Guava
PRE-AndMessage => HOLD-Guava    (11_Guava)

NORM-Papaya
ON-Papaya
PRE-AndMessage => HOLD-Papaya    (11_Papaya)

NORM-Mango
ON-Mango
PRE-AndMessage => HOLD-Mango    (11_Mango)

NORM-Pineapple
ON-Pineapple
PRE-AndMessage => HOLD-Pineapple    (11_Pineapple).
```

The queries to compute the intersection of A = {Guava, Papaya, Mango} and B = {Mango, Pineapple} are shown in Figure 4.2.

When the query is finished, $(A \cap B)$ is left on the message list in the ON state. In this example, the set B was added directly to the message list, but the intersection can be computed even if B is being generated simultaneously (e.g., from a graph search).

The number of classifiers required for this operation is linear with respect to the number of elements in the universe. One classifier is required for every element. The time complexity is constant (3 time steps).

4.2.5 Set Complementation

Set complementation in this context is always with respect to the finite universe U. Complementation is a unary operator, and, therefore, the form of the query is slightly different from those of union, intersection, and set difference. The query begins by placing (or generating through a previous computation) a set on the message list in the

Time Step	Message List	Activating Classifier
T0:	→ ON-Guava	
	→ ON-Papaya	
	→ ON-Mango	
	→ PRE-AndMessage	
	→ NORM-Mango	
	→ NORM-Pineapple	
T1:	ON-Guava	(1)
	ON-Papaya	(1)
	ON-Mango	(1)
	PRE-AndMessage	(8)
		(11Mango)
	HOLD-Mango	
	→ Pre-QuiescentMessage	
T2:	PRE-ResetMessage	(9)
	PRE-SaveMessage	(10)
	ON-Guava	(1)
	ON-Papaya	(1)
	ON-Mango	(1)
	PRE-AndMessage	(8)
	HOLD-Mango	(2)
T3:	ON-Mango	(4)

FIGURE 4.2 Example Intersection Operation

ON state. The "Not" message is added to the message list and the result (complement of the ON set) is left on the message list in the ON state. The original set is lost through this operation. Since this is a unary operation, the operand is assumed to have been completely computed at the time of the query. This means that the query can be completed automatically without any additional input from the command processor.

The complementation operation makes direct use of negated condition classifiers. As in the case of the intersection operator, there is a schema of classifiers that must be generated for each element in the universe. These classifiers place a message in the HOLD state for every element that is not in the ON state. The additional classifiers complete the processing by removing all ON messages and then changing all HOLD messages (the result) into ON messages. The classifiers to perform this operation are shown below:

```
PRE-NotMessage => PRE-ResetMessage   (12)

PRE-NotMessage => PRE-SaveMessage   (13)

for all name_i in U,

  ~ ON-name_i
    PRE-NotMessage => HOLD-name_i   (14_i).
```

As an example of complementation, consider the universe U defined above. Four additional classifiers would be generated:

```
~ ON-Guava
  PRE-NotMessage => HOLD-Guava   (14_Guava)

~ ON-Papaya
  PRE-NotMessage => HOLD-Papaya   (14_Papaya)

~ ON-Mango
  PRE-NotMessage => HOLD-Mango   (14_Mango)

~ ON-Pineapple
  PRE-NotMessage => HOLD-Pineapple   (14_Pineapple).
```

The queries for computing the complement of {Guava, Pineapple} are shown in Figure 4.3.

The number of classifiers required for this operation is linear (one classifier per element) in the number of elements in the universe. The time complexity is constant (two time steps).

4.2.6 Set Difference

To compute A – B, the set A is put in the HOLD state, B is computed (or added directly in the NORM state), and the result is formed as the computation of B proceeds. The

Time Step		Message List	Activating Classifier
T0:	→	ON-Guava	
	→	ON-Pineapple	
	→	PRE-NotMessage	
T1:		HOLD-Papaya	(14_{Papaya})
		HOLD-Mango	(14_{Mango})
		ON-Guava	(1)
		ON-Pineapple	(1)
		PRE-ResetMessage	(12)
		PRE-SaveMessage	(13)
T2:		ON-Papaya	(4)
		ON-Mango	(4)

FIGURE 4.3 Example Complementation Operation

elements in the HOLD state are only allowed to remain on the message list while there is no corresponding message in the NORM state. When the computation of B is finished, all remaining messages in the HOLD state (the answer) are transformed into the ON state, and the query terminates.

The additional classifiers needed for this operation are:

```
  PRE-SetDiffMessage
~ PRE-QuiescentMessage => PRE-SetDiffMessage  (15)

  PRE-SetDiffMessage
  PRE-QuiescentMessage => PRE-SaveMessage  (16)

  PRE-SetDiffMessage
  PRE-QuiescentMessage => PRE-ResetMessage  (17)

  for all name_i in U,

      HOLD-name_i
    ~ NORM-name_i
      PRE-SetDiffMessage => HOLD-name_i  (18_i).
```

Four additional classifiers would be generated for the example universe U:

```
  HOLD-Guava
~ NORM-Guava
  PRE-SetDiffMessage => HOLD-Guava  (18_Guava)

  HOLD-Papaya
~ NORM-Papaya
  PRE-SetDiffMessage => HOLD-Papaya  (18_Papaya)

  HOLD-Mango
~ NORM-Mango
  PRE-SetDiffMessage => HOLD-Mango  (18_Mango)

  HOLD-Pineapple
~ NORM-Pineapple
  PRE-SetDiffMessage => HOLD-Pineapple  (18_Pineapple).
```

Using the sets A = {Mango, Pineapple, Papaya} and B = {Pineapple} the computations for $A - B$ are shown in Figure 4.4.

This operation requires one additional classifier for each element in the universe and takes three time steps to compute.

4.2.7 Memory Operations

There are four operations that control the memory: PUSH, POPAND, POPOR, and CLEARMEM. The PUSH operation takes all messages that are in the ON state at the time PUSH is invoked, adds those messages to the memory, and leaves the ON messages intact. POPAND computes the intersection of the set in memory and the current active set (in the ON state) on the message list. The resulting set is left in the ON state. Similarly, POPOR computes the union of the ON and MEM sets. CLEARMEM removes all messages from memory. Since there is only one level of memory, every PUSH should have a subsequent CLEARMEM before the next PUSH. The classifiers for these operations are:

```
  ON-nil
  PRE-PushMessage => MEM-nil  (19)
```

```
PRE-PushMessage => PRE-ResetMessage  (20)

MEM-nil
PRE-PopOrMessage => ON-nil  (21)

PRE-PopOrMessage => PRE-ClearMemMessage  (22)

PRE-PopAndMessage => PRE-ResetMessage  (23)

PRE-PopAndMessage => PRE-ClearMemMessage  (24)

PRE-PopAndMessage => PRE-SaveMessage  (25)

For all name_i in U,

   MEM-Name_i
   ON-Name_i
   PRE-PopAndMessage => HOLD-Name_i  (26).
```

An example of how the memory operations work is shown in Figure 4.5. In this example, the set A = {Pineapple, Banana} is added to the message list and PUSHed. The set B = {Guava} is added to the message list, and A is POPORed to form (A ∪ B) = {Pineapple, Banana, Guava}.

The PUSH, POPOR, and POPAND operations each take two time steps, and the CLEARMEM operation takes one time step. POPAND requires one classifier for every element of U, and the other operations are all constant with respect to the size of the universe.

Time Step		Message List	Activating Classifier
T0:	→	HOLD-Mango	
	→	HOLD-Pineapple	
	→	HOLD-Papaya	
	→	PRE-SetDiffMessage	
	→	NORM-Pineapple	
T1:		HOLD-Mango	(18_{Mango})
		HOLD-Papaya	(18_{Papaya})
		PRE-SetDiffMessage	(15)
	→	PRE-QuiescentMessage	
T2:		HOLD-Mango	(18_{Mango})
		HOLD-Papaya	(18_{Papaya})
		PRE-SaveMessage	(16)
		PRE-ResetMessage	(17)
T3:		ON-Mango	(4)
		ON-Papaya	(4)

FIGURE 4.4 Example Set Difference Operation

Time Step	Message List	Activating Classifier
T0:	→ ON-Pineapple	
	→ ON-Banana	
T1:	ON-Pineapple	(1)
	ON-Banana	(1)
	→ PRE-PushMessage	
T2:	ON-Pineapple	(1)
	ON-Banana	(1)
	MEM-Pineapple	(19)
	MEM-Banana	(19)
	PRE-ResetMessage	(20)
T3:	MEM-Pineapple	(3)
	MEM-Banana	(3)
	→ ON-Guava	
	→ PRE-PopOrMessage	
T4:	ON-Pineapple	(21)
	ON-Banana	(21)
	ON-Guava	(1)
	MEM-Pineapple	(3)
	MEM-Banana	(3)
	PRE-ClearMemMessage	(22)
T5:	ON-Pineapple	(1)
	ON-Banana	(1)
	ON-Guava	(1)

FIGURE 4.5 Example Memory Operation

4.2.8 Arithmetic Operations

Included in this section are classifiers that perform operations on numbers. For KL-ONE, numeric processing was only required for the last six bits of the classifier word. That is, the six lowest-order bits of the messages on the message list are interpreted as a base-two positive integer. Thus, the operations have only been implemented for numbers in the range [0,63]. However, the schemata used to generate the classifiers are completely general and can be used for larger numbers (within the 32 bit word size restriction of the simulated machine) by changing the value of one variable. The operations described here are: finding the maximum or minimum of a set of numbers, comparing two numbers, and adding two numbers. All of these operations use the technique of processing each bit separately. In the comparison operator, all of the bits are processed in parallel, while in the other two, they are processed sequentially, with control messages providing the sequencing. While these operations do show how a classifier system can cycle through its bits, the algorithms here are somewhat clumsy. If a classifier system were required to perform a lot of numerical processing, some extensions to the classifier system architecture would be appropriate. Riolo's CFS implementation contains some of these extensions [101].

4.2.9 Finding Maximum and Minimum Values

The algorithms for computing maxima and minima from sets of numbers takes the same number of time steps as there are bits in the numbers. Three classifiers are required for each bit in the numbers. First, the classifiers for finding the maximum are described.

On the first time step, the first bit position (high-order bit) of each number is read by two classifiers. If there are any numbers with 1 in the first bit position, they are written to the message list at the next time step and all numbers with a 0 in the first bit position are filtered out (not written to the message list at the next time step). If there are no numbers with 1 in the first bit position, then all the numbers with 0 (this will be all the numbers) are written to the next message list. The classifiers for bit position one are:

```
 NUM-nil-nil-nil-nil-1#####
 PRE-MaxSort1 => NUM-nil-nil-nil-nil-1#####

 NUM-nil-nil-nil-nil-0#####
~NUM-nil-nil-nil-nil-1#####
 PRE-MaxSort1 => NUM-nil-nil-nil-nil-0#####.
```

These classifiers recognize messages whose tag fields are set to NUM and they interpret the last six bits of the message as the number that is being compared. Thus, the middle twenty-three bits do not have any effect on the processing.

The first classifier handles the case when there is at least one number with a one in the high-order bit, and the second classifier handles the case when there is not. The MaxSort1 message ensures that bit position one is only checked on the first time step.

On successive time steps, bit positions 2 through n (where n is the number of bits in the numbers) are examined in the same way.[4] A special group of classifiers controls the propagation of MaxSort messages between time steps. They have the form,

```
For every bit position i,

    PRE-MaxSort_i => PRE-MaxSort_i+1.
```

The classifiers for computing the minimum are similar. However, instead of filtering out the smallest set of numbers at each time step, they filter out the largest. The classifiers for bit position one are:

[4]In the KL-ONE implementation, the last bit position is handled slightly differently. Because the MAXIMUM and MINIMUM functions are part of a larger query, the final message(s) is slightly modified to facilitate the next query. Specifically, the classifiers that control the last bit position set the compare field on the output message. This saves an additional step before the next query in the Concept Subsumption test.

```
  NUM-nil-nil-nil-nil-0#####
  PRE-MinSort1 => NUM-nil-nil-nil-nil-0#####

  NUM-nil-nil-nil-nil-1#####
~ NUM-nil-nil-nil-nil-0#####
  PRE-MinSort1 => NUM-nil-nil-nil-nil-1#####.
```

The form of the control classifiers is:

```
For every bit position i,

    PRE-MinSorti => PRE-MinSort(i+1).
```

The full set of classifiers for six-bit numbers is shown in Appendix D along with a sample query.

4.2.10 Comparison of Two Numbers

The algorithm described here takes two messages (marked with a NUM tag and with the Compare field of one set to AFIELD and of the other set to BFIELD) and the Compare as input. It returns true if the numeric part of the AFIELD message is greater than or equal to the numeric part of the BFIELD message and false otherwise. The computation takes three time steps and requires three classifiers per bit position in the number.

The comparison takes place in two phases. First, each bit position is checked (simultaneously) to see if the bit values for the two numbers agree at that position. If they do agree, a special message (tagged as CFIELD) is written with a one in that bit position and zeroes at all other positions. During the second step, another set of classifiers looks for the first (highest-order) position where the numbers differ. If, in this position, the AFIELD number's value is greater than BFIELD's value, a True message is written. Otherwise a False message is written. If all positions are equal, a True message is written. The (annotated) classifiers for the six-bit comparator are shown below:

(1) These two classifiers handle the control messages for the operation. When the Compare message is placed on the message list these classifiers ensure that the Compare1 and Compare2 messages appear at the next two successive time steps. These two messages in turn determine which group of classifiers are potentially active in the next two time steps, thereby sequencing the computation.

```
PRE-Compare => PRE-Compare1   (50)

PRE-Compare1 => PRE-Compare2   (51)
```

(2) This classifier keeps the two operands on the message list for one time step so that they can be processed by the level-two group of classifiers.

```
NUM-nil-nil-nil-nil-nil
PRE-Compare => NUM-nil-nil-nil-nil-nil   (52)
```

(3) Each classifier in this group checks one bit position to see if both operands have a "1" at that position.

```
PRE-Compare
NUM-nil-nil-nil-AFIELD-1#####  (53)
NUM-nil-nil-nil-BFIELD-1##### => NUM-nil-nil-nil-CFIELD-100000

PRE-Compare
NUM-nil-nil-nil-AFIELD-#1####  (54)
NUM-nil-nil-nil-BFIELD-#1#### => NUM-nil-nil-nil-CFIELD-010000

PRE-Compare
NUM-nil-nil-nil-AFIELD-##1###  (55)
NUM-nil-nil-nil-BFIELD-##1### => NUM-nil-nil-nil-CFIELD-001000

PRE-Compare
NUM-nil-nil-nil-AFIELD-###1##  (56)
NUM-nil-nil-nil-BFIELD-###1## => NUM-nil-nil-nil-CFIELD-000100

PRE-Compare
NUM-nil-nil-nil-AFIELD-####1#  (57)
NUM-nil-nil-nil-BFIELD-####1# => NUM-nil-nil-nil-CFIELD-000010

PRE-Compare
NUM-nil-nil-nil-AFIELD-#####1  (58)
NUM-nil-nil-nil-BFIELD-#####1 => NUM-nil-nil-nil-CFIELD-000001
```

(4) Each classifier in this group checks one bit position to see if both operands have a "0" at that position.

```
PRE-Compare
NUM-nil-nil-nil-AFIELD-0#####  (59)
NUM-nil-nil-nil-BFIELD-0##### => NUM-nil-nil-nil-CFIELD-100000

PRE-Compare
NUM-nil-nil-nil-AFIELD-#0####  (60)
NUM-nil-nil-nil-BFIELD-#0#### => NUM-nil-nil-nil-CFIELD-010000

PRE-Compare
NUM-nil-nil-nil-AFIELD-##0###  (61)
NUM-nil-nil-nil-BFIELD-##0### => NUM-nil-nil-nil-CFIELD-001000

PRE-Compare
NUM-nil-nil-nil-AFIELD-###0##  (62)
NUM-nil-nil-nil-BFIELD-###0## => NUM-nil-nil-nil-CFIELD-000100

PRE-Compare
NUM-nil-nil-nil-AFIELD-####0#  (63)
NUM-nil-nil-nil-BFIELD-####0# => NUM-nil-nil-nil-CFIELD-000010

PRE-Compare
NUM-nil-nil-nil-AFIELD-#####0  (64)
NUM-nil-nil-nil-BFIELD-#####0 => NUM-nil-nil-nil-CFIELD-000001
```

(5) These are the second level of classifiers. Each classifier checks one bit position to see if it is the first place where the two numbers differ. If it is and the AFIELD number is larger, the True message is written.

```
PRE-Compare1
NUM-nil-nil-nil-AFIELD-1#####
NUM-nil-nil-nil-BFIELD-0##### => PRE-True  (65)

PRE-Compare1
NUM-nil-nil-nil-CFIELD-100000
```

```
NUM-nil-nil-nil-AFIELD-#1####
NUM-nil-nil-nil-BFIELD-0#### => PRE-True   (66)

PRE-Compare1
NUM-nil-nil-nil-CFIELD-1#####
NUM-nil-nil-nil-CFIELD-010000
NUM-nil-nil-nil-AFIELD-##1###
NUM-nil-nil-nil-BFIELD-##0### => PRE-True   (67)

PRE-Compare1
NUM-nil-nil-nil-CFIELD-100000
NUM-nil-nil-nil-CFIELD-010000
NUM-nil-nil-nil-CFIELD-001000
NUM-nil-nil-nil-AFIELD-###1##
NUM-nil-nil-nil-BFIELD-###0## => PRE-True   (68)

PRE-Compare1
NUM-nil-nil-nil-CFIELD-100000
NUM-nil-nil-nil-CFIELD-010000
NUM-nil-nil-nil-CFIELD-001000
NUM-nil-nil-nil-CFIELD-000100
NUM-nil-nil-nil-AFIELD-####1#
NUM-nil-nil-nil-BFIELD-####0# => PRE-True   (69)

PRE-Compare1
NUM-nil-nil-nil-CFIELD-100000
NUM-nil-nil-nil-CFIELD-010000
NUM-nil-nil-nil-CFIELD-001000
NUM-nil-nil-nil-CFIELD-000100
NUM-nil-nil-nil-CFIELD-000010
NUM-nil-nil-nil-AFIELD-#####1
NUM-nil-nil-nil-BFIELD-#####0 => PRE-True   (70)

PRE-Compare1
NUM-nil-nil-nil-CFIELD-100000
NUM-nil-nil-nil-CFIELD-010000
NUM-nil-nil-nil-CFIELD-001000
NUM-nil-nil-nil-CFIELD-000100
NUM-nil-nil-nil-CFIELD-000010
NUM-nil-nil-nil-CFIELD-000001 => PRE-True   (71).
```

(6) The first classifier keeps the True message on the list for one additional time step. This last time step is required so that a False message can be emitted if there is no True message. This is the job of the second classifier (number 73).

```
 PRE-Compare2
 PRE-True => PRE-True   (72)

 PRE-Compare2
~PRE-True => PRE-False   (73).
```

An example comparison of two numbers is shown in Figure 4.6 with the numbers 6 and 10 (in base two representation):

Time Step	Message List	Activating Classifier
T0:	→ NUM-0000000000-00000-00-AFIELD-001010	
	→ NUM-0000000000-00000-00-BFIELD-001000	
	→ PRE-Compare	
T1:	NUM-0000000000-00000-00-AFIELD-001010	(52)
	NUM-0000000000-00000-00-BFIELD-001000	(52)
	PRE-Compare1	(50)
	NUM-0000000000-00000-00-CFIELD-001000	(55)
	NUM-0000000000-00000-00-CFIELD-100000	(59)
	NUM-0000000000-00000-00-CFIELD-010000	(60)
	NUM-0000000000-00000-00-CFIELD-000100	(62)
	NUM-0000000000-00000-00-CFIELD-000001	(64)
T2:	PRE-Compare2	(51)
	PRE-True	(69)
T3:	PRE-True	(72)

FIGURE 4.6 Example Comparison of Two Numbers

4.2.11 Binary Addition

The algorithm for adding two numbers takes the same number of time steps as there are bits in the numbers. If the numbers being added each have n bits, then the number of classifiers that is required is linear in the number of bits:

$$12 * (n - 1) + 7.$$

Processing is from the low-order to the high-order bits with one set of control flow classifiers sequencing the operation, two overhead classifiers to keep the original numbers on the message list, and the remainder devoted to processing each bit position.

The control flow classifiers are of the form:

```
For every bit position i < n (here, n=6)

    PRE-Add_i -> PRE-Add_{i+1}.
```

The classifiers that keep the original messages on the message list are:

```
  NUM-nil-nil-nil-AFIELD-######
~ PRE-Add6 => NUM-nil-nil-nil-AFIELD-######

  NUM-nil-nil-nil-BFIELD-######
~ PRE-Add6 => NUM-nil-nil-nil-BFIELD-######.
```

The classifiers to process the first bit are:

```
NUM-nil-nil-nil-AFIELD-#####0
NUM-nil-nil-nil-BFIELD-#####0
Add1 => NUM-nil-nil-nil-CFIELD-#####0

NUM-nil-nil-nil-AFIELD-#####0
NUM-nil-nil-nil-BFIELD-#####1
Add1 => NUM-nil-nil-nil-CFIELD-#####1

NUM-nil-nil-nil-AFIELD-#####1
NUM-nil-nil-nil-BFIELD-#####0
Add1 => NUM-nil-nil-nil-CFIELD-#####1

NUM-nil-nil-nil-AFIELD-#####1
NUM-nil-nil-nil-BFIELD-#####1
Add1 => NUM-nil-nil-nil-CFIELD-#####0

NUM-nil-nil-nil-AFIELD-#####1
NUM-nil-nil-nil-BFIELD-#####1
Add1 => Carry.
```

One classifier is required to check for every combination of 1's and 0's in the low-order bit. Two decisions must be made: (1) what is the proper bit value for the low-order bit, and (2) is a carry generated? These issues are handled by separate classifiers. In all cases, the result value for the low-order bit must be determined—the first four classifiers are responsible for this. The result bit value is written out in the message labelled with CFIELD. In only one case (both low-order bits set to one) is there a carry generated—this is written out by the fifth classifier as a special message on the message list.

For the remaining bits, more classifiers are required because of the possibility of a carry coming into that bit position. There are four possible combinations of bit values and for each of these the presence or absence of a carry must be accounted for. This means that eight (2^3) classifiers are required for each bit position to determine the result value. In four of these situations, a carry message must be generated indicating the need for four more classifiers. However, if corresponding bits in the operands are set to one, it does not matter whether or not an incoming carry message is present (a new carry message must be generated, regardless). Thus, one less classifier is required (for example, see Classifier 23 in Appendix E).

On successive time steps (controlled by the clocking classifiers), each bit position is processed, a carry message is generated (if needed), and the result of that bit is accumulated in the CFIELD message. Appendix E gives a complete listing of the classifiers required for addition, and shows two examples of the system processing addition operations.

4.2.12 Inheritance

A major part of many semantic network systems is the idea of a multi-level structure in which concepts "inherit" properties from other concepts that are located at higher levels in the structure. This kind of structure is central to default hierarchies such as NETL, to completely defined systems such as KL-ONE, and to learning classifier systems that build hierarchical models [73]. Consequently, it is worthwhile considering the techniques that can be used to implement structured inheritance in classifier systems. Examples of these techniques appear in Chapter 5 using KL-ONE definitions, but the techniques presented are completely general and could be used to implement any similar system.

There are at least two distinct techniques that can be used to implement inheritance structures with classifier systems. One technique uses don't cares (#) to represent a concept's generality (level in the network), while the other technique represents the inheritance links explicitly as classifiers. The first technique is called "feature detection" and the second "tagging."

In the feature detection method each concept in the network is assigned a unique string. The universal top element (THING) is assigned the string that is all don't cares. Concepts one level below THING have one bit specified (0 or 1) and don't cares everywhere else, concepts two levels below THING have two bits specified, etc. Finally at the lowest level, instances are completely specified (no don't cares). Using this method, classifiers are built to represent links between concepts and their local properties (roles, slots, etc.) by using the concept's assigned string as the condition part of the classifier and the encoded local property as the action part. Thus, there is one classifier for every link between a concept and a local property.

If the structure is a binary tree, then each level in the tree is assigned one bit position. A one in that bit position denotes the left (for example) branch and a zero the right branch. A don't care in that position implies that the concept is located at a higher level. If the structure is a lattice (concepts can have multiple ancestors), then one bit position must be allocated for every concept in the structure (instead of one for every level). This is because a concept could be descended from both a left and a right branch at any level and would then need to have the corresponding bit position set to both one and zero which is impossible.

In this style of representation, the inheritance links (ISA, SUPERC, VC, etc.) are not represented explicitly. The implicit representation is achieved by the activation pattern of the classifier set. That is, when a lower-level node (say an instance) is activated by some incoming message, all the more general nodes (from which inheritance takes place) are also activated in the same time step) because of the don't care coding. A detailed description of this technique appears in Chapter 5 in the context of the KL-ONE PRIMITIVE construct.

Three major issues surround the analysis of the two representation techniques: (1) modeling capabilities, (2) space and time tradeoffs, and (3) learnability (e.g., stability and redundancy). The term "modeling" refers to the operations that can be performed easily within the representation. For example, in the feature-detection method it is difficult to index directly into the network structure (e.g., access a particular node in the network) without augmenting the representation. The feature-detection method also fits nicely with the theory of how classifier systems build up hierarchical models through learning [73].

The advantage of this first approach is the speed at which inheritance relations can be computed; the disadvantage is the amount of space (one bit in every classifier for every concept in the network) that must be allocated to support the representation for structures that allow concepts with multiple parents such as KL-ONE and NETL. The feature detection method provides an efficient method for retrieving information about primitive features that are part of a concept's definition. However, the primitive features cannot be separated from their structures, and under some conditions this method leads to space inefficiencies.

The tagging method for representing inheritance structures does not use the don't care coding, and consequently, it makes no use of the shared features of different concepts in computing inheritance relations. Each concept in the network is numbered (assigned a unique binary code). Inheritance links are represented as classifiers by having the condition part be the binary code for the concept the link comes from (the more specific concept) and the action part be the concept the link goes to. Local properties can be represented in the way described above. However, it is now necessary to represent the distinction between inheritance links and property attachment links. This can easily be accomplished by using a tag field and assigning each link type in the network a different tag. A detailed description of this second method appears in Chapter 5 in the context of KL-ONE SUPERC links.

The second method takes time proportional to the depth of the network to compute inheritance relations, but only requires $\log_2 C$ bit positions (where C is the number of concepts in the network) in every classifier for the encoded representation on the concept name. Further, the tagging method allows direct access to every node in the network.

The two methods have different implications for learning [7]. To summarize, Riolo and Goldberg have both performed experiments showing that feature-detection representations (called default hierarchies) can be learned. Riolo showed that they can form and be maintained by a variant of the bucket brigade algorithm [100]. Goldberg's experiments with a simulated gas pipeline operation provide evidence that such classifiers can also be discovered by the genetic algorithm. Holland et al. proposed a set of triggered learning heuristics that let a classifier system construct representations similar to those of the tagging method [73]. For example, they describe a triggered heuristic that couples classifiers—causing the message emitted by one classifier to satisfy the condition of another—if the classifiers are active simultaneously or nearly simultaneously. These triggered learning rules facilitate the formation of tags.

An important component of many default hierarchies is "exceptions." That is, the high-level default describes typical instances, and lower-level information describes refinements and exceptions to the default. Although KL-ONE does not allow exceptions, they can be implemented naturally in learning classifier systems by using the feature-detection method, and relying on the bidding mechanism to activate the more specific rule. For example, an exception to the default "all dogs bark" could be encoded as follows:

```
DOG-# => BARKS

DOG-BASENJI => DOESN'T BARK
```

In this example, the first classifier would be activated unless the dog were a basenji. Since the second classifier is more specific, the exception classifier would be activated in the exceptional case (when the dog is a basenji).

4.3 Summary

This chapter has presented both theoretical results and algorithms for classifier systems. In the theoretical section, some important issues for parallel computation were raised in the context of classifier systems. These include: flexibility, definitional problems, and computational tradeoffs. In the empirical section, parallel algorithms for Boolean operations, some numerical operations, and inheritance were shown.

5 Classifier System Implementation of KL-ONE

This chapter describes the KL-ONE representation in classifier systems. The mapping from KL-ONE to classifier system production rules (classifiers) is described in the first section, and the algorithms for querying a KL-ONE knowledge structure are presented in the second. Each subsection describes the parallel algorithms as independently of classifier systems as possible before showing the implementation in classifier systems. Thus, even though the emphasis is on classifier systems, the parallel algorithms could be implemented on any machine that supported parallel graph search, Boolean operations, sorting, and arithmetic.

As discussed in Chapter 2, the following notation has been adopted for classifiers: each separate condition is placed on a different line, different fields within a condition are separated by hyphens, "~" indicates a negated condition, and conditions are separated from actions by placing "=>" between the last condition and the action. Similarly, each message is placed on a separate line, and message lists (from one time-step of the classifier system) are separated from one another by a blank line. When a message is added to a message list from the external command processor, it is prefixed by the symbol "->" in the left margin. The first condition of a classifier is used for passing information through don't cares in the action part of the classifier.

All of the examples were generated by the program. However, in some cases minor changes have been made to the output and noted. In particular, the numeric fields (of both output messages and conditions of classifiers) have been modified from the base-two representation generated by the program to base-ten representation. Also, the program does not print out the tag field for predefined messages and conditions. In the exposition, the value of the tag field (PRE) is sometimes included to make the operation of the classifier system more clear.

5.1 Representation

The mapping from KL-ONE to classifiers is presented in two parts. First, there is a high-level overview of how classifiers are used to represent each major part of KL-ONE, and second, a more detailed description is provided.

5.1.1 Overview

In the classifier system implementation, every KL-ONE network is considered to have a set-theoretic universe associated with it. The elements of this universe are the concepts and roles that form the network. This representation allows important KL-ONE queries to be computed using Boolean operations on collections of concepts and roles.

When new concepts and roles are defined (using CONCEPTSPEC and ROLESPEC), they must be added to the universe. At the present time two classifiers are generated for each element in the universe. These classifiers are generated when the element (concept or role) is first mentioned. Only two classifiers are required for each element because not all of the defined Boolean operations are used in the accessing algorithms. The algorithms use only union, intersection, and set difference. If all of the operations (union, intersection, complementation, set difference, and memory operations) were used, four classifiers would be required. A full description of the Boolean operations is provided in Chapter 4.

If a role is ever mentioned in a role chain definition, two more classifiers are generated. These are used in the comparison of two role chains (when checking for subsumption of Role Value Maps).

Each SuperC link between two concepts (defined using SPECIALIZES) is mapped into two classifiers. This allows traversals of the network in both directions. One classifier allows propagations from the more specific to the more general concept, and the other classifier allows propagations from general to specific. These directions are referred to as "UP" and "DOWN" even though they are actually defined by the relation "SUBSUMES" which partially orders the concepts of the network. Each Differentiates link (defined using DIFFERENTIATES) between two roles is similarly mapped into two classifiers.

Every Role and Role Value Map (defined using ROLE, <, >, or =) that is mentioned in a concept definition is assigned one classifier that associates the named concept with the role or Role Value Map.

Each value restriction that is mentioned (using VRCONCEPT) is mapped into one classifier. This classifier associates the local concept (the concept at which the value restriction is defined), the role, and its value restriction.

MAX and MIN are mapped into one classifier each. NUMBER is mapped into two classifiers, since (NUMBER x) is a syntactical abbreviation for (MAX x) (MIN x). These classifiers associate the role to which the number restriction applies with the integer that defines the restriction. If the MIN restriction is missing, the lower bound is assumed to be zero, and if the MAX restriction is missing, the upper bound is assumed to be infinity.

Role chains require three classifiers for every link in the chain. These are used to synchronize the comparison between two role chains.

5.1.2 Detailed Description

The symbol table contains one entry for every term mentioned in a KL-ONE network. The symbol table is initialized with all the system predefined values before the terms for a particular network are added. The initialization information includes all predefined messages and field values. Each symbol table entry consists of seven fields: SYM, TYP, VAL, KIND, INU, INRC, and PRIM. The field SYM contains the name of the term the entry represents. This can be any Lisp atom. The TYP field identifies the entry as either a concept or a role. For system-defined values such as field names (NUM, PRE, etc.) this field is set to nil. The VAL field contains the unique bit pattern used to represent the term by the classifiers. The VAL field produces a packed encoding of the particular set of terms named in any given KL-ONE network. The KIND field distinguishes between different field types (see below), such as TAG, LINK, DIRECTION, etc. The field INU maintains a record of which symbols have been added to the universe. The first time a symbol is mentioned in a definition, two classifiers are generated for Boolean operations.

This field indicates whether or not these classifiers have been constructed. Likewise, the INRC field maintains a record of which roles have been used in role chain definitions, since the classifiers for this operation only need to be generated once. The PRIM field contains the bit pattern for the term that represents its primitive characteristics (see below for details).

The implemented classifier system is based on a word size of thirty-two bits. This implies that all the messages on the message list and all the conditions and actions of the classifiers are thirty-two bits long. This restriction places upper limits on the absolute size of the networks that can be represented. In a real system, this problem could be circumvented by the analog of double-precision arithmetic. When the size of the network exceeded the capacity of a thirty-two bit system, the system could be automatically promoted to sixty-four bits and the existing representations changed accordingly. This facility was not included in the simulation, and therefore, true upper bounds do exist. They are detailed below:

Total number of concepts and roles together: 1024
Maximum value of a number restriction: 63
Maximum number of distinct primitive characteristics of concepts: 11
Maximum number of distinct primitive characteristics of roles: 11
Maximum number of Role Value Maps: 64.

For the purposes of encoding, the thirty-two bits have been conceptually grouped into fields as shown below. The description of the KL-ONE encoding is then presented in terms of fields and field values, rather than using bit values. Note that each field value has a corresponding bit pattern which is stored in the symbol table, and that ultimately each condition and action is represented as a thirty-two bit string. The word "nil" denotes don't care for an entire field. A nil in a classifier is a true don't care; a nil in a message is any bit pattern.

Since classifiers are used in many different ways in this system, there are several different ways in which the bits are interpreted. Tagging ensures that there is no ambiguity about which interpretation is used. The type definition facilities of Pascal-like languages provide a natural way to express the the conceptual interpretations:

```
type
   tag = (NORM,ON,HOLD,MEM,NUM,RVM,PRE);
   boolcontrol = NORM .. MEM;
   link = (SUPERC,ROLE,DIFF,VRLINK,MAX,MIN,LEFT,RIGHT);
   direction = (UP,DOWN);
   compare = (AFIELD,BFIELD,CFIELD);
   name = string;
   message = string;
   numeric = 0 .. 63;
   primitive = 1 .. 11;


   classifier pattern = record
   case tag : tagfield

      boolcontrol : /* Structural Variant */
         (tagfield name link direction primitive);
```

```
        NUM : /* Numeric Variant */
            (tagfield name nil direction compare numeric);


        RVM : /* Role Value Map Variant */
            (tagfield name link direction compare numeric);


        PRE : /* PreDefined Variant */
            (tagfield message);
    end;
```

In the implementation, the various fields are assigned the following bit positions:

```
tag : 0 - 2
name : 3 - 12
link : 13 - 18
direction : 19 - 20
primitive : 21 - 31
compare : 21 - 25
numeric : 26 - 31
message : 3 - 31.
```

This definition defines four patterns for constructing classifiers: structural, numeric, Role Value Map, and predefined. The structural pattern is by far the most important. It is under the control of the Boolean operations (tag field is one of NORM, ON, HOLD, or MEM) and is used to represent concepts and roles. The numeric pattern is used for processing the number restrictions MAX, MIN, and NUMBER. The Role Value Map (RVM) pattern is used only for RVMs, and the predefined pattern is used for control purposes. The predefined pattern has no nils in it and adds constants to the system.

The structural pattern is broken into five fields: tag, name, link, direction, and primitive. The tag field contains the control information for the Boolean operations, the name field contains the coded name of a concept or role, the link field specifies which link type is being traversed (SUPERC, DIFF, etc.), the direction determines whether the traversal is up or down, and the primitive field contains the inherited "primitiveness" for the concept or role.

The Numeric pattern has six fields: tag, name, link, direction, compare, and number. In most cases the name, link, and direction fields are not relevant to the numeric processing and will be filled with nils. The tag field is always set to NUM, and the compare field is one of AFIELD, BFIELD, or CFIELD. The compare field is used to distinguish operands in arithmetic operations. The number field contains the binary representation of the number being processed. Since this field is limited to six bits, the system only processes numbers between 0 and 63.

The Role Value Map pattern is broken into the same six fields described for numeric patterns. However, the tag field is set to RVM instead of NUM. The remaining fields are used as follows: name is not used (nil), link is used to differentiate the "left" role chain of the Role Value Map from the "right" role chain, direction is used to control role comparison in the role chain; only the AFIELD and BFIELD values are used for the compare field, and the numeric field contains the unique identification number of the Role Value Map being processed.

The Predefined pattern has the value PRE in the tag field. The rest of the pattern (29 bits) is assigned to one field. These bits are always completely defined (even in conditions and actions) as they refer to unique constant messages. These messages provide internal control information and are used to initiate queries from the command processor.

The precise mapping from KL-ONE to the classifier system is shown in Appendix F. The following seven sections correspond to the major constructs of the language: concepts and roles, primitives, concept specialization, role differentiation, value restrictions, number restrictions, and role constraints.

5.1.3 Concepts and Roles

Whenever a new concept or role name is mentioned for the first time, either using CONCEPTSPEC or ROLESPEC explicitly or by embedding it in another definition, it is assigned a unique bit pattern that is stored in the symbol table. This corresponds to the NAME field. Since the name field is allowed ten bits, there are $2^{10} = 1024$ different role and concept names allowed in any one network.

Concept and role names constitute a universe of elements over which the Boolean operations are defined. The INU (in universe) field of the symbol table maintains a record of elements in the universe. A T value in the INU field indicates that the concept or role is already a member of the universe and a nil value indicates that it is not. In the context of the classifier system, adding an element to the universe corresponds to generating the following two classifiers[1]:

```
  NORM-Name-nil-nil-nil
  ON-Name-nil-nil-nil
  PRE-And => HOLD-Name-nil-nil-nil

  NORM-Name-nil-nil-nil
~ ON-Name-nil-nil-nil
  PRE-SetDiff => HOLD-Name-nil-nil-nil.
```

Here, "Name" denotes the name of the concept or role being added to the Universe.

When a role is associated with a concept (using ROLE), a classifier is constructed to represent the association. For example, in the definition (CONCEPTSPEC Person (ROLE Arm)) the following classifier is constructed:

```
nil-Person-nil-nil-nil
PRE-rolemess => nil-Arm-DIFF-nil-nil.
```

5.1.4 Primitives

The PRIMITIVE construct places an additional constraint on SPECIALIZES and DIFFERENTIATES links. For example, in the definition,

```
(CONCEPTSPEC A PRIMITIVE (ROLE Arm))
(CONCEPTSPEC B (ROLE Arm)),
```

the use of PRIMITIVE indicates that there is something special about A above and beyond the explicit definition that "all A's have arms." Thus, the system cannot infer that B specializes A, even though B meets the explicit requirements (that is, all B's have

[1]When the program prints out classifiers, the tag field is not printed for PreDefined patterns. Thus, the condition "PRE-And" is actually printed as "And" by the program. The tag field is printed for these examples to emphasize which pattern variant is being used. However, sample queries to the classifier system are reproduced exactly (without the tag field for PreDefined patterns).

arms) for being an A. The only way that this can be determined is by mentioning it explicitly:

```
(CONCEPTSPEC B (SPECIALIZES A)).
```

In this case B inherits the primitive characteristics of A, and in the future no other concept will be subsumed by B unless it exhibits at least the same primitive characteristics as B (in this case the same as A). In the current example, this could happen in one of two ways:

```
(CONCEPTSPEC C (SPECIALIZES A)) or
(CONCEPTSPEC C (SPECIALIZES B)).
```

Since the use of the PRIMITIVE statement does not add any links or nodes to the network, no new classifiers are generated for this statement. Instead, the inherited primitive characteristics are collected during the parsing phase for every concept and stored in the symbol table (using the PRIM field). One bit position is assigned for every new "kind" of primitiveness that is introduced to the system. Because of the network's lattice structure, a concept (or role) can inherit any combination of concept (or role) primitiveness. Thus, one bit is required to represent each different kind of primitiveness in the network. However, the primitive characteristics of concepts are completely distinct from those on roles.

The PRIM field is constructed by discovering which primitives are inherited by this node, placing a "1" in the bit positions corresponding to the inherited primitive characteristics and don't cares ("#") in all the other positions. When classifiers are generated for SPECIALIZES or DIFFERENTIATES links, the primitive information is included in the classifier to control propagations through the network. The notation "(PRIM x)" is used to indicate the primitive field of the term x.

5.1.5 Concept Specialization and Role Differentiation

Two classifiers are generated for every explicit specialization in the network. This allows traversals through the network in either the UP (specific to general) or DOWN (general to specific) direction. The classifiers form the link between the concept that is being specialized and the specializing concept. For example, in the definition, (CONCEPTSPEC B (SPECIALIZES A)), the following two classifiers would be generated[2]:

```
NORM-A-SUPERC-DOWN-(PRIM B) => NORM-B-SUPERC-DOWN-(PRIM B)

NORM-B-SUPERC-UP-(PRIM B) => NORM-A-SUPERC-UP-(PRIM A).
```

There are two classes of propagations in the DOWN direction. The first traverses all subsumees of the node (or nodes) from which the propagation originates. The second kind of propagation is a selective traversal that only visits those nodes whose PRIM fields are compatible with that specified on the originating message. This latter class of propagation is used in the FindMSS algorithm and ensures that only those concepts whose primitive characteristics are compatible with the incoming concept are visited.

[2]Here and in the following examples the program produces the actual values for the primitive field and not "(PRIM x)."

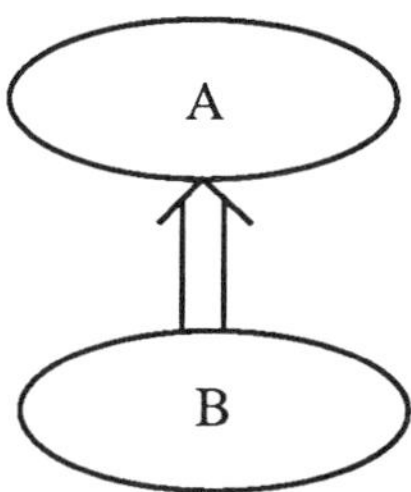

FIGURE 5.1 Concept Specialization

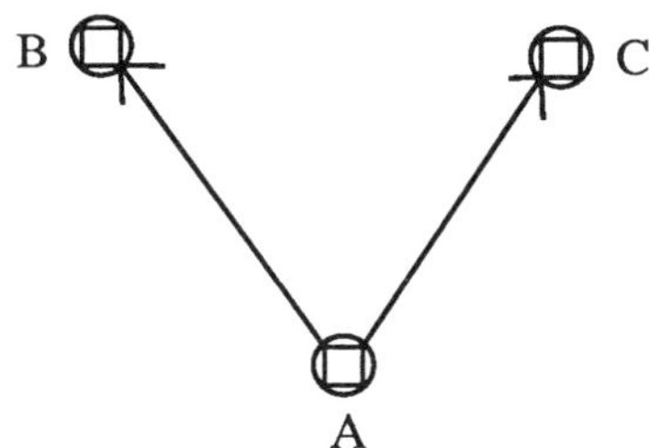

FIGURE 5.2 Role Differentiation

For this reason, the input message must satisfy the primitive requirements for the lower (more specific) concept in the DOWN direction. This is why "(PRIM B)" appears in the condition of the first classifier, rather than "(PRIM A)." As a result, the search through the lattice is restricted to concepts that share the same primitive definitions with the concept being considered. In the UP direction this restriction is not required because the most specific primitive characteristics are passed along to the higher concepts in the network. It is still possible to activate all of the nodes (concepts) beneath a given one regardless of primitives by setting the eleven bits of the primitive field to "1" in the initial message. Although this feature operation is not used in the MSS and SUBSUMES algorithms, it might be useful in other queries. This is done by setting the eleven bits of the primitive field to "1" in the initial message. Since the primitive fields in the classifiers use #s to express the absence of primitive characteristics, a message with all primitive bits set to "1" will override the effect of the primitive field.

Differentiation is handled similarly. The value DIFF in the link field ensures that concepts and roles will not be confused. This separation allows the same eleven bits in the PRIM field to be used for concepts and for roles. As an example of differentiation, consider the definition, (ROLESPEC A (DIFFERENTIATES B) (DIFFERENTIATES C)), shown in Figure 5.2.

Two links are specified by this definition, and the following four classifiers would be generated:

```
NORM-B-DIFF-DOWN-(PRIM A) => NORM-A-DIFF-DOWN-(PRIM A)

NORM-A-DIFF-UP-(PRIM A) => NORM-B-DIFF-UP-(PRIM B)

NORM-C-DIFF-DOWN-(PRIM A) => NORM-A-DIFF-DOWN-(PRIM A)

NORM-A-DIFF-UP-(PRIM A) => NORM-C-DIFF-UP-(PRIM C).
```

These classifiers control propagations along DIFF links. They are used whenever it is necessary to determine whether one role DIFFERENTIATES another.

5.1.6 Value Restrictions

One classifier is constructed for each explicitly mentioned value restriction. The classifier associates the local concept and the relevant role with their value restriction. The control message, VR, ensures that the classifier is only activated when the system is looking for value restrictions. This prevents interference with other parts of the system. For example, consider the definition (CONCEPTSPEC Athlete (ROLE Specialty (VRCONCEPT Sport))), shown in Figure 5.3.

The following classifier is produced for the value restriction:

```
nil-Athlete-nil-nil-nil
nil-Specialty-nil-nil-nil
PRE-VR => nil-Sport-SUPERC-nil-nil.
```

5.1.7 Number Restrictions

There are three grammatical constructs included in this category: MAX, MIN, and NUMBER. One classifier is constructed for MAX and one for MIN. Since (NUMBER x) is simply a grammatical shorthand for (MAX x)(MIN x), there are two classifiers generated for NUMBER. For example, consider the definition (CONSCEPTSPEC Person (ROLE Arm (NUMBER 2))), shown in Figure 5.4. This says that a Person has exactly two Arms and is equivalent to (CONCEPTSPEC Person (ROLE Arm (MAX 2) (MIN 2))).

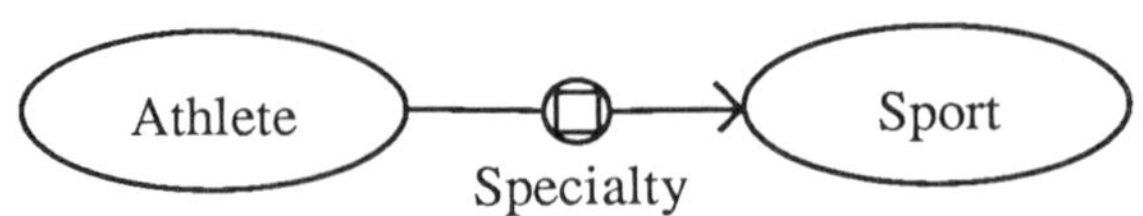

FIGURE 5.3 Value Restrictions

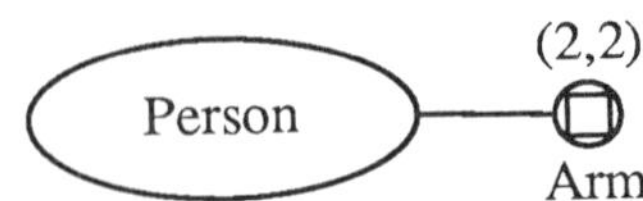

FIGURE 5.4 Number Restrictions

The following two classifiers would be generated for the number restriction[3]:

```
nil-Arm-nil-nil-nil
nil-Person-nil-nil-nil
PRE-Max => NUM-nil-maxlink-nil-nil-2

nil-Arm-nil-nil-nil
nil-Person-nil-nil-nil
PRE-Min => NUM-nil-minlink-nil-nil-2.
```

5.1.8 Role Value Maps

The representation of Role Value Maps (RVM) in classifiers transforms every RVM to one canonical form ($\subseteq$)[4] by the following equivalences:

```
(RoleChainA ⊇ RoleChainB) ≡ (RoleChainB ⊆ RoleChainA),

(RoleChainA = RoleChainB) ≡ ((RoleChainA ⊆ RoleChainB)
   AND (RoleChainB ⊆ RoleChainA)).
```

Each Role Value Map is assigned a unique number. Since equal (=) RVMs are transformed into two RVMs, they are assigned two different numbers. In the implementation, six bits are assigned to this number.

The use of a canonical form for Role Value Maps allows the system to inherit the two parts of an "=" RVM from two different concepts. Thus it would be possible for a concept to inherit ($A \subseteq B$) from one concept and ($B \subseteq A$) from another. This would then be equivalent to ($A = B$) and allow the concept to be classified under a concept with the restriction ($A = B$).

In the KL-ONE syntax, the first of the two Role Chains defined in a Role Value Map is interpreted as the "left hand side" of the relation and the second Role Chain as the "right hand side." Propagations from Role Value Maps along Role Chains are referred to as being either in the "LEFT" or the "RIGHT" direction.

The parser ensures that each Role Chain is at least one role long (a syntactic requirement). The system assumes that each role chain is traversable (that each role in the chain is associated with the value restriction of the previous role in the chain). One classifier is constructed to associate the role constraint with the concept from which it is defined. This classifier allows the system to discover the local role constraints at a given concept. For example, consider the definition, (CONCEPTSPEC Snail (= House Shell)), shown in Figure 5.5.

This role constraint, which says that a snail's shell is the same as its house, would be assigned a unique identifying number, say 32. The following classifier would be constructed:

```
nil-Snail-nil-nil-nil
PRE-RVMCheck => RVM-Snail-nil-nil-nil-32.
```

Two classifiers are generated for each role that appears in a role chain. These allow synchronization between propagations across corresponding role chains in a subsumption

[3]The program prints out the base-two representation for the value of the numeric field. Here, it has been changed to the base-ten representation for clarity.
[4]In KL-ONE syntax, "<" stands for "$\subseteq$" and ">" stands for "$\supseteq$."

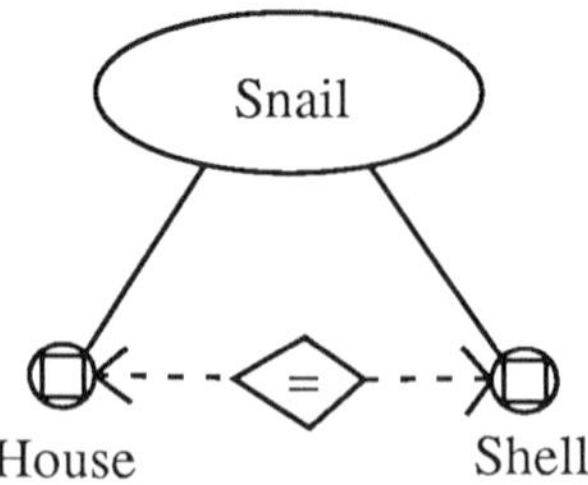

FIGURE 5.5 Role Value Maps

test. The two classifiers are generated only once, even if a role appears in many different role chains. The INRC (in role chain) field of the symbol table records which roles have been mentioned in a role chain. Using the above example, two classifiers would be generated for Shell and two for House. The classifiers for Shell are:

```
RVM-Shell-LEFT-nil-AFIELD-nil
nil-Shell-DIFF-UP-BFIELD-nil
PRE-LeftDelay => PRE-LeftUnDelay

RVM-Shell-RIGHT-nil-AFIELD-nil
nil-Shell-DIFF-UP-BFIELD-nil
PRE-RightDelay => PRE-RightUnDelay.
```

The remaining classifiers are designed to facilitate the subsumption test for Role Value Maps. The subsumption test is discussed in full detail in the next section, but some preliminary comments are appropriate before showing their representation in classifiers. Two computational principles of the classifier system are illustrated by the subsumption test for Role Value Maps: synchronization and additional parallelism through tagging.

The synchronization problem arises in the following way. Assume that the right branches of two Role Value Maps are being checked. The roles of each role chain must be in one-to-one correspondence with each other. If there are four roles in one role chain there must also be four roles in the other. The corresponding roles in each chain need to be compared in a pairwise fashion. That is, the third member of the (hypothetically) subsumed role chain must differentiate the third member of the subsuming role chain, and similarly for every other pair in the two role chains. The DIFFERENTIATES relation can take anywhere from one to n time-steps, where n = the depth of the network, to confirm, and the propagation along the subsumed role chain must be delayed until the corresponding member of the subsuming role chain has been reached via the DIFFs links. This is a synchronization problem because there are two different propagations being carried out simultaneously that must be synchronized at each link. The Delay message is used to hold up the propagations until the UnDelay message is emitted; the propagations are then allowed to continue to the next link.

An additional layer of parallelism has been added to the system through tagging. In this context tagging allows both sides of a Role Value Map (LEFT and RIGHT) to be checked simultaneously. Thus, during a subsumption test between two Role Value Maps, there will be four separate propagations carried out simultaneously with two independent

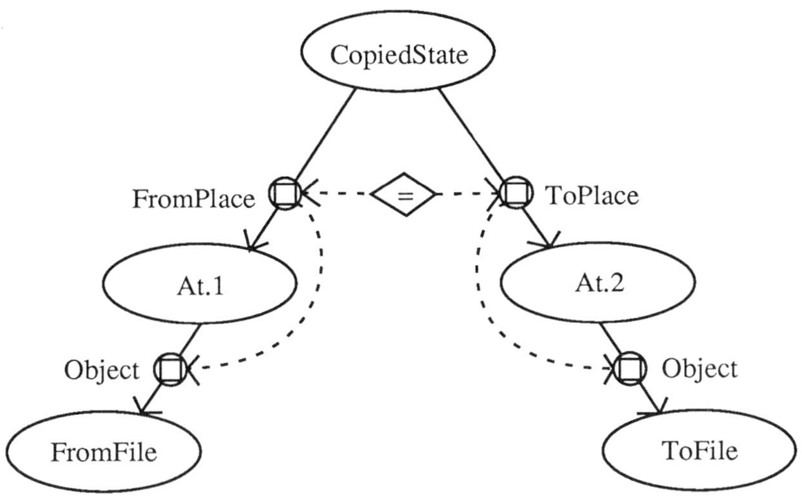

FIGURE 5.6 Copied State Example

synchronizations. The left and right sides of a Role Value Map are not symmetric in that the Differentiation relationship between corresponding roles in the Role Chains are inverted for the left side The role of a subsuming left Role Chain must differentiate the role of a subsumed one. The AFIELD and BFIELD designators are used to control which direction the Differentiation check goes, and the LEFT and RIGHT designators are used to keep the two role chain tests from interfering with each other. This construction illustrates how tagging (LEFT and RIGHT function as tags) can be used to implement additional layers of parallelism.

Since the number of classifiers quickly becomes very large, a minimal piece of a larger model of file copying will be used to illustrate the construction. This particular example expresses the requirement that the new file (ToFile) will be identical with original file (FromFile). Consider the following network, shown in Figure 5.6:

```
(CONCEPTSPEC CopiedState
   (ROLE FromPlace (VRCONCEPT At.1
      (ROLE Object (VRCONCEPT FromFile))))
   (ROLE ToPlace (VRCONCEPT At.2
      (ROLE Object (VRCONCEPT ToFile))))
   (= (FromPlace Object) (ToPlace Object))).
```

First, the Role Value Map is transformed into two maps, (< (FromPlace Object) (ToPlace Object)) and (> (ToPlace Object) (FromPlace Object)), and each map is assigned a unique number, say 33 and 34 respectively. We will only consider the first map, number 33. The following classifiers would be constructed:

```
nil-CopiedState-nil-nil-nil
PRE-RVMCheck => RVM-CopiedState-nil-nil-33

RVM-CopiedState-LEFT-nil-BFIELD-33
RVM-LeftUnDelay => NORM-FromPlace-DIFF-UP-BFIELD-33

RVM-CopiedState-LEFT-nil-BFIELD-33
```

```
PRE-LeftUnDelay => RVM-FromPlace-LEFT-nil-BFIELD-33

RVM-CopiedState-LEFT-nil-AFIELD-33
PRE-LeftUnDelay => RVM-FromPlace-LEFT-nil-AFIELD-33

RVM-FromPlace-LEFT-nil-BFIELD-33
PRE-LeftUnDelay => NORM-Object-DIFF-UP-BFIELD-33

RVM-FromPlace-LEFT-nil-BFIELD-33
PRE-LeftUnDelay => RVM-Object-LEFT-nil-BFIELD-33

RVM-FromPlace-LEFT-nil-AFIELD-33
PRE-LeftUnDelay => RVM-Object-LEFT-nil-AFIELD-33.
```

In addition to the classifiers generated for every defined Role Value Map, there is an overhead set of general-purpose classifiers that are needed for querying the system about Role Value Maps. These are automatically included with every classifier system representation of a network. They are described in Appendix G.

5.2 Algorithms

This section describes the algorithms for finding the set of Most Specific Subsumers (MSS) in a given KL-ONE network for a concept that has not yet been classified in that network. Included as a subpart of the MSS test is the algorithm for deciding whether or not one concept SUBSUMES another (SUBSUMESP). The algorithm is formulated as a sequence of queries to the classifier system that represents the network. The queries are initiated by placing a set of messages on the message list, allowing the system to iterate for a pre-determined number of cycles, and then reading the new set of messages from the final message list. In the current implementation, the algorithms rely to some extent on the embedding language (Lisp). That is, some of the algorithms take advantage of the control structures and data management facilities of Lisp beyond using it to formulate the queries to the classifier system. The parts of the algorithm that have been implemented in Lisp are either intrinsically sequential or they could be made parallel by using additional tagging. While in principle many of these operations could be performed by the classifier system, the simulation would be much more inefficient, because the classifier system is an awkward way to implement sequential processing. This is similar to the Connection Machine which provides a separate "front-end processor" for handling sequential operations. Only those operations which most benefit from parallelism or illustrate interesting principles have been implemented in classifiers.

The embedding language (Lisp) is used in four ways: (1) to translate symbolic queries into binary messages and translate them back after the query, (2) to invoke the classifier system, (3) to store the results of queries (for example, a list of messages) that will be needed again later, and (4) to control the overall flow of the algorithm between different sequences of queries. The necessity and appropriateness of these four uses of Lisp are discussed in Chapter 3.

Again, all examples were produced by the program except where noted.

The remainder of this section is divided into five parts that correspond to natural divisions of the algorithm: Most Specific Subsumer, Concept Subsumption, Value Restrictions, Number Restrictions, and Role Value Maps. Each part of the algorithm is described by first stating the requirements for the subsumption test (giving one or more examples) and then showing how the test is made using the classifier system.

5.2.1 Most Specific Subsumers

An important set of concepts defined for any incoming concept is the set of its Most Specific Subsumers (MSS). The MSS relation is defined as follows:

```
For any concepts A and B, A MSS B iff
    A SUBSUMES B, and
    there does not exist a concept C, such that
    A SUBSUMES C and C SUBSUMES B.
```

In principle, the set of all subsumers would be just as useful for the purposes of classification as the MSS set. However, any reasonable implementation must limit the number of explicit links in the system once the knowledge base becomes large. The MSS set is useful in this context because it allows the incoming concept to be classified (and added to the network) with a minimal number of links.

The algorithm for finding the MSS set for an incoming concept C starts at the top element (Thing) and conducts a breadth-first search of the network, checking each concept in the search to see if it SUBSUMES C. Starting at the top element of the structure, the set of "immediate subcs" (those concepts that are one level below the current level in the network) is computed and each member of this set is tested to see whether or not it SUBSUMES C. The immediate subcs are found by following SuperC links in the DOWN direction for one time step. Those concepts that pass the subsumption test are placed on the OKList. The OKList is then used to generate a new set of immediate subcs (union of the immediate subcs of each member of the OKList) which in turn is used to generate a new OKList. The procedure is iterated until the OKList is empty.

Whenever a concept on the OKList has no immediate subcs that pass the concept subsumption test, that concept is known to be MSS-related to C. In other words, it meets the criteria for a Most Specific Subsumer: (1) the concept SUBSUMES C, and (2) there does not exist a more specific concept that also SUBSUMES C. Hence, the concept is placed on the MSSList.

If the KL-ONE network structure were a tree, it would be sufficient to ignore those concepts that fail the subsumption test. The tree could be pruned by taking only those concepts that pass the subsumption test and using them to generate the next set of immediate subcs. However, since the KL-ONE network structure allows nodes to be descended from more than one parent, pruning is more complicated. Once a concept X has failed the subsumption test, it is known that every concept subsumed by X will also fail the subsumption test (by transitivity). However, it is possible to reach a descendent of X via a different path of successful subsumption tests. Since the concept subsumption test is expensive, it is desirable to eliminate as many as possible. So, before asking the subsumption question about some concept, the algorithm determines that the concept is not a specialization of any node that is known to have failed the subsumption test.

The set of nodes that have failed the subsumption test may be thought of as casting a shadow on the rest of the network. Any node that falls in the shadow will also fail the subsumption test. Three alternatives were considered for computing this shadow.

The first method would maintain a list of all the nodes in the shadow. Every time a node failed the subsumption test, its contribution to the shadow (all of its subsumees) would be computed and added to the list. If the complete list were maintained, it would then be cheap (one time step using the classifier system) to decide whether or not a given node were in the shadow. However, the size of the shadow would grow exponentially with the number of failed nodes if the network structure were branching out. In a large network maintaining the complete list is infeasible.

A second possibility would be to propagate the "wave front" of the shadow one step at a time in synchronization with the nodes being considered by the breadth first search. The term "wave front" refers to the leading edge of a propagation through the network. In many of the computations of the classifier system, some portion of the network is traversed (in parallel) and all visited nodes remain on the message list until the end of the traversal. In this case, a node would be on the message list only when it was being traversed. Since the nodes being checked for concept subsumption are at an equal depth in the network, the shadow could be propagated one step at a time in synchronization with the rest of the search. When a new list of subcs was generated, the algorithm could easily determine (one time-step) which ones were in the shadow's wave front.

This method fails when there are two paths of different length to a node and one of the paths falls in the shadow and the other does not, a situation illustrated by the following example, shown pictorially in Figure 5.7:

```
(CONCEPTSPEC A (SPECIALIZES Thing))
(CONCEPTSPEC B (SPECIALIZES Thing))
(CONCEPTSPEC C (SPECIALIZES B))
(CONCEPTSPEC D (SPECIALIZES A) (SPECIALIZES C)).
```

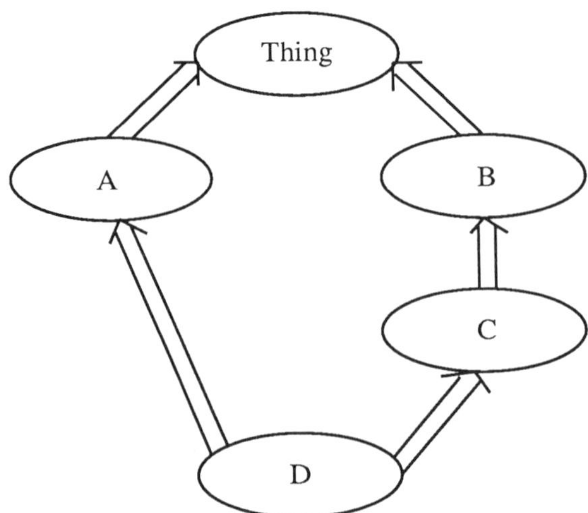

FIGURE 5.7 Shadow Example

Suppose the incoming concept X were subsumed by A and not by B. Then at the next iteration, D would be tested to see if it subsumed X. This test should not take place since D is subsumed by B. However, at this time step the wave front of the shadow would only be at C. Thus, the second alternative would fail in some cases.

A third method, the one chosen for the algorithm, maintains a list of the upper bounds of the shadow (called the NotOKList). It is then easy to determine for any node whether or not it is in the shadow by propagating up and checking to see if the propagation intersects the cover set of the shadow. This test takes time proportional to the depth of the concept in the network, but it is guaranteed to eliminate all concepts that fall within the shadow. Because the test to see if a concept falls within the shadow takes much less time than the SUBSUMESP test, it is included in the high-level search.

When the MSS algorithm is computing the next set of immediate subcs, some concepts can be pruned based on their primitive characteristics. Elimination of these concepts from the immediate subcs list further reduces the number of concepts that must be tested for subsumption. As discussed previously, the primitive information is encoded in each classifier that represents a SUPERC link. When computing immediate subcs, the messages that initiate the propagation down one set of links are set to the primitive field of the incoming concept. If an incoming concept X does not have at least the same primitive characteristics as the potential subsumer A, then A's classifier will not be activated and it will not even be considered. This is correct since A cannot possibly subsume X if X does not have all the primitive characteristics that A has.

The algorithm assumes that all subparts of the description have been previously classified in the network. This assumption precludes complete classification of cyclic descriptions such as (CONCEPTSPEC Person (ROLE Mother (VRCONCEPT Person))).

A temporary classifier list (TempClassList) is used to maintain the links between the incoming concept and the current set of subsumers during the search. Initially, the concept is assumed to specialize Thing. It may also have explicit SPECIALIZES links in its definition, but these will be located in the permanent classifier list rather than TempClassList. As the search moves down through the network, the classifiers linking the incoming concept with Thing are replaced by links to more specific concepts that are known to subsume the incoming concept. TempClassList is updated every time the search moves down one level in the network. The purpose of this list is to make the test for concept subsumption more efficient by preventing redundant checking as discussed in the next section.

The details of how the algorithm is expressed as queries to the classifier system are most easily presented in the context of an example. Since the FindMSS level of the algorithm does not directly consider Roles, Role Value Maps, Number Restrictions, or Value Restrictions, the example shown here uses a minimal amount of definitional machinery. The SPECIALIZES and PRIMITIVE constructs are emphasized because they are central to this level of the algorithm. The other parts of the language are encapsulated in the test for concept subsumption. To reiterate, a query takes the form of messages posted to the global message list by the external command processor (these messages are preceded by "->"). The state of the global message list at each time step of the sequence of queries is shown.

Consider the following network, shown pictorially in Figure 5.8:

```
(CONCEPTSPEC Person PRIMITIVE
   (SPECIALIZES Thing)
   (ROLE Limb (VRCONCEPT Legs))
   (ROLE Sex (VRCONCEPT Gender)))
(CONCEPTSPEC Legs PRIMITIVE (SPECIALIZES Thing))
(CONCEPTSPEC Gender PRIMITIVE (SPECIALIZES Thing))
(CONCEPTSPEC Male PRIMITIVE (SPECIALIZES Gender))
(CONCEPTSPEC Female PRIMITIVE (SPECIALIZES Gender))
(CONCEPTSPEC Man (SPECIALIZES Person)
   (ROLE Sex (VRCONCEPT Male)))
(CONCEPTSPEC Woman (SPECIALIZES Person)
   (ROLE Sex (VRCONCEPT Female)))
(CONCEPTSPEC Young PRIMITIVE (SPECIALIZES Thing))
(CONCEPTSPEC YoungMan (SPECIALIZES Person)
   (ROLE Sex (VRCONCEPT Male))
   (ROLE Age (VRCONCEPT Young)))
(CONCEPTSPEC HighRiskDriver (SPECIALIZES Person)
   (ROLE Sex (VRCONCEPT Male))
   (ROLE Age (VRCONCEPT Young))).
```

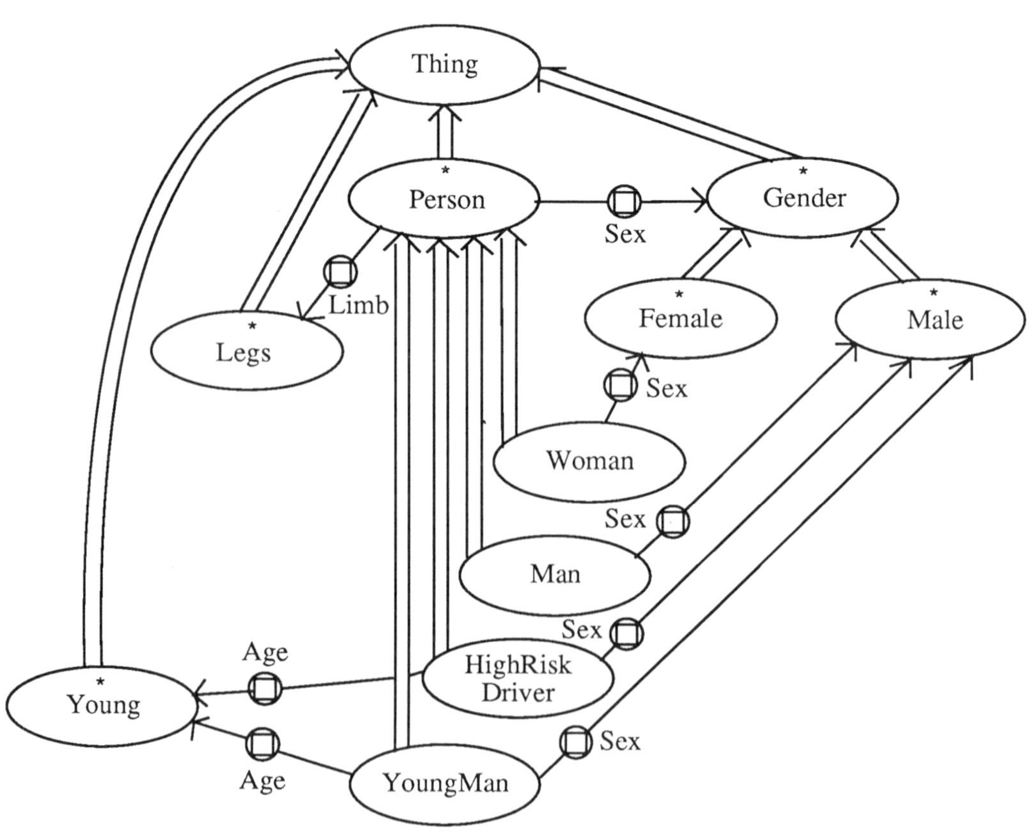

FIGURE 5.8 Example of Most Specific Subsumers Algorithm

Assume that all concepts except YoungMan have been classified and that YoungMan is an incoming concept to be classified. The classifiers that represent this network appear in Appendix I together with a pictorial representation of the network. To find the Most Specific Subsumers (FindMSS) for YoungMan the algorithm proceeds as follows:

(1) Put the immediate subcs of Thing on the TempOKList. Person is the only concept on this list. This is because all four of the concepts that are directly beneath Thing (Gender, Person, Young, and Legs) are primitive specializations. Since the primitive characteristics of YoungMan are only compatible with those of Person, Person is the only concept that is considered.

Time Step		Message List
T0:	→	NORM–Thing–SUPERC–DOWN–10000000000
T1:		NORM–Person–SUPERC–DOWN–10000000000

(2) Create classifiers to represent the fact that YoungMan specializes Thing, and place them on the TempClassList. Set OKList to Thing and NotOKList to nil. This is handled by Lisp and is not a classifier system operation.

(3) Check to see if Person is in the shadow of the elements of NotOKList. A query is formed (to compute the intersection of the NotOKList and all nodes above the concept Person) and the classifier system is iterated for one time step before the Quiescent message is generated (since the current depth of the search in the network is one):

Time Step		Message List
T2:	→	NORM–Person–SUPERC–UP–10000000000
	→	And
T3:		NORM–Thing–SUPERC–UP–10000000000
		And
	→	Quiescent
T4:		Reset
		Save
T5:		

Since the NotOKList is empty this is a degenerate test (no members of the NotOK-List to put on the message list at time T2), and the final message list will be empty. Thus, Person is not in the shadow.

(4) Check to see if Person SUBSUMES YoungMan (SUBSUMESP). The answer is yes and Person will be on the next OKList. The SUBSUMESP test is discussed at length in the next section. Therefore, the output is not reproduced here.

(5) Before the old OKList is replaced, it is necessary to determine whether any of its members are in the MSS set. That is, if a concept is on the OKList, but will have no descendents on the OKList at the next time step, then it is in the MSS set. This test can be thought of as:

(a) let A = old OKList (Thing)

(b) let B = immediate subcs of A (Person)

(c) let B' = B - NotOKList (Person)

(d) let A' = immediate supercs of B' (Thing)

(e) A - A' = new MSS elements (O).

Time Step		Message List
T28:	→	NORM–Person–SUPERC–UP–10000000000
T29:		NORM–Thing–SUPERC–UP–10000000000
	→	HOLD–Thing–SUPERC–UP–00000000000
	→	SetDiff
T30:		SetDiff
	→	Quiescent
T31:		Save
		Reset
T32:		

(6) Generate a new TempOKList. This consists of the immediate subcs of OKList (Person): (Woman, Man, YoungMan, HighRiskDriver).

Time Step		Message List
T33:	→	NORM–Person–SUPERC–DOWN–10000000000
T34:		NORM–Man–SUPERC–DOWN–10000000000
		NORM–Woman–SUPERC–DOWN–10000000000
		NORM–YoungMan–SUPERC–DOWN–10000000000
		NORM–HighRiskDriver–SUPERC–DOWN–10000000000

(7) Generate a new TempClassList. This creates the SUPERC links between YoungMan and all of the members of OKList (Person). In this particular case, the new classifiers duplicate the classifiers that were generated during the definition of YoungMan.

Since duplicate messages are removed, this duplication does not affect the performance of the classifier system.

(8) Check to see if the concept Man is in the shadow, and since it is not, perform the test for Man SUBSUMES YoungMan. This succeeds and the concept Man becomes the first member of the new OKList. The queries for checking the shadow are shown below. Again, the queries for the SUBSUMESP test are not shown here.

Time Step		Message List
T35:	→	NORM–Man–SUPERC–UP–10000000000
	→	And
T36:		NORM–Person–SUPERC–UP–10000000000
		And
T37:		NORM–Thing–SUPERC–UP–10000000000
		And
	→	Quiescent
T38:		Reset
		Save
T39:		

(9) Check to see if the concept Woman is in the shadow, and since it is not, perform the test for Woman SUBSUMES YoungMan. This fails and Woman becomes the first member of the new NotOKList.

Time Step		Message List
T116:	→	NORM–Woman–SUPERC–UP–10000000000
	→	And
T117:		NORM–Person–SUPERC–UP–10000000000
		And
T118:		NORM–Thing–SUPERC–UP–10000000000
		And
	→	Quiescent
T119:		Reset
		Save
T120:		

(10) Check to see if HighRiskDriver is in the shadow, and since it is not, perform the test for HighRiskDriver SUBSUMES YoungMan. This succeeds and HighRiskDriver becomes a member of the new OKList. This is the first time that the NotOKList has been non-empty.

Time Step		Message List
T174:	→	ON–Woman–SUPERC–UP–10000000000
	→	NORM–HighRiskDriver–SUPERC–UP–10000000000
	→	And
T175:		NORM–Person–SUPERC–UP–10000000000
		ON–Woman–SUPERC–UP–10000000000
		And
	→	Quiescent
T176:		On–Woman–SUPERC–UP–10000000000
		Reset
		Save
T177:		

(11) Check to see if any members of the old OKList (Person) should be added to the MSS set. The queries to the classifier system that perform the test for step 12 are shown below.

Time Step		Message List
T307:	→	NORM–HighRiskDriver–SUPERC–UP–10000000000
	→	NORM–Man–SUPERC–UP–10000000000
T308:		NORM–Person–SUPERC–UP–10000000000
		NORM–Person–SUPERC–UP–10000000000
	→	HOLD–Person–SUPERC–UP–10000000000
	→	SetDiff
T309:		NORM–Thing–SUPERC–UP–10000000000
		SetDiff
	→	Quiescent
T310:		Save
		Reset
T311:		

The final message list is empty because Person was the only candidate to become a MSS member, and it is specialized by both Man and HighRiskDriver which are on the new OKList.

(12) Update the OKList. It will consist of the concepts Man and HighRiskDriver.

(13) Generate a new TempOKList. This is empty as determined by the following query:

Time Step		Message List
T312:	→	NORM–HighRiskDriver–SUPERC–DOWN–10000000000
	→	NORM–Man–SUPERC–DOWN–10000000000
T313:		

(14) Check to see if any members of the old OKList (Man and HighRiskDriver) should be added to the MSS list. Since both concepts have no descendants and they both subsume the concept YoungMan, they will be added to the list.

Time Step		Message List
T314:	→	HOLD–HighRiskDriver–SUPERC–UP–10000000000
	→	HOLD–Man–SUPERC–UP–10000000000
	→	SetDiff
T315:		HOLD–Man–SUPERC–UP–10000000000
		HOLD–HighRiskDriver–SUPERC–UP–10000000000
		SetDiff
	→	Quiescent
T316:		HOLD–Man–SUPERC–UP–10000000000
		HOLD–HighRiskDriver–SUPERC–UP–10000000000
		Save
		Reset
T317:		ON–Man–SUPERC–UP–10000000000
		ON–HighRiskDriver–SUPERC–UP–10000000000.

(15) The final MSSList consists of HighRiskDriver and Man.

5.2.2 Concept Subsumption

The expressive power of KL-ONE makes it impossible to compute a complete answer to the question, "does concept A Subsume concept B." Specifically, there may be implications of a particular network structure that are relevant in determining concept subsumption but do not appear explicitly in the network. This has led to the distinction between sound and complete classification procedures. The subsumption algorithms used in KL-ONE are not complete in the sense that there are certain circumstances in which the algorithm will not discover the concept subsumption between two concepts for whom the relation holds. They may be sound because the algorithms are guaranteed to not find concept subsumption in cases where it does not exist.

For example, the inclusion of number restrictions raises the possibility of combinatorial analyses of great complexity. As a very simple example, consider the following definitions:

```
(ROLESPEC Sibling (MAX 3))
(ROLESPEC OlderSibling (DIFFERENTIATES Sibling) (MIN 2))
(ROLESPEC Sister (DIFFERENTIATES Sibling) (MIN 2)).
```

From these definitions it can be inferred that there is at least one Sibling who is both an OlderSibling and a Sister (that is, an older sister). If a concept were being classified that used Sibling in its definition, this information could be relevant to the subsumption test if there were concepts that used OlderSibling or Sister in its definition. Combinatorial inferences of this sort have not been included in previous classification algorithms and are not included here.

In previous implementations, the gap between soundness and completeness has been resolved by making explicit those facts that can be discovered efficiently, or are very important, and ignoring the rest. Since the class of facts that can be discovered efficiently using parallel techniques may not be the same as those for the existing sequential algorithms, the question of which classes of inferences should be performed by a parallel algorithm has not been emphasized here. For example, the parallel implementation can test for explicit links between two concepts or two roles very quickly, but it is relatively expensive to add specific checks for unusual conditions (such as cyclic descriptions). There are some tests that the classifier system implementation does not make that the sequential version does,[5] and likewise, there are some tests that the classifier system makes that the sequential version does not.[6] One of the advantages of structured inheritance networks such as KL-ONE is the compact representation of a large body of knowledge that can be stored efficiently. Decisions made about the design of KL-ONE ensure that certain types of knowledge (properties of concepts and relations between them) are readily available and that other types are not (for example, complex combinatorial relations). Thus, the question of which inferences should be made explicit should be part of the design of the language. These issues are discussed in more detail in [17] and are not the major focus of this study.

The definition of concept subsumption that has been implemented is substantially the same as that used in NIKL. The major differences are those mentioned in the two earlier footnotes.

For any concepts A and B, A SUBSUMES B iff

(1) B has at least the same primitive characteristics as A, AND
(2) For every role r_i of A,

[5]For example, when comparing concepts, the parallel algorithm requires corresponding roles to be identical. However, in some cases (when the value and number restrictions are related in special ways) it is enough for the role of the subsuming concept to DIFFERENTIATE the role of the subsumed concept. The sequential algorithm looks for this case.

[6]When comparing two Role Value Maps, the sequential algorithm requires the corresponding Role Chains to be identical, but the parallel algorithm allows the weaker condition of differentiation.

(a) r_i is a role of B, AND

(b) The Value Restriction of r_i at A SUBSUMES the Value Restriction of r_i at B, AND

(c) The Number Restriction of r_i at B is a subset of the Number Restriction of r_i at A, AND

(3) For every Role Value Map rvm_j of A, there exists a Role Value Map rvm_k of B such that

(a) rvm_j SUBSUMES rvm_k.

The parallel algorithm for concept subsumption is not concerned with the first requirement of the definition because FindMSS guarantees that the potential subsumee has the appropriate primitive characteristics. This is because the check for primitives happens automatically in FindMSS because of the way primitives are encoded.

The tests for the second two requirements must take into account all inherited restrictions as well those that are locally defined. Restrictions for a particular concept are inherited from all of its superconcepts.

The technique used to discover a concept's inherited information involves traversing UP SuperC links from that concept to the top of the network. The traversal keeps all visited nodes on the message list. At the end of the traversal (the number of time steps is the same as the depth of the concept in the network), a single message is added to the message list to produce the relevant information. In the typical case, RoleMessage would be added to the message list and all of the inherited roles would be available at the next time step. There are at least two other possible techniques for determining a concept's inherited information. A minor modification of the above traversal would avoid keeping the visited superc nodes on the list for more than one time step. The roles (or Role Value Maps) that are attached to each concept could be generated when the traversal passes through that concept. However, this would complicate the algorithm (more classifiers would be required to keep track of which nodes were in the traversal and which nodes were roles to be inherited). Also, it is not clear that this would make the algorithm substantially more efficient.[7] Another possibility would involve a radically different representation. If the direction of the classifiers were from roles (and Role Value Maps) to the concepts to which they were attached, more unusual algorithms for finding subsumers could possibly be employed. However, this organization would make it more difficult to handle exceptions to the standard inheritance patterns, such as the complicated algorithm described for testing subsumption between Role Value Maps (see Section 5.1.7).

One possibility for checking Part 2 of the definition would be to generate all the inherited roles for the subsuming concept (A), and then check the subsumed concept (B) for each role to make sure that it met the requirements of the definition. However,

[7]It would depend on the average number of roles and role value maps that were added at each concept. If the average were greater than one, there would be no savings. If the average were less than one, then there could be fewer messages on the global message list during the traversal, which would presumably increase the efficiency of the underlying machine.

this approach can lead to a large amount of unnecessary computation. In many cases both concepts (A and B) will inherit restrictions from the same superconcepts. These shared restrictions will always satisfy the definition and therefore do not need to be considered.

The first step of the algorithm is to produce a list of superconcepts whose restrictions do need to be checked for the potential Subsumer. This list excludes all the common superconcepts of A and B and is called the SupConceptList. The purpose of maintaining the temporary classifier list during the MSS search is to minimize the size of SupConceptList by knowing the maximum number of shared superconcepts. This prevents redundant checking by removing previously checked restrictions (those checked at a previous step in the MSS search) from consideration.

The only roles (of Part 2 of the definition) and Role Value Maps (of Part 3) that must be tested are those that are explicitly restricted at a concept on SupConceptList. A list of these roles can be produced in one time step from the SupConceptList, and is called SupRoleList.

An example of how the SupConceptList is computed using the classifier system is shown below. The example is based on the network described for MSS Subsumption. Given that network, suppose that the system is trying to decide whether or not Man SUBSUMES YoungMan and suppose that it is already known that YoungMan is subsumed by Person and HighRiskDriver. The following sequence of queries produces the SupConceptList:

Time Step		Message List
T40:	→	Or
	→	NORM–Man–SUPERC–UP–10000000000
T41:		NORM–Person–SUPERC–UP–10000000000
		ON–Man–SUPERC–UP–10000000000
		Or
T42:		NORM–Thing–SUPERC–UP–10000000000
		ON–Man–SUPERC–UP–10000000000
		ON–Person–SUPERC–UP–10000000000
		Or
T43:		ON–Man–SUPERC–UP–10000000000
		ON–Person–SUPERC–UP–10000000000
		ON–Thing–SUPERC–UP–10000000000
		Or
	→	Quiescent

(continued)

Time Step		Message List
(continued)		
T44:		ON–Man–SUPERC–UP–10000000000
		ON–Person–SUPERC–UP–10000000000
		ON–Thing–SUPERC–UP–10000000000
	→	SetHold
	→	Reset
T45:		ON–Man–SUPERC–UP–10000000000
		ON–Person–SUPERC–UP–10000000000
		ON–Thing–SUPERC–UP–10000000000
T46:		HOLD–Man–SUPERC–UP–10000000000
		HOLD–Person–SUPERC–UP–10000000000
		HOLD–Thing–SUPERC–UP–10000000000
	→	SetDiff
	→	NORM–YoungMan–SUPERC–UP–10000000000
T47:		HOLD–Thing–SUPERC–UP–10000000000
		HOLD–Person–SUPERC–UP–10000000000
		HOLD–Man–SUPERC–UP–10000000000
		NORM–Person–SUPERC–UP–10000000000
		SetDiff
		NORM–Person–SUPERC–UP–10000000000
T48:		HOLD–Thing–SUPERC–UP–10000000000
		NORM–Thing–SUPERC–UP–10000000000
		HOLD–Man–SUPERC–UP–10000000000
		SetDiff
T49:		HOLD–Man–SUPERC–UP–10000000000
		SetDiff
	→	Quiescent
T50:		HOLD–Man–SUPERC–UP–10000000000
		Save
		Reset
T51:		ON–Man–SUPERC–UP–10000000000.

In the case of the potential Subsumee, it is necessary to maintain the list of all subsuming concepts and all roles that are restricted at concepts in this list. Since some of the inherited restrictions may be redundant, it is possible that the inherited information from a shared superconcept may be relevant in a test involving an unshared superconcept. For this reason, two lists are generated for the potential subsumee, the list of all subsuming concepts and the list of all roles restricted at these concepts. The lists are called SubConceptList and SubRoleList respectively.

Once the four lists (SupConceptList, SupRoleList, SubConceptList, SubRoleList) have been generated, the algorithm iterates through SupRoleList testing each role for conditions 2a, 2b, and 2c of the definition. The tests for Value Restrictions (2b) and Number Restrictions (2c) are described in the next two sections.

If the requirements for role subsumption are met, the algorithm then proceeds to the test for Role Value Maps. A list of role value maps for A is generated from the SupConceptList by placing those concepts on the message list and adding one message (RVMCheckMessage) to produce the local Role Value Maps. The subsumption test for Role Value Maps is described in a later section.

5.2.3 Value Restrictions

A role defines an ordered relation between two concepts. Value Restrictions limit the range of a role in the context of a particular concept. The domain of a role is defined to be the most general concept at which it is defined, and likewise the range is the most general value restriction. If no value restriction is mentioned for some role, its range is the top element Thing. Even if the domain concept for a role is not mentioned explicitly in the network definition, it is implicitly defined as shown by the following example:

```
(CONCEPTSPEC A (ROLE x (VRCONCEPT C)))
(CONCEPTSPEC B (ROLE x (VRCONCEPT D))).
```

In this example A and B are not related to each other, but they are both part of the domain of x. If these are the only places where x appears in the network, the actual domain for x is an unmentioned concept that is the common superconcept (union) of A and B.

Value restrictions on the range of a role are always with respect to the concept at which they are defined. Thus the expression VR(A,r_i) refers to the value restriction for the role r_i at concept A. A value restriction can be defined locally using the VRCONCEPT construct, or it can be inherited from the subsuming concepts that place value restrictions on r_i. Just as with domains and ranges, the actual value restriction for a concept may not be explicitly defined in the network. However, in the subsumption test, it is necessary to determine its components. The complete value restriction of a role at a concept is defined to be the conjunction of all value restrictions of the inherited concepts and any locally defined value restriction. The conjunction of a set of concepts is their common subconcept.

In the following example, shown pictorially in Figure 5.9, the value of VR(ThunderShower,Behavior) is the conjunction of Thunder and Rain:

```
(CONCEPTSPEC Storm (ROLE Behavior (VRCONCEPT Weather)))
(CONCEPTSPEC ThunderStorm (SPECIALIZES Storm)
   (ROLE Behavior (VRCONCEPT Thunder (SPECIALIZES Weather))))
(CONCEPTSPEC DownPour (SPECIALIZES Storm) (ROLE Behavior
   (VRCONCEPT Rain (SPECIALIZES Weather))))
(CONCEPTSPEC ThunderShower (SPECIALIZES ThunderStorm)
   (SPECIALIZES DownPour)).
```

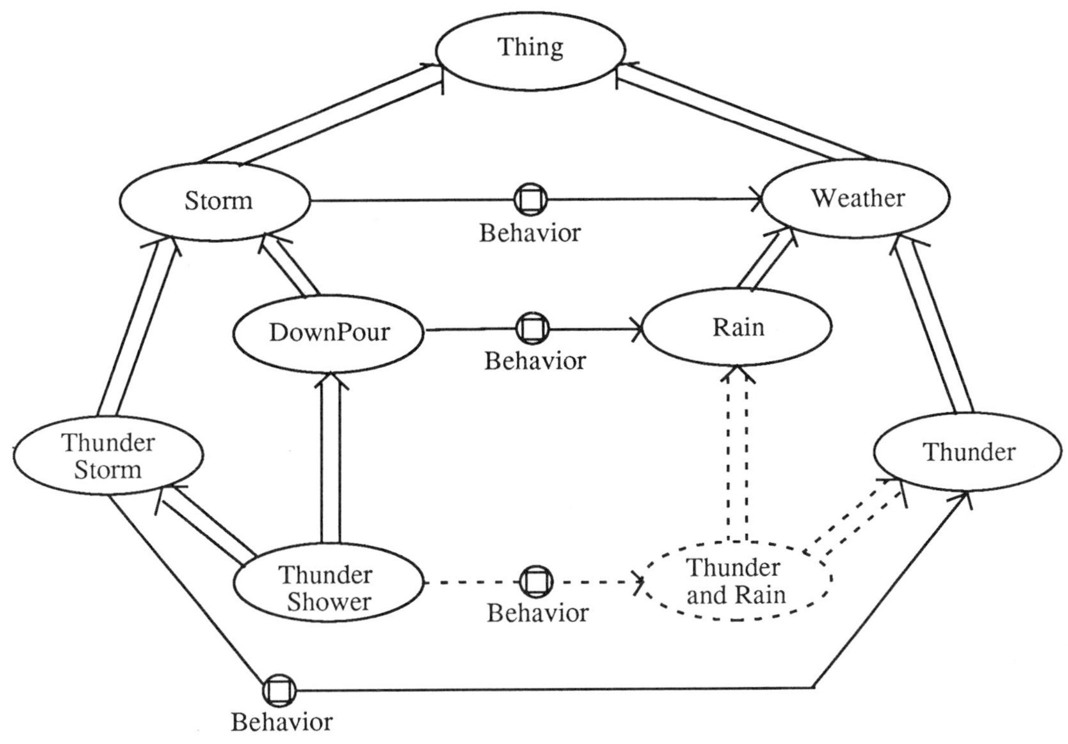

FIGURE 5.9 Example Value Restriction

The classifier system finds the value restriction for a concept by first taking the set of relevant superconcepts (see discussion of SupConceptList or SubConceptList) and then adding the role message for the appropriate role (Behavior in the above example) and the "VR" message. After one time step, all of the relevant value restrictions are on the message list. The actual value restriction is the conjunction of the most specific concepts on this list. The concept representing the inferred value restriction is never constructed. It is sufficient for the purposes of the test to generate the set of concepts that define the value restriction.

Returning to the previous example and assuming that ThunderShower's relevant concepts are DownPour, Thunderstorm, and Storm, the algorithm would compute VR(ThunderShower,x) as follows:

(1) Place ThunderShower, DownPour, ThunderStorm, and Storm on the initial message list as shown in step 2. In the context of the concept subsumption test (in function FindVR1), these messages will already be on the message list as the result of a previous query.

(2) Add the Behavior and VR messages and run the classifier system for one time step. It is also necessary to add the "reset" message which halts a propagation UP from the initial message list in subsequent time steps. After one time step, the messages on the list represent the value restrictions of Behavior at the concepts on the initial message list.

Time Step	Message List
T0:	NORM–ThunderShower–SUPERC–UP–00000000000
	NORM–DownPour–SUPERC–UP–00000000000
	NORM–ThunderStorm–SUPERC–UP–00000000000
	NORM–Storm–SUPERC–UP–00000000000
	→ NORM–Behavior–DIFF–UP–00000000000
	→ VR
	→ Reset
T1:	NORM–Part–DIFF–UP–00000000000
	ON–Weather–SUPERC–UP–00000000000
	ON–Thunder–SUPERC–UP–10000000000
	ON–Rain–SUPERC–UP–01000000000
	→ ResetNorm
	→ SetHold
	→ Reset.

(3) Get the most specific of these concepts. The method for obtaining these most specific concepts can be thought of as:

(a) let A = the original set (Rain, Thunder, and Weather).

(b) let B = immediate subsumers of A (Weather and Thing).

(c) let B′ = all subsumers of B (Weather and Thing).[8]

(d) A − B′ = the desired set (Rain and Thunder).

The queries to the classifier system that perform this test are as follows:

Time Step	Message List
T2:	NORM–Weather–SUPERC–UP–00000000000
	NORM–Thunder–SUPERC–UP–10000000000
	NORM–Rain–SUPERC–UP–01000000000
	HOLD–Weather–SUPERC–UP–00000000000
	HOLD–Thunder–SUPERC–UP–10000000000
	HOLD–Rain–SUPERC–UP–01000000000

(continued)

[8]Since subsumption and differentiation are partially ordered, they are reflexive.

Time Step		Message List
(continued)		
T3:		NORM–Weather–SUPERC–UP–10000000000
		NORM–Weather–SUPERC–UP–01000000000
		NORM–Weather–SUPERC–UP–00000000000
		HOLD–Weather–SUPERC–UP–00000000000
		HOLD–Thunder–SUPERC–UP–10000000000
		HOLD–Rain–SUPERC–UP–01000000000
	→	SetDiff
T4:		HOLD–Thunder–SUPERC–UP–10000000000
		HOLD–Rain–SUPERC–UP–01000000000
		SetDiff
T5:		HOLD–Thunder–SUPERC–UP–10000000000
		HOLD–Rain–SUPERC–UP–01000000000
		SetDiff
	→	Quiescent
T6:		HOLD–Thunder–SUPERC–UP–10000000000
		HOLD–Rain–SUPERC–UP–01000000000
		Save
		Reset
T7:		ON–Thunder–SUPERC–UP–10000000000
		ON–Rain–SUPERC–UP–01000000000.

This sequence of queries demonstrates how the value restriction is found for one concept.

In checking for subsumption of role restrictions, the value restrictions for both the Subsumer and the Subsumee are compared. This is, in effect, another test for concept subsumption, since both value restrictions are concepts, or possibly a concept that conjoins several concepts. In theory, it would be possible at this point to call recursively the concept subsumption routine with the two value restrictions. However, if all concepts that have been previously defined in the network have also been classified, it suffices to see if the value restriction of the Subsumee SPECIALIZES the value restriction of the Subsumer. Since the concept representing the inferred value restriction may not be explicitly present in the network, the parallel algorithm uses the list of concepts that form the value restriction. If A is the value restriction set for the Subsumer and B is the value restriction set for the Subsumee, B specializes A iff every a_i in A is specialized by some b_j in B. This is formulated to the classifier system as the following set of queries:

```
let B′ = all superc′s of B
let C = B′ - A.
```

If C is empty, then B specializes A.

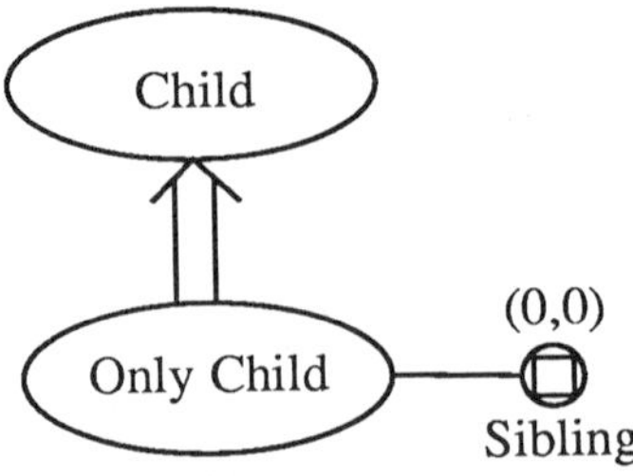

FIGURE 5.10 Example Number Restriction

5.2.4 Number Restrictions

Number restrictions place limitations on the minimum and maximum number of role fillers an instance may have. There are two types of number restrictions: MAX and MIN. For example, an only child is defined to be a child with no siblings. This could be expressed in KL-ONE (see Figure 5.10) as

```
(CONCEPTSPEC OnlyChild (SPECIALIZES Child)
   (ROLE siblings (MAX 0) (MIN 0)).
```

Number restrictions in KL-ONE are limited to the natural numbers. The default MIN restriction for a concept is zero and the default MAX restriction is infinity. MIN restrictions are processed separately from MAX restrictions, but both are handled similarly. They are inherited according to the same rules as value restrictions with one exception. The intersection of several value restrictions (concepts) is the concept that represents the conjunction of those concepts. The intersection of several MAX restrictions is the minimum of them, and the intersection of several MIN restrictions is the maximum of them. Note also that taking the minimum of a set of MAX restrictions (and the maximum of a set of MIN restrictions) produces the same result as taking the intersection of a set of intervals over the natural numbers. Thus, the difference in treatment between value and number restrictions is one of method rather than substance. There is one substantive difference, however. It is always possible to form the conjunction of a set of concepts, but it is not always possible to find a non-empty intersection of a set of number restrictions. In the implementation it is possible to define a concept with a MAX restriction of six and a MIN restriction of ten. This is one example of how concepts can be defined in KL-ONE that would never have an extension in any imaginable world.

The parallel algorithm for finding number restrictions is similar to that for value restrictions. It generates the set of MAX restrictions for a given concept by placing the message "MAX" on the message list instead of "VR." The minimum of this set is found using the MinSort set of classifiers that are described in Chapter 4. This produces one value which is the MAX restriction for this concept. A similar procedure is followed for MIN restrictions.

To test for subsumption, the maximum and minimum restrictions are found for the potential Subsumer and Subsumee. The two maximum restrictions and the two minimum restrictions are compared using the Compare classifiers and queries that will be described elsewhere. If the MAX restriction of the Subsumer is greater than or equal to the MAX restriction of the Subsumee, and likewise if the MIN restriction of the Subsumer is less than or equal to the MIN restriction of the Subsumee, the subsumption criteria have been met.

5.2.5 Role Value Map Subsumption

The subsumption algorithms for the classifier system assume that Role Value Maps are always in the canonical form, "<." However, by way of introduction, the "=" case will also be considered.

For a concept defined with an "=" Role Value Map A to SUBSUME a concept with an "=" Role Value Map B, A and B must have identical role chains. As an example, consider a concept PersonA whose cousins are the same as her good friends, a concept PersonB whose first cousins are the same as her best friends, and a concept PersonC whose relatives are the same as her friends. The KL-ONE descriptions of these concepts (also shown in Figure 5.11) are:

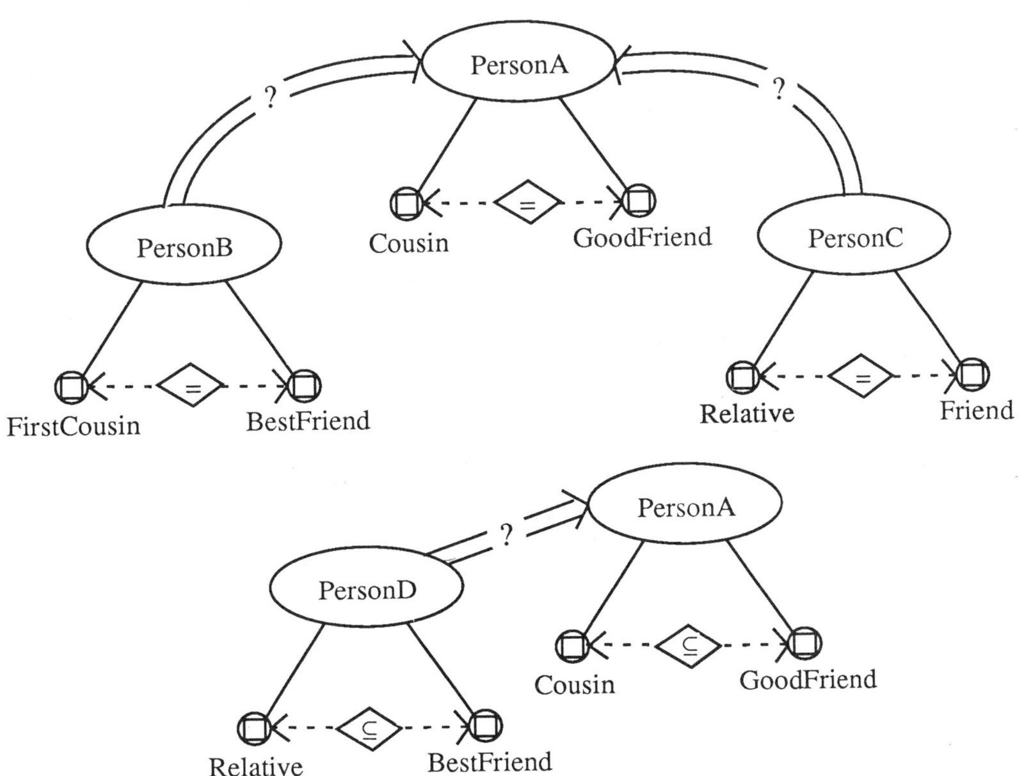

FIGURE 5.11 Subsumption of Role Value Maps

```
(CONCEPTSPEC PersonA (ROLE Cousin) (ROLE GoodFriend)
   (= Cousin GoodFriend))
(CONCEPTSPEC PersonB (ROLE FirstCousin) (ROLE BestFriend)
   (= FirstCousin BestFriend))
(CONCEPTSPEC PersonC (ROLE Relative) (ROLE Friend)
   (= Relative Friend)).
```

This example illustrates the reason that identical corresponding Role Chains are required for subsumption. Intuitively, the subsumed RVM cannot be more specific, as in the case of PersonB, because the fact that all PersonB's first cousins are her best friends does not imply that all of her cousins are good friends. Likewise, the subsumed RVM cannot be more general, as in the case of PersonC, since the fact that all of one's relatives are friends says nothing about whether all of one's cousins are good friends. Therefore, the role chains must be identical.

The requirement for identical Role Value Maps could easily be checked in the classifier system using a much less complicated set of classifiers than those generated for subsets. Specifically, the identical Role Value Maps test could be accomplished without performing the test for Differentiation or any synchronization. Since the subset relation is the more general case, it was selected for implementation, and identity maps are processed as a special case of subset maps.

By rearranging the above KL-ONE example, it is easy to see that the requirement for identical Role Chains can be relaxed in the subset case. Consider the following definition:

```
(CONCEPTSPEC PersonA' (ROLE Cousin) (ROLE GoodFriend)
   (< Cousin GoodFriend))

(CONCEPTSPEC PersonD (ROLE Relative) (ROLE BestFriend)
   (< Relative BestFriend)).
```

Further, assume that the set of BestFriends is a subset of the set of GoodFriends (the role BestFriend DIFFERENTIATES the role GoodFriend) and assume that the set of Cousins is a subset of the set of Relatives (the role Cousin DIFFERENTIATES the role Relative). This means that the definitions

```
(ROLESPEC BestFriend (DIFFERENTIATES GoodFriend))
(ROLESPEC Cousin (DIFFERENTIATES Relative))
```

exist elsewhere in the network. In this case PersonD is subsumed by PersonA′, since the definition that all of PersonD's relatives are also best friends implies that all of PersonD's cousins are also good friends. It is sufficient for the subsumee that a role (e.g., Relatives) that is differentiated by the corresponding role of the subsumer (e.g., Cousins) is a subset (<) of a role (e.g., BestFriends) that DIFFERENTIATES the corresponding role of the subsumer (e.g., GoodFriends). This is an example of the kind of information that can be implicit in a network even if it is not explicitly mentioned. Thus, Part 2 of the following definition requires reasoning about implicit rather than explicit knowledge.

Requirement 3a of the definition for concept subsumption can now be refined as follows:

RVM_j SUBSUMES RVM_k iff

(1) Every role in the first (LEFT) Role Chain of RVM_j DIFFERENTIATES the corresponding role in the first Role Chain of RVM_k, AND

(2) Every role in the second (RIGHT) Role Chain of RVM_k DIFFERENTIATES the corresponding role in the second Role Chain of RVM_j.

The definition assumes that RVM_j and RVM_k are in the canonical form "<."

This definition establishes the two conditions that must be met for subsumption: (1) that the corresponding role chains be in one-to-one correspondence and (2) that the proper DIFFERENTIATES relation holds between the corresponding roles. These requirements must be met for both sets of role chains (first and second). The classifiers that have been designed to represent Role Value Maps allow both requirements to be checked simultaneously for both sets of Role Chains. In order to exhibit the full Role Value Map subsumption algorithm, it is necessary to extend the example to include a role chain. For brevity, the role chain will only contain two roles, but this is sufficient to show how the synchronization works. Consider the following network (shown pictorially in Figure 5.12):

```
(CONCEPTSPEC PersonWithGodParents (ROLE GodFather)
   (ROLE GodMother))
(ROLESPEC Relative PRIMITIVE))
(ROLESPEC Cousin (DIFFERENTIATES Relative))
(ROLESPEC GoodFriend PRIMITIVE)
(ROLESPEC BestFriend (DIFFERENTIATES GoodFriend))
(CONCEPTSPEC Person PRIMITIVE (ROLE Cousin) (ROLE GoodFriend))
(CONCEPTSPEC PersonA
   (ROLE Cousin (VRCONCEPT PersonWithGodParents))
   (SPECIALIZES Person)
   (< (Cousin GodFather) GoodFriend))
(CONCEPTSPEC PersonD
   (SPECIALIZES Person)
   (ROLE Relative (VRCONCEPT PersonWithGodParents))
   (ROLE BestFriend)
   (< (Relative GodFather) BestFriend))).
```

The classifiers relevant to RVM subsumption for this example are shown in Appendix H. The queries to test RVM subsumption between PersonA and PersonD are shown and annotated below.

(1) Find all Role Value Maps that need to be checked by adding the "rvmcheck" and "reset" messages to SupConceptList. The result is one Role Value Map (identified by "1").

Time Step		Message List
T0:	→	ON–PersonA–SUPERC–UP–(PRIM PersonA)
	→	RVMCheck
	→	Reset
T1:		RVM–PersonA–SUPERC–UP–nil–1.

(2) Find all Role Value Maps that pertain to the subsumee (PersonD) by adding the appropriate messages to SubConceptList. The result is also one map (identified by "2").

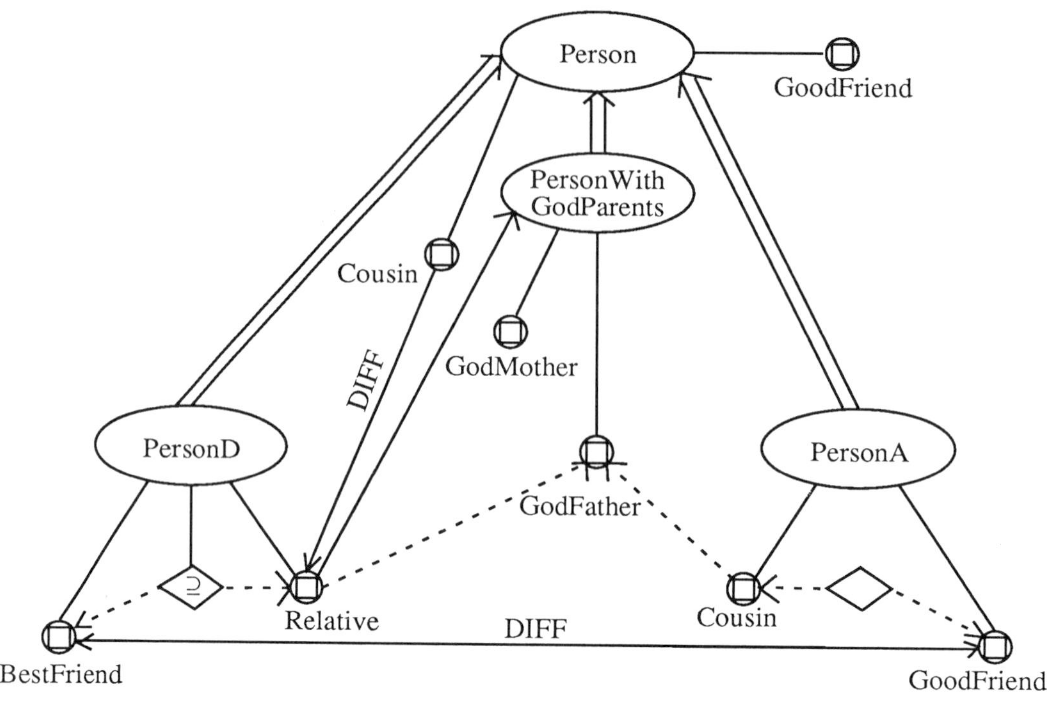

FIGURE 5.12 Example of Role Value Map Subsumption

Time Step	Message List
T2:	→ ON–PersonD–SUPERC–UP–(PRIM PersonD) → ON–Person–SUPERC–UP–(PRIM Person) → ON–Thing–SUPERC–UP–(PRIM Thing) → RVMCheck → Reset
T3:	RVM–PersonD–SUPERC–UP–nil–2.

(3) Begin the propagation with one message for all four role chains that are being considered. The first link of the chain is reached by a traversal from the concept at which the the chain originates to the chain's first role. There will be four separate propagations, one for each side of the Role Value Maps. They are uniquely identified by direction (LEFT and RIGHT) and by the designators (AFIELD and BFIELD). AFIELD and BFIELD designators control which role chain initiates propagations up DIFFERENTIATES links. The propagation always begins from the role that is traversed by a message with BFIELD set. On the lefthand role chains, this will be the subsuming chain; on the righthand chains, it will be subsumed chain. The Undelay messages are added so that the traversal can proceed to the next (in this

case the first) link of the chain. The RVMCheck2 message is present throughout this sequence of queries to prevent interference with other general purpose classifiers. The initial message list is set up here, and system runs the entire test with no additional reading or writing from the external command processor.

Time Step		Message List
T4:	→	RVM–PersonA–LEFT–nil–BFIELD–1
	→	RVM–PersonA–RIGHT–nil–AFIELD–1
	→	RVM–PersonD–LEFT–nil–AFIELD–2
	→	RVM–PersonD–RIGHT–nil–BFIELD–2
	→	LeftUndelay
	→	RightUndelay
	→	RVMCheck2

(4) The delay message is now set on both sides, so that traversal across the chain will be held up until the relations between the various roles have been established. In this example, it will be established for both sides in one time step. However, it is possible that it would take different amounts of time for each side. In this case, the right and left sides would proceed independently, not being forced to wait for the slower of the two. The propagation up DIFFERENTIATES links is initiated from the Cousin and BestFriend roles. The four roles stay in a "holding pattern" until the DIFFERENTIATES tests are completed and Undelay messages placed on the message list.

Time Step	Message List
T5:	NORM–Cousin–DIFF–UP–BFIELD–1
	RVM–Cousin–LEFT–nil–BFIELD–1
	RVM–GoodFriend–RIGHT–nil–AFIELD–1
	RVM–Relative–LEFT–nil–AFIELD–2
	NORM–BestFriend–DIFF–UP–BFIELD–2
	RVM–BestFriend–RIGHT–nil–BFIELD–2
	RightDelay
	LeftDelay
	RVMCheck2
T6:	NORM–Relative–DIFF–UP–BFIELD–1
	NORM–GoodFriend–DIFF–UP–BFIELD–2
	RightDelay
	LeftDelay
	RVMCheck2
	RVM–GoodFriend–RIGHT–nil–AFIELD–1
	RVM–BestFriend–RIGHT–nil–BFIELD–2
	RVM–Cousin–LEFT–nil–BFIELD–1
	RVM–Relative–LEFT–nil–AFIELD–2

(5) Both tests are successfully completed and the undelay messages placed on the list. The propagation up DIFFERENTIATES links continues (through Part) but does not interfere in the computation. (This could be a problem in deep networks and should probably be changed.) The classifiers producing the delay messages have no *a priori* way to know that the delay message is not needed until after the undelay message has appeared. Therefore, it will take one more time step for the classifiers to be turned off.

Time Step	Message List
T7:	NORM–Part–DIFF–UP–BFIELD–1
	NORM–Part–DIFF–UP–BFIELD–2
	RightUndelay
	LeftUndelay
	RightDelay
	LeftDelay
	RVMCheck2
	RVM–GoodFriend–RIGHT–nil–AFIELD–1
	RVM–BestFriend–RIGHT–nil–BFIELD–2
	RVM–Cousin–LEFT–nil–BFIELD–1
	RVM–Relative–LEFT–nil–AFIELD–2

(6) The Undelay messages allow the propagation to continue to the next set of roles. However, on the right side this is the end of the chain. One classifier checks to see if both right role chains are terminated in the same time step. Three conditions must be met: (1) the RightDelay message is on, (2) there is no AFIELD message in the right direction, and (3) there is no BFIELD message in the right direction. If these conditions are met, the role chain test has proceeded to completion for the right side and the "RightOK" message is emitted. On the left side, both role chains pass through the same role (GodFather). This does not interfere with the processing as the AFIELD and BFIELD designators keep the two chains distinct.

Time Step	Message List
T8:	NORM–GodFather–DIFF–UP–BFIELD–1
	RVM–GodFather–LEFT–nil–BFIELD–1
	RVM–GodFather–LEFT–nil–AFIELD–2
	RightUndelay
	LeftUndelay
	RVMCheck2
	RVM–GoodFriend–RIGHT–nil–AFIELD–1
	RVM–BestFriend–RIGHT–nil–BFIELD–2
	RVM–Cousin–LEFT–nil–BFIELD–1
	RVM–Relative–LEFT–nil–AFIELD–2

(continued)

Time Step	Message List
(continued)	
T9:	NORM–Part–DIFF–UP–BFIELD–1 NORM–GodFather–DIFF–UP–BFIELD–1 RVM–GodFather–LEFT–nil–BFIELD–1 RVM–GodFather–LEFT–nil–AFIELD–2 RightDelay LeftDelay RVMCheck2
T10:	NORM–Part–DIFF–UP–BFIELD–1 LeftUndelay LeftUndelay RightDelay LeftDelay RVMCheck2 RightOK RVM–GodFather–LEFT–nil–BFIELD–1 RVM–GodFather–LEFT–nil–AFIELD–2

(7) The differentiation test is completed for the left side (GodFather DIFFERENTIATES GodFather) and the traversal continues. Since GodFather is the last role in both role chains, the left side traversal is terminated successfully, and the "LeftOK" message is emitted.

Time Step	Message List
T10:	RightDelay LeftUndelay RVMcheck2 RightOK RVM–GodFather–LEFT–nil–BFIELD–1 RVM–GodFather–LEFT–nil–AFIELD–2
T11:	RightDelay LeftUndelay RVMcheck2 RightOK RVM–GodFather–LEFT–nil–BFIELD–1 RVM–GodFather–LEFT–nil–AFIELD–2
(continued)	

Time Step	Message List
(continued)	
T12:	RightDelay LeftDelay RVMCheck2 RightOK
T13:	RightDelay LeftDelay RVMCheck2 RightOK LeftOK

(8) When both the LeftOK and RightOK messages appear, a classifier is activated that puts the "True" message on the list. The message list then stays in the same state until the QuiescentRVM message is added which removes all the extraneous messages, leaving either a True message (if the test was successful as in this case) or a False message (if unsuccessful).

Time Step	Message List
T14:	RightDelay LeftDelay RVMCheck2 Rightok LeftOK True
T15:	True RightDelay LeftDelay RVMCheck2 RightOK LeftOK True
(continued)	

Time Step		Message List
(continued)		
T16:		True
		RightDelay
		LeftDelay
		RVMCheck2
		RightOK
		LeftOK
		True
T17:	→	QuiescentRVM
		True
		RightDelay
		LeftDelay
		RVMCheck2
		RightOK
		LeftOK
		True
T18:		True
		True.

The command processor reads the True message off the final message list and is able to conclude that the Role Value Map of A SUBSUMES the Role Value Map of D. If the subsumption test had failed during the course of the computation, the False message would have appeared on the final message list.

5.3 Summary

This chapter has shown how KL-ONE networks can be represented using the classifier system. In addition, it has demonstrated how to use the classifier system representation to find the set of Most Specific Subsumers for an incoming concept in which all of the concept's subparts have been previously classified. The parallel algorithms for finding MSS nodes have been divided into five natural parts and presented independently. To see how the five parts work together, the major example (from the MSS section) has been extended in Appendix J and the algorithm has been run on this example. The program output for this example is also in Appendix K.

6 Analysis of Results

This chapter discusses the complexity of the parallel KL-ONE operations described in Chapter 5. In sequential systems, two measures of complexity, space and time, are commonly used. With the introduction of parallelism, however, two additional measures are relevant. These are: the number of processors in the system (in sequential systems this is always one) and the amount of inter-processor communication (in sequential systems there is none because there is only one processor). The discussion of complexity for KL-ONE uses all four measures (length of computation, size of each processor, number of processors, and amount of inter-processor communication). For classifier systems the four measures are interpreted as: the number of time steps required to complete a computation, the number and length of conditions for each classifier, the number of classifiers used to represent a KL-ONE network, and the size of the message list that is used to send messages from one classifier to another. Each of the four components is discussed and then the results are compared with an idealized sequential algorithm.

The following assumptions are made about the behavior of the classifier system (see Chapter 4): (1) all positions in a condition are matched against all bits in a message simultaneously, (2) one condition is matched against all messages on the message list simultaneously, (3) all conditions of one classifier are matched simultaneously, (4) all classifiers in a classifier system are matched simultaneously, and (5) all classifiers are allowed to post their output messages to the message list simultaneously. In addition, I make the assumption that the time it takes each classifier to be matched against the message list is insignificant compared to the time it takes to process the output messages. Thus, the size of the message list (degree of inter-processor communication) does not significantly affect the time complexity of the system. If the size of the message list were the same order of magnitude as the number of classifiers, this assumption would be unreasonable. However, both for the deterministic algorithms of Chapters 4 and 5 and for learning classifier systems, the message list is restricted to a small fraction of the total number of classifiers. The implications of relaxing this final assumption are explored in the section on computational tradeoffs.

For the purposes of comparison with sequential algorithms, it is necessary to assume that the networks being processed are large enough to make redundant storage of data infeasible. This removes the possibility of optimizations peculiar to either algorithm influencing the overall complexity, such as local storage of inherited properties. We are primarily concerned with the amount of improvement that can generally be expected from using parallelism as well as the specific improvements obtained through this implementation. Also, the intent of structured inheritance networks is that they be used to represent and organize large amounts of information. For small systems, other organizations might be more appropriate.

Several assumptions are made about the topology of a typical network. These assumptions have a direct effect on the comparison of parallel and sequential algorithms. They are discussed in detail in the fourth section of this chapter.

Finally, a number of "technical" assumptions are mentioned in this chapter that are implementation artifacts and not deep philosophical points. Thus, assumptions about the minimum number of primitive characteristics in the system and the depth of the role lattice are included for completeness, but they are not crucial to the system's overall complexity.

The following definitions are used throughout this chapter.

C = the number of concepts in the network;

D = the depth of the network (this corresponds to how many SUPERC links it takes to reach Thing from the lowest concept in the search);

E = the mean fan–out per concept (this is the mean number of subconcepts (SUBCs) for every concept in the network);

F = the mean fan–in per concept (this is the mean number of superconcepts (SUPCs) for every concept in the network);

L = the current level of depth in the network (this will range from 1 to D);

R = the mean number of new roles or additional restrictions to existing roles that are defined at every concept;

S = the mean number of new Role Value Maps (RVMs) that are defined at each concept. An "=" RVM counts as two subset("<")RVMs;

T = the length of the longest role chain;

A = the number of SUPERC links in the network (this can be approximated by $(E - F) \times C$);

B = the number of primitive marks in the network;

V = the number of value restrictions in the network;

M = the number of MAX restrictions in the network;

N = the number of MIN restrictions in the network;

P = the number of Role Value Maps in the network;

Q = the number of role chain links in the network;

K = the number of overhead classifiers associated with each network (for this implementation, $K = 94$).

6.1 Time of Computation

The number of time steps that the classifier system iterates is interpreted as the measure of its time complexity for a given operation. Thus, a "time step" is defined to be one cycle of the classifier system, during which a message list is matched against the classifier list and all of the classifiers that are matched write their output messages back to the refreshed message list.

The calculations make the simplifying assumption that the depth of the "role lattice" is less than or equal to the depth of the concept lattice. The organization of concepts into a lattice is an often-emphasized feature of KL-ONE (see Chapter 2). Less frequently mentioned is the corresponding partially ordered structure for roles. We assume that the latter structure is no deeper than the former. As a result of this assumption, the time to search the role lattice, which is implicitly part of the SubsumesP operation, is expressed in terms of D instead of some the depth of the role lattice. This is a reasonable assumption because the emphasis in most KL-ONE networks is on defining concepts rather than roles. Hence, it is expected that the number of different concepts and their depth is much greater than the number of different roles.

The number of time steps for the entire SubsumesP test is most easily calculated by considering the various subparts of the test. The worst-case time complexity of the SubsumesP subparts is[1]:

SubsumesP: $(3 \times D) + (R \times [\text{RoleSubsumesP}]) + [\text{RVMSubsumesP}] + 12$;

RoleSubsumesP (the test to determine whether the role restriction at one concept subsumes the role restriction at another concept): $(3 \times D) + 17 + [\text{NRSubsumesP}]$;

NRSubsumesP (the test to determine whether the number restriction of a role at a concept subsumes the number restriction of the same role at another concept): $(2 \times D) + 22$;

RVMSubsumesP (the test to determine whether the RVMs at one concept are subsumed by the RVMs at another concept): $S^2 \times ((T \times D) + 1)$.

Combining these results yields the following formula for the time complexity of SubsumesP:

$$3D + 5RD + S^2TD + 39R + S^2 + 12.$$

Since R, S, and T are fixed for a given network (by definition), the time complexity for SubsumesP is linearly proportional to D. However, it is important to know how the magnitudes of R, S, and T compare with that of D. In the absence of empirical data, the answer is somewhat speculative, but it is possible to make the following observations. First, it seems likely that R and S will be small constants (possibly near 1) for most networks. High values of R and S would indicate a structure in which definitions of new concepts were not composed from simpler components (more general concepts). Instead, most concepts would have complex local definitions and correspondingly fewer connections (SuperC links) to other concepts. Second, T (the length of the longest role chain) will probably be small but not as small as R and S. As discussed earlier, the emphasis in most networks is on defining concepts and using roles to support these definitions. In this context, it seems unlikely that the composition of roles into role

[1]The notation "[Operation]" refers to the time complexity of the operation that appears between the brackets.

chains will be useful beyond some relatively small number. Since this is one place where the capability of the parallel algorithm exceeds that of the sequential version, it would be easy to reduce the S^2TD term were the length of role chains ever a problem.

The search for MSS nodes as implemented in the classifier system is essentially a breadth-first search through the network. At each level of the search for the MSS set for concept X, all of the concepts for that level are submitted to the SubsumesP test with two exceptions: (1) any concepts that are "primitively incompatible" with X are not checked, and (2) any concepts that are in the "shadow" (see Chapter 5) are not checked. These two exceptions are explained below.

Any concepts whose primitive marks are incompatible with those of X are not considered for the SubsumesP test. The primitive information is "compiled" into classifiers that represent the network (see Chapter 5 for details). This has the effect of blocking the traversal through the network at nodes whose primitive information is not compatible with that of the concept being classified. This is a maximally efficient way to eliminate concepts from the search that are primitively incompatible with X. However, this could create space problems if there were an excessive number of different primitive marks. In any reasonably constructed network the number of primitive marks should be small with respect to the total number of concepts in the network. In cases where the proportion of primitive marks is high, the network can be best thought of as a feature detector, with each primitive mark acting as one feature. For this kind of behavior, the full representational power of KL-ONE would not be required. The property that gives KL-ONE its expressive power is the ability to compose definitions of new concepts from existing ones. The overall effect of primitive marks on the performance of the algorithm should be insignificant, except perhaps in the upper regions of the network. I therefore make this assumption in my calculations and do not account for primitives. If primitive marks were considered, the measure of the performance of the algorithm would be improved.

The second exception involves networks in which concepts have more than one SUPC (the structure is not a tree). A tree can be pruned by using only those concepts that pass the subsumption test to generate the next set of SUBCs. When the structure is not a tree, pruning is more complicated. Once a concept Y fails the subsumption test, it can be inferred (by transitivity) that all of Y's descendents will also fail the subsumption test. However, it may be possible for one of Y's descendents to be tested for subsumption as the result of a different path of (successful) SUPERC links. In Chapter 5, the notion of a "shadow" was introduced to describe the effect that failed subsumption tests should have on the pruning of the structure to be searched. The implemented algorithm is able to use a parallel operation to determine whether or not a concept is in the "shadow" of nodes that have already failed the subsumption test. This allows the parallel algorithm to check the shadow in L time steps, rather than in the same number of time steps as the number of nodes above X in the network.

In the implementation, all of the nodes at a given level that need to be checked for subsumption (those that have primitive marks which are compatible with X and are not specializers of a concept that has already failed) are checked one at a time, or sequentially. By adding one field to the definition of classifier record it would be possible to perform all of these tests simultaneously by adding one additional level of parallelism. Conceptually, this can be viewed as having n different message lists available if n is the number of nodes that need to be checked. If it were possible to add arbitrarily many message lists (that is, to expand the size of the one global list) with no appreciable cost, then it would no longer be so important to determine whether or not a node was in the shadow. One conceptual message list would be required for every node at a given level. The algorithm would still process each level sequentially but all nodes that were at the same level would be processed simultaneously. If, on the other hand, the possible increase in the number of message lists is limited to a small, finite number, then checking the shadow is worthwhile and might limit the number of concepts to be checked at each level to a small constant.

With this additional layer of parallelism, which is fairly easy to add, the complexity of the MSS search (with the SubsumesP test embedded in it) would be $\mathbf{O}(D^2)$, and the maximum size of the message list would be increased by a constant factor. If it were assumed that arbitrarily many message lists were available, eliminating the check for the shadow, the complexity of the complete MSS operation would be $\mathbf{O}(D)$.

6.2 Number and Size of Processors

The number of processors (classifiers) and their size is interpreted as the measure of the space requirements for the system. There are three components that contribute to the system's space complexity: the number of classifiers, the number of conditions in each classifier, and the length of each condition. According to the first component, the number of classifiers required to represent a KL-ONE network is directly proportional to the length of the definition. That is, a constant number of classifiers is generated for each KL-ONE construct that appears in the definition. With the exception of a few overhead classifiers (the predefined classifiers that are loaded in with every network), the classifiers in the implemented system never have more than three conditions. Thus, the number of conditions can be considered as constant and discarded from the calculations. The length of each condition increases as the logarithm of the total number of concepts and roles in the network and linearly with the number of primitive marks. As discussed above, this requirement on primitives is not serious because it is reasonable to expect a very small proportion of primitives in most networks.

The number of classifiers generated for any network is given below:

$$N_1 = 2(C + R) + 2A + R + S + V + M + N + P + 3Q + K. \tag{6.1}$$

The length of each classifier used to represent this network is given by the formula[2]:

$$N_2 = \log_2(C + R) + B + 11. \tag{6.2}$$

The number of conditions per classifier used in this representation is never greater than 3.

Combining these three measures produces a formula for the total space requirements of the system:

$$N_3 = N_1 N_2. \tag{6.3}$$

[2]More precisely, B should be replaced by max(B,8) since 8 is the lower bound of bits needed for non-"structural" record variants (see Chapter 5). These bits are needed even if the number of primitive marks in the system is less than 8.

Equation 6.1 is the most pertinent as a standard of comparison with the sequential algorithm. Equation 6.2 is analogous to the number of bytes that are available at each memory location in a conventional memory. In principle, the word-size requirements would be expected to increase with large enough networks on a conventional computer in the same way that they do for the classifier system. Since the requirements increase very slowly in both cases, they will not have a significant effect on the design of either system. Therefore, Eq. 6.1 is the appropriate measure of space complexity for this system. Based on this measure, the classifier system implementation uses a number of processors that is directly proportional to the size of the input definition.

6.3 Inter-Processor Communication

For a classifier system, the obvious measure of inter-processor communication is the size of the global message list. Analysis of the size requirements for the message list is based on the assumption that the message list must be big enough to accommodate the largest message list ever generated in the course of a computation, even if the actual size is much less for most time steps. It is also assumed that every classifier must read every message at every time step. Several proposals have been made for relaxing the second assumption should the classifier system be implemented in hardware, but the implications of this are not explored here.

The maximum-size message list required to perform the MSS and SubsumesP computations is related to the structure of the particular network. First, some boundary conditions are discussed, then a formula for the general case is given, and finally there is a discussion of message list size for networks that conform to a "reasonable" set of assumptions.

Two extreme network structures that need to be considered are a tree ($F = 1$) and a network in which all the fan-out happens at the top node and, for all other nodes, E (fan-out) is equal to one. This second case can be thought of as an inverted tree with one additional node on top of it. In the first case (a tree), the maximum message list size will be proportional to the depth of the tree (D), which is approximately $\log_E C$. This can be seen intuitively by considering that the basic propagation through the network is in the UP direction. If the fan-in (F) is one, there will be only one node added to the message list at every time step. If the propagation runs for D time steps, there will be a maximum of D messages collected on the message list at the end of the propagation.

In the case of an inverted tree, the maximum message list size will be C. That is, a typical UP propagation will result in every concept in the network (to the depth of D) being placed on the message list. Fortunately, this kind of network structure is highly unlikely (see below).

In general, the maximum size of the message list required for a network is given by:

$$\text{maximum size} = \begin{cases} (F - E)^D & \text{if } E < F; \\ D & \text{Otherwise.} \end{cases}$$

There is little to be gained, either computationally or conceptually, by organizing data into a structured inheritance network unless E is generally greater than F. A network in which the only important distinctions between classes are made at the highest levels loses the advantages of inheritance and the ability to refine general concepts into more specific subcases. In the extreme case of an inverted tree, all possible distinct classes would be enumerated at the highest level, and the lower-level concepts would represent the possible subsets of the initial enumeration. Organizing the data strictly into a tree fails to take advantage of the compositional power of combining two concepts to form a third (for example, the concept WindSurfing can be formed as the conjunction of Sailing and Surfing). It is reasonable to assume that in most useful cases, the fan-out (E) will be greater than the fan-in (F). With this assumption, the size of the message list will be proportional to the depth of the network. This assumes that the fan-out and fan-in are relatively constant at different depths in the network and can be reasonably approximated by the averages E and F. This is probably not a reasonable assumption and possible refinements of it are discussed later.

6.4 Comparison with Sequential Algorithm

Since a careful complexity analysis of the original sequential algorithm does not exist, it is difficult to discuss the improvements obtained by the parallel algorithm. Furthermore, the "standard" classification algorithm was formulated as a Lisp program[85] and used many shortcuts (for example, taking advantage of modern hardware that offers large real memory spaces to store many "inherited" properties locally).

As a basis for comparison, an idealized sequential algorithm is described and compared with the results obtained by using parallelism. The parallel implementation described here can be viewed as an idealized version as well. There are several tricks that could be used to make the parallel version more efficient if it were intended to be used on real networks. For example, it would be possible to accomplish the equivalent of storing relevant properties locally by using very long classifiers (one bit for every concept in the network). While it is possible to imagine a hardware classifier system with long enough words to make this approach reasonable for many real networks, it is an unfair assumption from the point of view of studying the amount of improvement that can be generally expected from using parallelism to solve the problem. Thus, I make the assumption that the algorithms (both sequential and parallel) are being designed to run on networks that are large enough to exceed the capacity of the underlying hardware to support redundant storage of data. This is equivalent to the assumption that the space complexity of both algorithms is proportional to the size of the network definition. For the purposes of comparison, this is a reasonable assumption.

The implication of this assumption for a sequential algorithm is that any SubsumesP operation will require a visit to every node that can be reached along SUPERC links in the UP direction to collect the inherited information (in Fahlman's terminology, to compute the Virtual Copy). Thus, the time complexity for the SubsumesP operation will at least be proportional to the number of nodes "above" the concept in the network.

In the context of idealized algorithms, the parallel version described in Chapter 5 makes significant improvements over the sequential version. At the level of SubsumesP operations, the parallel version captures the fan-in factor (F) in all of its propagations up through the network. This is exactly the improvement that can be expected from the introduction of parallelism. Likewise, at the level of the search for an MSS set, the parallel version takes advantage of the fan-out factor (E) at every node that it visits and shows concomitant improvement over the sequential version. While the above results appear to achieve significant improvements, it is worthwhile examining how much difference this order of speedup would make in the sorts of networks that are actually constructed.

Unfortunately, it is difficult to determine a realistic value for the expected improvement without detailed knowledge of typical network configurations. In particular, typical values would be needed for all of the variables that have been used to define the formulas as well as estimates for more subtle factors, such as the rate of increase of the shadow as the search moves down through the network. This is difficult to estimate *a priori*, since it depends on the "tangledness" of the network and on the proportion of successful subsumption tests at each level. In spite of these difficulties, it is possible to make some predictions based on a few relatively simple assumptions. The remainder of this section is devoted to these speculations.

In the previous section, it was argued that most real networks will have a higher fan-out than fan-in (E > F). This simple assumption has several important consequences. First, it guarantees that the size of the message list will stay within reasonable bounds. Second, the number of nodes visited by both algorithms (parallel and sequential) in the course of the SubsumesP operation can be approximated by $k(F \times D)$. This can be seen by noticing that at every time step of an UP propagation to collect inherited properties, it is necessary to visit on average all of the F concepts that can be reached by traversing one SUPERC link in the UP direction. Because E > F, however, there will be on average only one concept from which to initiate the traversal (k refers to the number of times that such a propagation must take place). If at each level, F nodes are visited, then the total number number of nodes will be $F \times L$. In the context of a MSS search some improvements could be made on this figure, but just as in the case of the parallel algorithm, the reduction in k would not change the complexity class. Furthermore, the parallel algorithm can store intermediate results advantageously any place that the sequential algorithm can. Thus, the parallel version could match any speedups obtained by the sequential version through a reduction of k.

In addition to visiting every node to compute the virtual copy, more computations are required to combine these properties reasonably. As pointed out in Chapter 5, this is where large amounts of computation (undecidable in the general case [94]) would be required to reason completely about the inherited properties. Also, it is at this level that the strategy of the standard sequential algorithm would be expected to begin diverging from the parallel one. That is, the parallel techniques used for some specialized computations could well be an artifact of the particular parallel representation, and there might be other good ways for the sequential algorithm to proceed. The techniques used to reason about number restrictions, for example, are very different in the parallel and sequential case. In the absence of a a detailed analysis of sequential classification algorithms, I will consider only the high-level MSS search and the highest level (collection of inherited properties) of the SubsumesP operation, keeping in mind that the comparison is ignoring a large part of the sequential algorithm.[3]

[3]However, all of the figures given for the parallel version include the lower-level operations as well.

The obvious sequential MSS algorithm would be a breadth-first search that checked the shadow for the same nodes as the parallel version. The implemented parallel algorithm would have the advantage of checking the shadow in parallel. Thus, if the number of nodes above X at any given level were C, the sequential version would take C time steps to establish that X was not in the shadow, while the parallel version would take L time steps. With the assumption of $E > F$, this would mean a reduction from $C \simeq (D \times F)$ to D time steps.

If the extra layer of parallelism were added to the implemented version, all of the concepts at the same level in the network would be visited simultaneously. This would result in some increased efficiency, but the savings would probably not be the entire fan-out factor. This is because some percentage of the nodes to be visited would be ruled out by failed subsumption tests (or inherited failure from the shadow) from nodes that were higher in the network. The advantage in terms of time over a sequential algorithm that would be gained is related to the average number of subsumption tests that must be conducted at each level of the search. This in turn is related to the average fraction of successful subsumption tests at each level.

For example, if every SubsumesP test were successful, adding the extra layer of parallelism would reduce the time to check level L from $(k+m)((E-F)^L - (E-F)^{L-1})$ to $(k + m)$ where k is the time it takes to conduct one SubsumesP test and m is the time it takes to check the shadow. At the other extreme, if only one SubsumesP test were successful at every level, additional parallelism would reduce the time at each level from $((m + k)E - kG)$ to $(k + m)$, where G stands for the average number of nodes that fall within the shadow at every level of the search. Over the course of a search of depth D, this would mean a reduction from $O(D \times E)$ to $O(D)$ time steps for MSS and SubsumesP in the worst case (the least favorable for the parallel version) and a reduction from $O(D(E-F)^D)$ to $O(D)$ in the best case. It is meaningless to try to characterize the expected case without some empirical evidence about how fast the shadow expands.

The factors E and F were defined to be averages over an entire network. The previous estimates that were based on these averages are valid only if the fan-in and fan-out are fairly uniform at different depths in the network. In fact, this will probably not be the case. Consider Fahlman's characterization of typical knowledge bases which was described in [36]:

> The proposed network, on the other hand, can perform many deductions in time proportional to the length of the longest branch of the search-tree, regardless of how many nodes the tree may contain overall. For short, bushy trees (knowledge bases consist mostly of short, bushy trees), the speed-up could be huge: a tree that is five or ten links deep might contain millions of nodes in its branches, so a million-fold speed increase is possible. (p. 11)
>
> As I mentioned earlier, the VC hierarchy is a tangled one. That means simply that a node may have more than one immediate parent, as well as an arbitrarily large number of offspring. To put it another way, the tree branches upwards as well as downwards.... In the familiar non-tangled hierarchy or tree structure, a node may have thousands of descendants, but only a single strand of ancestors. Therefore, to find some property of X it is only necessary to trace up this single strand. In the tangled hierarchy, the descendents still fan out, but now the ancestors do as well. The hierarchy containing the ancestors of X can spread out to very considerable

dimensions before it again converges toward the top-level THING node. (pp. 20–21)

It is the combination of "short bushy trees" and "ancestors of X spreading out to very considerable dimensions" for which the previous assumptions do not account fully. The first condition implies that the depth of a typical network is small relative to the total number of nodes. This in turn suggests that the fan-out is much greater in the upper regions of the network than the fan-in. The second condition points to the central issue for discussing SubsumesP: how many nodes are visited during the time that X is "spreading out to very considerable dimensions before again converging"? The extent of the "considerable dimension" is the same extent to which the parallel algorithm will show actual improvements over the sequential version. The improvements can be characterized by assuming some depth D_{mid}, above which the effective fan-in is close to 1 and below which the fan-in is significant. For simplicity, let D_{mid} be the number of levels from the lowest level of the search (normally, the bottom of the network). The exact location of D_{mid} will vary from network to network and its relevance to each concept's sub-lattice will also vary, but in general it will indicate that region of the network in which the parallel algorithm shows the most dramatic improvement. The structure above D_{mid} can be ignored since it will be cheap for everyone to compute VC's in this region, and the possible gains in the lower regions can be considered. In the lower regions the effective fan-in factor will be referred to as F_{eff}. The term "effective fan-in" means the difference between the fan-in and the fan-out for this region of the network. It is assumed that this will have a positive value. Now, consider the cost of visiting all of the nodes in the sub-lattice above some concept X at depth D up to the level of D_{mid}. Sequentially, this is ${F_{eff}}^{D_{mid}}$ and in parallel it is D_{mid}. This figure can be interpreted as the expected improvement of parallel over sequential algorithms for the SubsumesP part of the classification problem.

When the MSS search is added into the calculations, further improvements are realized. From the top level down to $D_{mid}(D - D_{mid}$ levels), the only significant improvements will come from the additional layer of parallelism that would allow all nodes at one level to be checked simultaneously. The SubsumesP test in this region would not be significantly faster for the parallel version than the sequential one. With the assumption that the network closely resembles a tree (with fan-out E_{eff}) in the region between the top element and D_{mid}, the expected reduction in time would be from $E(\text{eff})^{(D-D_{mid})}$ to $(D - D_{mid})$. In the lower regions of the network, the MSS search adds another factor of $({F_{eff}}^{D_{mid}})$ which is the expected number of nodes that the sequential version would visit. A parallel version that checked all nodes at one level simultaneously would add a factor of D_{mid}. Thus, the total expected time for the sequential MSS version is:

$$\left({E_{eff}}^{(D-D_{mid})} + \left({F_{eff}}^{D_{mid}2}\right)\right).$$

The total expected time for the parallel algorithm is:

$$(D - D_{mid})(D_{mid})^2.$$

The above sorts of arguments can also be applied to the size of the message list. It is thus expected that the size of the message list will be large between D and D_{mid} and then grow very slowly from D_{mid} to the top. However, the message list will be processing only one sub-lattice at a time and not the entire network, so it can be expected to stay within reasonable bounds. That is, in the expected case, the set of virtual copies will make up a small fraction of the entire network.

6.5 Computational Tradeoffs

One consideration ignored by the previous discussion is the assumption that the size of the message list does not affect the time complexity. That is, it was assumed that the time it takes each production rule (classifier) to be matched against the message list is insignificant compared to the time it takes to process the output messages. This is probably an unrealistic assumption because each classifier's structure is so simple that the time spent matching the message list constitutes the major processing task at each time step.[4] It might be more realistic to consider the time complexity measure to be the product of the size of the message list and the number of time steps. With this assumption, the worst-case time complexity for the parallel algorithm is $O(D^3)$ which is still an improvement over the sequential case for large networks. However, this figure is unrealistically harsh on the parallel algorithm because in the vast majority of time steps the actual number of messages to be processed is much less than D.

Previously, I mentioned "shortcuts" that involve redundant storage of data. This is an instance of time-versus-space tradeoffs. By using a representation similar to that developed for primitive marks at every concept, it would be possible to collect inherited information in a constant number of time steps. This would effectively reduce the time complexity for MSS to a constant term. However, each classifier would have as many bits as there were concepts in the network.

This is a similar issue to that of adding additional layers of parallelism. For every layer that is added, the computational time is reduced, but the length of each processor is increased. For example, in Chapter 4, the check for Role Value Maps is conducted with one additional layer of parallelism. This reduces the time for that particular operation by 1/2, and one additional field (LEFT,RIGHT) is added to every structural classifier. In general, the length of each classifier will be increased by $\log_2 X$ where X represents the degree of parallelism to be obtained.

6.6 Summary of Results

The complexity results for both the idealized sequential algorithm and the implemented parallel algorithm are summarized below. These results are based on the following assumptions:

(1) The number of distinct primitive marks in a network is insignificant when compared to the total number of concepts in that network;
(2) The depth of the role lattice is never greater than the depth of the concept lattice;
(3) There are at least 8 primitive marks in the network;
(4) Each production rule (classifier) reads every message on the message list at every time step;

[4]This is because this version of the classifier system does not employ the bucket brigade (see Chapter 2).

(5) The networks under consideration are large enough to make redundant storage of data infeasible;
(6) The average fan-out (E) is greater than the average fan-in (F) for most networks;
(7) The processing time of each production rule (classifier) is independent of the number of messages on the message list.

The number of time steps in the parallel algorithm for the SubsumesP test is O(D). The MSS test (incorporating SubsumesP) is $O(D^2)$. The number of processors is directly proportional to the size of the network definition. The maximum size of the message list is in the worst case O(C), but in the expected case ($E > F$), the maximum size is O(D).

Comparison with the sequential algorithm is difficult for two reasons: (1) the detailed complexity of analysis of the implemented sequential algorithm was not available, and (2) the amount of improvement over the sequential case is dependent on the configuration of each particular network. However, with assumption of $E > F$, best and worst case improvements can be identified. In the best case (every subsumption test is positive), the parallel algorithm reduces the search time from $(k+m)(E-F)^D$ to $(k+m)D$. The first factor reduces to $O(DF)(E-F)^D$ and the second to D^2. In the worst case (only one subsumption test positive at every level), the parallel algorithm reduces the search time from $D(Em+k)$ to D. These factors reduce to $O(D^2E)$ and O(D) respectively.

By refining the characterization of network structures from one in which E and F are constant at every depth to one in which E is high (and F low) above some D_{mid} and F is significant below D_{mid}, the above estimates can be refined. If any savings in the upper part of the network are ignored, which is probably insignificant compared to the middle part, the improvement of parallel over sequential can be expressed as a reduction from $({F_{eff}}^{D_{mid}})$ to D_{mid} for SubsumesP. By considering both regions of the network and including the MSS test, the complexity of the sequential algorithm could be expected to be:

$$O\left({E_{eff}}^{(D-D_{mid})} + \left({F_{eff}}^{(D_{mid})^2}\right)\right).$$

The time complexity of the parallel algorithm is:

$$O\left((D-D_{mid})(D_{mid})^2\right).$$

These estimates are based on the highest two levels (MSS and SubsumesP) of the algorithm. It is probable that more benefits are accrued in the lower levels.

The complexity analysis has suggested several general constraints on KL-ONE network topology. First, the ratio of primitive to composite concepts in the network should be relatively small. If it is not small, then the network will be behaving primarily as a feature-detection system. KL-ONE's strength lies in the ability to build large complex networks of concepts by recombining and composing a few primitives. A second constraint arises by considering how many nodes an incoming concept is classified beneath at each level of the network. Again, if the average concept classifies beneath all the nodes at a level, then the upper levels in the network are not providing useful discriminations. On the other hand, if incoming concepts classify beneath only one concept at each level, then the resulting network will be a tree instead of a lattice. Much of the richness and complexity of KL-ONE arise from the lattice structure of the networks. Finally, the ratio of fan-out to fan-in at different levels of the network will have an affect on both of the previous constraints. A reasonable network would be one in which the effective fan-out in the upper regions of the network is relatively high (allowing discrimination) and fan-in increases in the lower regions (recombination and composition).

7 Conclusions

Classifier systems are interesting from several perspectives: as a computational model of cognition, as a model of fine-grained parallel processing, as a tool for solving real-world problems, and as a programming language in which correct programs can be learned as well as programmed. The work described in the previous chapters incorporates each of these themes to varying degrees, but concentrates on the message-passing layer of classifier systems and its role as a model of parallel computation. The conclusions to be drawn from this work naturally fall into three categories: classifier systems, KL-ONE, and parallelism. For each area, the major results are summarized along with directions for future research.

7.1 Classifier Systems

Several interesting properties of classifier systems have been demonstrated. First, we have seen that classifier systems are a powerful and flexible representation system. Theorem 1 proves that a deterministic classifier system can compute any finite function. Flexibility is demonstrated by Theorems 1 and 2, which together show that any finite function can be computed either in one time step or spread out over many time steps (with only one classifier active at every time step). In most situations an intermediate representation is most appropriate, in which many classifiers are active at the same time but the computation takes more than one time step. One advantage of these intermediate representations is that the total number of processors can be substantially reduced.

The algorithms that are described in Chapters 4 and 5 fall largely into this intermediate category. They were designed to allow computations in a minimal number of time steps with the constraint that there not be an unreasonably large number of classifiers and that each classifier be of reasonable size. In addition, many classifiers are used in more than one operation.

General techniques for controlling the behavior of a classifier system were described in Chapter 4. Tagging, in which one field of the classifier is used as a selector, is used to maintain groups of messages on the message list that are in distinct states. This allows the use of specialized operators that are defined for particular states. This specificity allows additional layers of parallelism to be added by processing more than one operation simultaneously. In these situations, the messages for each operation are kept distinct on the global message list by the unique values of their tags.

Negative conditions activate and deactivate various subsystems of the classifier system. Negative conditions are used to terminate computations and explicitly change the state of a group of messages when a "trigger" message is added to the list. The trigger condition violates the negative condition and that classifier is effectively turned off.

Computations that proceed one bit at a time illustrate two techniques: (1) using control messages to sequence the processing of a computation, and (2) collecting and combining information from independent messages into one message. Sequencing will always be useful when a computation is spread over multiple time steps instead of being performed in one step. Collection is important because in the classifier system it is easy to "parallelize" information from one message into many messages that can be operated on independently. This is most easily accomplished by having many classifiers that match the same message and operate on various fields within the message. The division of one message into its components takes one time step. However, the recombination of the new components back into one message (for example, an answer) is more difficult. The collection process must either be conducted in a pairwise fashion or a huge number of classifiers must be employed. The computational tradeoff for n is 2^n classifiers (one for each combination of possible messages) in one time step versus n classifiers (one for each bit) that are sequenced for n time steps. Intermediate solutions are also possible.

Synchronization techniques allow one operation to be delayed until another has finished. Synchronization can be achieved by combining tagging with negative conditions. It is demonstrated by the algorithm for Role Value Map subsumption in Chapter 5.

The techniques just described are illustrated by the algorithms that have been developed for set operations, the max and min functions, comparison of two numbers, binary addition, and formation of default hierarchies. The algorithms in turn have been combined and extended in Chapter 5 to a complex, sophisticated knowledge representation system, KL-ONE. For two cases (addition and default hierarchies) alternative representations have been discussed and arguments made for the particular representation that was chosen.

The implementation demonstrates that one very effective way of capturing a high degree of parallelism for languages like KL-ONE is to decompose them into fine-grained structures, such as that of the classifier system. It seems unlikely that this amount of parallelism could be achieved with a coarser decomposition. Since the KL-ONE algorithms were implemented via intermediate operations, such as Boolean set queries and parallel graph traversal, the results and algorithms could be applied to other fine-grained parallel systems. Likewise, the intermediate operations could be used to implement other knowledge-representation formalisms in classifier systems.

The implementation of a complex, high-level AI system using classifier systems addresses one common criticism—that the syntactic, low-level form of the rules is too far removed from high-level symbolic structures to be useful. The implementation demonstrates that a mapping between these two levels is possible and contributes to the growing body of research on how symbolic and subsymbolic paradigms are related (see for example [95]). Both symbolic and subsymbolic models contribute to our understanding of intelligent systems. Researchers in symbolic knowledge representation have described many aspects of human knowledge and proposed computational mechanisms by which they might be realized. This work provides a top-down account of what an intelligent agent must "know" in order to function. On the other hand, the subsymbolic approach proposes powerful and psychologically plausible models of learning.

The theoretical results combined with the implemented algorithms show that the classifier system formalism is a powerful and flexible representation system that provides an opportunity for either a "programmer" or a learning algorithm to optimize over the number of processors and the length of computation. The ability to support both programming and learning in one formalism is important for two reasons. First, learning is a time-consuming process. In many applications, it is desirable to integrate learning algorithms with pre-existing "programmed" knowledge, so that the system does not need to begin completely from scratch in all circumstances. In order to accomplish this, it is necessary for the learning algorithms and programmed representations to be compatible. Second, the compatibility of programming with learning in classifier systems can be a useful tool in understanding the behavior of learning classifier systems. When learning occurs in a low-level model like classifier systems, it can be very difficult to "decompile" the final structures to understand what was learned, how it is represented, and how it evolved. Riolo's studies of bucket-brigade behavior illustrate how the judicious use of programmed classifier systems can shed light on learning processes [99, 100].

Since this study did not incorporate learning algorithms, one obvious question is how many of the structures described here are learnable by the bucket brigade and genetic algorithm. Goldberg [50], Holland [71], and Riolo [100] have shown that the bucket brigade is capable of building up default hierarchies, using tags, negative conditions as triggers, and limited sequencing (chaining). Belew and Forrest have studied how the structures obtained in these studies compare with the structures produced by the deterministic algorithms of Chapters 4 and 5 [7].

This work is quite preliminary, however, and to date there are no significant classifier system applications that successfully combine programmed and learned knowledge. This is an important direction for future research, which would test the efficacy of the learning algorithms and determine which of the techniques from Chapters 4 and 5 are plausible in a learning context. While the particular algorithms that I have developed probably would not emerge directly, the general techniques are expected to appear in some form. In addition to the results of Goldberg, Holland, and Riolo, other structures might appear, including synchronization, more sophisticated uses of tags, more extensive sequencing, and in the context of knowledge representation, the formation of roles. Roles are more complex than "properties" for two reasons. First, they are two-place relations rather than one-place predicates, and second, relations between roles (DIFF links) are well defined.

A related question is how well classifier systems can learn symbolic representations. While learning classifier systems have demonstrated impressive performance in some domains, they typically construct fairly "flat" stimulus/response solutions. To claim that a learning classifier system was exhibiting symbolic behavior, it would need to construct internal representations (probably much simpler than the KL-ONE structures) and manipulate them to produce output. This is one of the most important problems currently facing classifier system research.

Finally, this study raises the question of how the deterministic classifier system should be viewed. Is it an architecture, a programming language, or something in between? It has been presented as a low-level programming language that is general enough to avoid commitment to one particular hardware implementation, but too specific and low level to be justified as a programming language. As a programming language, the requirements for classifier systems are threefold: (1) to be general enough to represent a wide variety of computational structures, (2) to express the natural parallelism in these structures, and (3) to be compatible with learning algorithms. The implementation has demonstrated the first two of these. As a fine-grained architecture for implementing AI systems, the requirements are somewhat different. Research on parallelism in AI is in its infancy. Therefore, it is desirable to have a model that allows experimentation with the principles of parallelism without committing to a specific hardware architecture. Classifier systems meet this requirement; they are sufficiently low level that we believe they could be implemented in hardware, and they are general enough to be efficiently implemented on top of a wide range of parallel machines. Likewise, they are flexible enough to implement a variety of high-level representations (e.g., other than KL-ONE), yet they make architectural commitments to certain universal properties of intelligent systems, such as reasoning about uncertainty, representing transitions in the environment, and learning.

7.2 KL-ONE

This study has also been about KL-ONE. The implementation described in Chapter 5 constitutes an existence proof that the use of parallelism to answer subsumption questions can result in dramatic speedups. Because the implemented subsumption algorithms (both sequential and parallel) are incomplete, these results do not violate the undecidability of complete subsumption. In general, a parallel implementation like that of Chapter 5 can be expected to reduce computations from $O({F_{eff}}^{D_{mid}})$ to $O(D_{mid})$. This is similar to the improvements hypothesized by Woods in [124]. It seems unlikely that significant improvements over this figure can be gained without a huge increase in one or more of the following: number of processors, size of processors, and amount of communication between processes. This is because either the data would have to be stored redundantly (longer classifiers) or many more inferences would have to be pre-computed (stored explicitly) which would increase the number of processors. These tradeoffs are not specific to classifier systems. Any fine-grained organization of knowledge that supports certain operations efficiently can be expected to exhibit similar characteristics. However, the implementation does show that it is possible to capture fan-out and fan-in (fan-out in the UP direction) using the same representation.

The study has raised several questions about KL-ONE. First, what is the ideal knowledge structure that can be built within a KL-ONE-like formalism? For example, what is a reasonable ratio of primitive to composite definitions; what would be an optimal number of nodes at every level that a concept successfully classifies beneath; what are optimal fan-out and fan-in rates at various depths in the network? In most cases, I would not expect to find universal answers to these questions, but it would be useful to refine and expand the arguments about typical network topologies that were begun in Chapter 6. Those arguments were necessarily based on fairly crude assumptions about the typical configuration of networks, which suggests a companion issue: the empirical investigation of what sorts of networks are actually built. It could turn out that certain parts of KL-ONE's definitional machinery are being used either inappropriately or disproportionately. Results of this nature could point in either of two directions. One possibility is that the basic ideas of structured inheritance networks need to be reworked. For example, it might turn out that the price of "true" inheritance is too high in many situations and that other organizations of knowledge should be considered. On the other hand, if the empirical tests indicated that the "typical" network was close to optimal (from the theoretical standpoint), this would be confirming evidence that the design of KL-ONE emphasizes the correct "epistemological primitives."

Another avenue to explore is the possibility of a more heuristic approach to classification, possibly one that lends itself directly to parallelism. Patel-Schneider has shown undecidability for complete classification [94]. Since the common implementations are necessarily incomplete, it might be useful to design subsumption algorithms entirely from the standpoint of heuristics rather than from the viewpoint of logical completeness. Specifically, it would be interesting to study in detail what the effect of removing (or simplifying) certain checks would have on the behavior (and usefulness) of the networks, especially with an eye toward parallelism. This might allow more novel approaches to parallel representations, such as those mentioned in Chapter 5.

7.3 Parallelism

The claim that fine-grained parallelism is interesting and unique because "the whole is greater than the sum of the parts" can be made at two levels. Simon in *The Sciences of the Artificial* [111] refers to these as "pragmatic" and "ultimate, metaphysical":

> Roughly, by a complex system I mean one made up of a large number of parts that interact in a nonsimple way. In such systems the whole is more than the sum of the parts, not in an ultimate, metaphysical sense but in the important pragmatic sense that, given the properties of the parts and the laws of their interaction, it is not a trivial matter to infer the properties of the whole. In the face of complexity an in-principle reductionist may be at the same time a pragmatic holist. (p. 195)

The classifier system implementation of KL-ONE is an example of fine-grained parallelism that illustrates "pragmatic holism." A complex system has been built up hierarchically in which "a large number of parts interact in a nonsimple way." The system is hierarchical because the KL-ONE system has been built out of simpler sets of classifiers (subassemblies in Simon's terminology) that were described in Chapter 4). These in turn were built up using general structures such as negative conditions, tagging etc. While the final construction is deterministic and fixed, it is also flexible. First, the components of the system are general-purpose algorithms that could be combined in other ways to build other special-purpose structures. Second, many of the processors (classifiers) are useful in more than one context.

The classifier system can be viewed as an "architecture of complexity." It fulfills both of Simon's criteria: hierarchy and robustness (built up from subassemblies). In this study, the set of subassemblies (the algorithms and techniques described in Chapter 4 form the basis of a highly complex structure, KL-ONE. These subassemblies illustrate the kind of complex behavior of which the classifier system is capable. The claim of robustness would be more compelling if the high-level behavior had been generated by learning algorithms. However, this level of complexity is well beyond the scope of most current research efforts that involve learning. In its place, the individual elements of a classifier system have been combined to form a complex hierarchical structure, resulting in the largest programmed classifier system and most sophisticated application to date.

Another theme of fine-grained parallelism is the explicit savings in time that can be gained through the use of many processors working in parallel. While the details of these savings are reported in Chapters 4 and 6, the question of implicit parallelism is addressed here. There is a correlate of the "implicit parallelism" of the genetic algorithm in the sense that a huge search space of schemata is implicitly explored by every individual in a population.

When tagging is used to add parallelism (see for example, the description of Role Value Maps in Chapter 5), the total number of messages passed through the system is at least as large as would be passed if the parallel "pieces" had been processed sequentially. Since the amount of time that each classifier spends processing a message once it has been activated is a small constant, one component of complexity for the classifier system is the number of messages passed through the global message list. Thus, while in principle any number of processes may be carried on in parallel using the tagging methodology, actual speedups to the system may not be realized when the processes are totally independent and there is no sharing of information. While this parallelism may be helpful (when the proper hardware is available to support it), true speedups (what I call implicit parallelism) occur when the messages on the global message list are interrelated and the classifiers can be active cooperatively, rather than independently. This is similar to Holland's argument for the advantages of implicit parallelism [67]. The completely defined messages on the global message list are analogous to the individuals of the genetic algorithm and the classifier list defines the space of schemata being searched. This search is efficient if completely defined messages explore many different schemata simultaneously. In terms of the classifier system, this corresponds to one message activating more than one classifier.

One example of classifiers working cooperatively in this sense is the discussion of default hierarchies in Chapter 4. The technique is to use one bit for every primitive feature in the system. When don't cares are used for some of the bit positions, a limited number of classifiers can be used to describe a very large number of individuals. For example, in the ideal case of a tree, thirty-two classifiers could be used to classify 2^{32} possible individuals. In this extreme case there are huge savings in representation by using the don't care coding technique. In the implementation, a similar technique is used for PRIMITIVEs. Even if in the general case representations are not nice neat trees or lattices in which thirty-two primitive features determined ahead of time discriminate all of the objects in the world, we can say that any system that builds up representations using this technique when it can (an emergent default hierarchy) will accrue huge savings that are "implicit" rather than "explicit."

The distinction between explicit and implicit parallelism points to the principles of emergent computation. The savings provided by implicit parallelism *emerge* from the interactions among components. This is in contrast with conventional parallelism in which code or data are decomposed into independent subunits, and interactions are managed explicitly (e.g., through synchronization). The savings here are explicit. The idea of emergent computation is to exploit interactions among primitive components to create useful computational systems. Emergent computations are potentially useful in several different ways. They might provide implementation efficiencies through implicit parallelism, flexibility for systems that must interact with complex and dynamic environments (such as on-line intelligent systems), or more natural representations and models of physical phenomena.

The risk of emergent computation is that interactions among components can result in highly unpredictable and complex behavior (e.g., chaos, self-organization, etc.). Thus, the challenge is to understand how to engineer emergent-computation systems so that they produce desired global behaviors. Since it is so hard to predict emergent behavior from the constituent pieces, a natural approach is one that incorporates learning, and in fact the best current examples of successful emergent behavior are systems that employ learning (see Chapter 2).

While the ideas of emergent computation are intuitively appealing, there are many questions to be answered before these principles will have an impact on the field of parallel processing and the modeling of intelligent systems. Most important is the question of how to define exactly what constitutes emergent phenomena. A start in this direction was made in [47], but the definitions need to be refined and made more rigorous. Related to this is the question of the role of parallelism. Since any parallel program can be implemented on a sequential machine, sequential machines should be capable in principle of exhibiting emergent behaviors also. However, it is much easier to imagine how interactions among processes can provide provable speed-ups in the parallel case than in the sequential one. Finally, the question of how to engineer emergent-computation systems is paramount. Should they be designed as an entire system or should each component be designed locally (as in local-level learning)? A related issue is how learning can manipulate systems with many components and interactions and avoid the pitfalls of unpredictable behavior that are associated with such systems.

APPENDICES

APPENDIX A. Backus Normal Form Description of Input Language

```
<expr-specification> ::= <concept-specification> |
   <role-specification> .

<concept-specification> ::= |
   ( CONCEPTSPEC <atom> |
   <list-of-spec-forms> )

<list-of-spec-forms> ::= |
   <spec-form> <list-of-spec-forms> |
   NIL

<spec-form> ::= |
   ( SPECIALIZES <concept-name-or-spec-list> ) |
   ( ROLE <atom> <role-spec-list> ) |
   PRIMITIVE |
   <role-constraint-form>

<concept-name-or-spec-list> ::= |
   <concept-name-or-spec> <concept-name-or-spec-list> |
   NIL

<concept-name-or-spec> ::= |
   <concept-specification>|
   <atom>

<role-spec-list> ::= |
   <role-spec> <role-spec-list> |
   NIL

<role-spec> ::= |
   ( DIFFERENTIATES <name-form-list> ) |
   ( VRCONCEPT <concept-name-or-spec> ) |
   ( NUMBER <integer> ) |
   ( MAX <integer> ) |
   ( MIN <integer> ) |

<role-constraint-form> ::= |
   ( <role-constraint-type> <role-chain> <role-chain> )

<role-constraint-type> ::= = !| > !| <

<role-chain> ::= |
   <role-name> <role-chain> |
   <role-name>

<role-name> ::= <atom>

<role-specification> ::= |
   ( ROLESPEC <role-name> <role-form-list> )
```

```
<role-form-list> ::=
   <role-form> <role-form-list> !||
   NIL

<role-form> ::= |
   ( DIFFERENTIATES <role-name-list> ) |
   PRIMITIVE

<role-name-list> ::= |
   <role-name> <role-name-list> |
   NIL
```

The non-terminals <atom> and <integer> denote lexical tokens, and NIL denotes the empty symbol.

APPENDIX B. Theorems

THEOREM 1 For every function F: ML $\rightarrow$ ML, there exists a Classifier Set CS that computes F in one time step.

PROOF Let M = $\{m_1, m_2, \ldots, m_t\}$, where $t=2^n$. This is the set of all possible messages.

Let ML = $\{ml_1, ml_2, \ldots, ml_s\}$, where $s=2^{2^n}$ and n = the number of bits in a message. This is the set of all possible message lists.

Let F = $\{\langle ml_i, ml_j\rangle : (ml_i, ml_j \in ML) \text{ AND } F(ml_i) = ml_j\}$. This is the given function.

Given these three sets, the set CS_F can be constructed to compute F by considering each ordered pair $\langle ml_i, ml_j\rangle$ separately. For each $\langle ml_i, ml_j\rangle \in F$ and $ml_k = M - ml_i$, such that

$$ml_i = \{m_{1i}, m_{2i}, \ldots, m_{ui}\},$$
$$ml_j = \{m_{1j}, m_{2j}, \ldots, m_{vj}\}, \text{ and}$$
$$ml_k = \{m_{1k}, m_{2k}, \ldots, m_{wk}\},$$

construct the following set CS_i of classifiers using the notation described in Chapter 2:

```
  m1i
  m2i
  ⋮
  mui
~ m1k
~ m2k
  ⋮
~ mwk => m1j (1)¹

  m1i
  m2i
  ⋮
  mui
~ m1k
~ m2k
  ⋮
~ mwk => m2j (2)

  ⋮

  m1i
```

[1]The numbers in parentheses are a unique classifier tag used only for this exposition. They are not part of the Classifier System formalism.

```
m2i
 ⋮
mui
~ m1k
~ m2k
 ⋮
~ mwk => mvj (v).
```

This set (the classifiers constructed for one i and one j) maps from one point (a message list) in the domain to one point (also a message list) in the range. Let CS_F be the union of all the CS_{ij}.

To show that CS_F computes F, it is necessary to show (1) that every point ml_i in the domain of F is mapped to $F(ml_i)$, and (2) that all points ml_j that are not in the domain of F are not processed by CS_F.

To show (1), assume that ml_i is in the domain of F and that $F(ml_i) = ml_j$. The set of classifiers CS_{ij} is responsible for this mapping. Each classifier in CS_{ij} will be activated when ml_i is on the message list. This is because the only positive preconditions to be met are that m_{1i} through m_{ui} (all the messages in ml_i) be present on the message list. Each classifier in CS_{ij} will produce one of the messages in ml_j. Since there is one classifier for each message, all the messages in ml_j will be produced.

Furthermore, no other messages will be produced. For if any were, they would be produced by a classifier that did not belong to CS_{ij}. Suppose it belonged to CS_{km}. Since F is a function, ml_i and ml_k differ by at least one message. Call this m_n. If $m_n \in ml_k$, then all of the classifiers in CS_{km} would have as one of their preconditions m_n. Since m_n would not appear on the message list when $F(ml_i)$ was to be computed, none of the classifiers in CS_{km} would be activated. If, on the other hand, $m_n \in ml_i$ and not of ml_k, then all of the classifiers in CS_{km} would have "$\sim m_n$" as one of its conditions. Since m_n would appear on the message list when $F(ml_i)$ was to be computed, none of the classifiers in cs_{km} would be activated.

To show (2) we use a similar argument. Suppose there exists a ml_k that is not in the domain of F. Then it must differ from any ml in the domain of F by at least one message. Suppose that ml_k differs from ml_i by m_n. Then, none of the classifiers in CS_{ij} will be activated (for the reasons given in the preceding paragraph). Q.E.D.

THEOREM 2 For every function F: ML $\rightarrow$ ML, there exists a Classifier Set CS' that computes F for which only one classifier is active at any one time step.

PROOF Since only one classifier at a time can be active (by assumption), the answer (a message list) will be emitted sequentially (one message per time step). Also, the clocking function will be performed by tags rather than separate messages (to ensure that classifier is active at a time). Input and output messages will be augmented with a tag field.

Assign each classifier in CS'_F a unique tag (or address) t. For each $\langle ml_i, ml_j \rangle \in F$, the preceding construction (see Theorem 1) is modified as follows[2]:

```
 nil || m1i
 nil || m2i

 ⋮

 nil || mui
~nil || m1k
~nil || m2k

 ⋮

~nil || mwk => t1 || m1j        (1)

 t1 || m1j => t2 || m2j         (2)

 t2 || m2j => t3 || m3j         (3)

 ⋮

 t(v-1) || m((v-1)j) => tv || mvj     (v).
```

Let CS_F be the union of all the CS'_{ij}.

To show that CS'_F computes F, it is necessary (as before) to show (1) that every point ml_i in the domain of F is mapped to $F(ml_i)$, and (2) that all points ml_j that are not in the domain of F are not processed by CS'_F.

To show (1), assume as before that ml_i is in the domain of F and that $F(ml_i) = ml_j$. Further, assume that each message in ml_i has been concatenated with the tag t_0. Only classifiers in CS'_{ij} can be activated (for the same reasons as before), and of these, only the first classifier will be activated by the modified ml_i, since the tag fields (set to t_0) of messages in ml_i will not match the tag fields of the other classifiers (set to t_1 through t_{v-1}). Thus, after the first time step one message will be emitted ($t_1 \| m_{1j}$). At the second time step, the message $t_2 \| m_{2j}$ will be emitted (since the condition part of classifier 2 will be matched by $t_1 \| m_{1j}$). This process will continue until the message $t_v \| m_{vj}$ is emitted on the vth time step.

Part 2 is shown using the same argument as that used for Theorem 1. Q.E.D.

[2]The notation "||" denotes the concatenation operator, and nil denotes don't care for the entire tag field.

APPENDIX C. Processing Compound Queries

LEMMA 1 Any boolean clause of the form

$$A = a_1 p_1 \wedge a_2 p_2 \wedge \ldots a_n p_n,$$

where each a_i is either the negation operator (NOT) or nil and each p_i is a set, can be computed using the Classifier System without using any memory (messages in the MEM state).[3]

PROOF Rearrange the terms so that all those with a_i=NOT come before those with a_i=nil. Then apply De Morgan's law to factor out the NOT's. This leaves a clause of the form Any compound query B can be put into Disjunctive Normal Form:

$$A = \mathrm{NOT}(p_i \vee p_i \vee \ldots \vee p_l) \wedge p_q \ldots \wedge p_n.$$

This can be processed in the Classifier System by first processing the OR clause. This requires no memory since one set at a time is "unioned" with the accumulating result. The accumulating result is kept in the ON state and the successive clauses are added in the NORM state. When the union of p_i through p_l has been computed, the result can be complemented which also requires no memory. Then this result can be intersected with p_q through p_n, processing one set at a time. Once again, this requires no memory.

LEMMA 2 Any compound query can be computed using no more than one level of memory.

PROOF Any compound query B can be put into Disjunctive Normal Form:

$$B = (A_1) \vee (A_2) \vee \ldots (A_n)$$

where each A_i is a clause of the same form as A in Lemma 1. B is computed by computing each A_i as shown in Lemma 1. The accumulated result $(A_1 \vee A_2 \vee \ldots \vee A_{i-1})$ is stored in memory. When A_i is computed, the POPAND operator can be used to compute $(A_1 \wedge A_2 \wedge \ldots \wedge A_i)$ which can be PUSHed and left in memory until A_{i+1} is computed.

[3]These lemmas were first outlined by Paul Grosso.

APPENDIX D. Finding Maximum and Minimum Values with the Classifier System

The classifiers to find the minimum or maximum of a set of numbers are shown. The numbers must have the tag field set to "NUM." The rightmost (low-order) six bits are interpreted as the numbers to be sorted. The remaining fields are ignored and can have any value.

(1) These are the control flow classifiers. They sequence the computation by controlling which other classifiers (in the groups below) are active in which time step.

```
MaxSort1 => MaxSort2   (1)

MinSort1 => MinSort2   (2)

MaxSort2 => MaxSort3   (3)

MinSort2 => MinSort3   (4)

MaxSort3 => MaxSort4   (5)

MinSort3 => MinSort4   (6)

MaxSort4 => MaxSort5   (7)

MinSort4 => MinSort5   (8)

MaxSort5 => MaxSort6   (9)

MinSort5 => MinSort6   (10)
```

(2) These are the classifiers that allow the highest numbers determined at each bit position) to stay on the message list.

```
  NUM-nil-nil-nil-nil-1#####
  MaxSort1 => NUM-nil-nil-nil-nil-1#####   (11)

  NUM-nil-nil-nil-nil-0#####
~ NUM-nil-nil-nil-nil-1#####
  MaxSort1 => NUM-nil-nil-nil-nil-0#####   (12)

  NUM-nil-nil-nil-nil-#1####
  MaxSort2 => NUM-nil-nil-nil-nil-#1####   (13)

~ NUM-nil-nil-nil-nil-#0####
  NUM-nil-nil-nil-nil-#1####
  MaxSort2 => NUM-nil-nil-nil-nil-#0####   (14)

  NUM-nil-nil-nil-nil-##1###
  MaxSort3 => NUM-nil-nil-nil-nil-##1###   (15)

  NUM-nil-nil-nil-nil-##0###
~ NUM-nil-nil-nil-nil-##1###
  MaxSort3 => NUM-nil-nil-nil-nil-##0###   (16)

  NUM-nil-nil-nil-nil-###1##
  MaxSort4 => NUM-nil-nil-nil-nil-###1##   (17)
```

```
  NUM-nil-nil-nil-nil-###0##
~ NUM-nil-nil-nil-nil-###1##
  MaxSort4 => NUM-nil-nil-nil-nil-###0##   (18)

  NUM-nil-nil-nil-nil-####1#
  MaxSort5 => NUM-nil-nil-nil-nil-####1#   (19)

  NUM-nil-nil-nil-nil-####0#
~ NUM-nil-nil-nil-nil-####1#
  MaxSort5 => NUM-nil-nil-nil-nil-####0#   (20)

  NUM-nil-nil-nil-nil-#####1
  MaxSort6 => NUM-nil-nil-nil-nil-#####1   (21)

  NUM-nil-nil-nil-nil-#####0
~ NUM-nil-nil-nil-nil-#####1
  MaxSort6 => NUM-nil-nil-nil-AFIELD-#####0   (22)
```

(3) These classifiers allow the lowest (determined at each bit position) numbers to stay on the message list.

```
  NUM-nil-nil-nil-nil-0#####
  MinSort1 => NUM-nil-nil-nil-nil-0#####   (23)

  NUM-nil-nil-nil-nil-1#####
~ NUM-nil-nil-nil-nil-0#####
  MinSort1 => NUM-nil-nil-nil-nil-1#####   (24)

  NUM-nil-nil-nil-nil-#0####
  MinSort2 => NUM-nil-nil-nil-nil-#0####   (25)

  NUM-nil-nil-nil-nil-#1####
~ NUM-nil-nil-nil-nil-#0####
  MinSort2 => NUM-nil-nil-nil-nil-#1####   (26)

  NUM-nil-nil-nil-nil-##0###
  MinSort3 => NUM-nil-nil-nil-nil-##0###   (27)

  NUM-nil-nil-nil-nil-##1###
~ NUM-nil-nil-nil-nil-##0###
  MinSort3 => NUM-nil-nil-nil-nil-##1###   (28)

  NUM-nil-nil-nil-nil-###0##
  MinSort4 => NUM-nil-nil-nil-nil-###0##   (29)

  NUM-nil-nil-nil-nil-###1##
~ NUM-nil-nil-nil-nil-###0##
  MinSort4 => NUM-nil-nil-nil-nil-###1##   (30)

  NUM-nil-nil-nil-nil-####0#
  MinSort5 => NUM-nil-nil-nil-nil-####0#   (31)

  NUM-nil-nil-nil-nil-####1#
~ NUM-nil-nil-nil-nil-####0#
  MinSort5 => NUM-nil-nil-nil-nil-####1#   (32)

  NUM-nil-nil-nil-nil-#####0
  MinSort6 => NUM-nil-nil-nil-nil-#####0   (33)

  NUM-nil-nil-nil-nil-#####1
~ NUM-nil-nil-nil-nil-#####0
  MinSort6 => NUM-nil-nil-nil-BFIELD-#####1   (34).
```

An example of how these classifiers find the maximum of a set of numbers is shown below:

Time Step	Message List	Activating Classifier
T0:	→ MaxSort1	
	→ NUM–nil–nil–nil–nil–011000	
	→ NUM–nil–nil–nil–nil–001011	
	→ NUM–nil–nil–nil–nil–011001	
	→ NUM–nil–nil–nil–nil–001100	
T1:	MaxSort2	2
	NUM–nil–nil–nil–nil–011000	12
	NUM–nil–nil–nil–nil–001011	12
	NUM–nil–nil–nil–nil–011001	12
	NUM–nil–nil–nil–nil–001100	12
T2:	MaxSort3	3
	NUM–nil–nil–nil–nil–011000	13
	NUM–nil–nil–nil–nil–011001	13
T3:	MaxSort4	4
	NUM–nil–nil–nil–nil–011000	15
	NUM–nil–nil–nil–nil–011001	15
T4:	MaxSort5	5
	NUM–nil–nil–nil–nil–011000	18
	NUM–nil–nil–nil–nil–011001	18
T5:	MaxSort6	6
	NUM–nil–nil–nil–nil–011000	20
	NUM–nil–nil–nil–nil–011001	20
T6:	num–nil–nil–nil–nil–011001	21

APPENDIX E. Binary Addition with The Classifier System

The classifiers for a six-bit adder are shown below. The classifiers process three input messages, two operands and the message signifying that the operands are to be added. The operand messages must have the tag field set to "NUM," and have the compare field set to "AFIELD" and "BFIELD" respectively. The rightmost (low-order) six bits are interpreted as the numbers to be added. The remaining fields are ignored and can have any value. The result is labelled with "CFIELD" in the compare field and has an "overflow" message if an overflow message has occurred.

(1) Control Flow Classifiers

```
Add1 => Add2  (1)

Add2 => Add3  (2)

Add3 => Add4  (3)

Add4 => Add5  (4)

Add5 => Add6  (5).
```

(2) Classifiers to keep original numbers on the message list. The second condition "turns off" these messages when the answer is ready.

```
  NUM-nil-nil-nil-AFIELD-######
~ Add6 => NUM-nil-nil-nil-AFIELD-######  (6)

  NUM-nil-nil-nil-BFIELD-######
~ Add6 => NUM-nil-nil-nil-BFIELD-######  (7)
```

(3) Classifiers for the first (low order) bit position.

```
NUM-nil-nil-nil-AFIELD-#####0
NUM-nil-nil-nil-BFIELD-#####0
Add1 => NUM-nil-nil-nil-CFIELD-#####0  (8)

NUM-nil-nil-nil-AFIELD-#####0
NUM-nil-nil-nil-BFIELD-#####1
Add1 => NUM-nil-nil-nil-CFIELD-#####1  (9)

NUM-nil-nil-nil-AFIELD-#####1
NUM-nil-nil-nil-BFIELD-#####0
Add1 => NUM-nil-nil-nil-CFIELD-#####1  (10)

NUM-nil-nil-nil-AFIELD-#####1
NUM-nil-nil-nil-BFIELD-#####1
Add1 => NUM-nil-nil-nil-CFIELD-#####0  (11)

NUM-nil-nil-nil-AFIELD-#####1
NUM-nil-nil-nil-BFIELD-#####1
Add1 => Carry  (12)
```

(4) Classifiers for the second bit position.

```
  NUM-nil-nil-nil-CFIELD-######
  NUM-nil-nil-nil-AFIELD-####0#
  NUM-nil-nil-nil-BFIELD-####0#
  Carry
  Add2 => NUM-nil-nil-nil-CFIELD-####1#   (13)

  NUM-nil-nil-nil-CFIELD-######
  NUM-nil-nil-nil-AFIELD-####0#
  NUM-nil-nil-nil-BFIELD-####0#
~ Carry
  Add2 => NUM-nil-nil-nil-CFIELD-####0#   (14)

  NUM-nil-nil-nil-CFIELD-######
  NUM-nil-nil-nil-AFIELD-####0#
  NUM-nil-nil-nil-BFIELD-####1#
~ Carry
  Add2 => NUM-nil-nil-nil-CFIELD-####1#   (15)

  NUM-nil-nil-nil-CFIELD-######
  NUM-nil-nil-nil-AFIELD-####0#
  NUM-nil-nil-nil-BFIELD-####1#
  Carry
  Add2 => NUM-nil-nil-nil-CFIELD-####0#   (16)

  NUM-nil-nil-nil-CFIELD-######
  NUM-nil-nil-nil-AFIELD-####0#
  NUM-nil-nil-nil-BFIELD-####1#
  Carry
  Add2 => Carry  (17)

  NUM-nil-nil-nil-CFIELD-######
  NUM-nil-nil-nil-AFIELD-####1#
  NUM-nil-nil-nil-BFIELD-####0#
~ Carry
  Add2 => NUM-nil-nil-nil-CFIELD-####1#   (18)

  NUM-nil-nil-nil-CFIELD-######
  NUM-nil-nil-nil-AFIELD-####1#
  NUM-nil-nil-nil-BFIELD-####0#
  Carry
  Add2 => NUM-nil-nil-nil-CFIELD-####0#   (19)

  NUM-nil-nil-nil-CFIELD-######
  NUM-nil-nil-nil-AFIELD-####1#
  NUM-nil-nil-nil-BFIELD-####0#
  Carry
  Add2 => Carry  (20)

  NUM-nil-nil-nil-CFIELD-######
  NUM-nil-nil-nil-AFIELD-####1#
  NUM-nil-nil-nil-BFIELD-####1#
~ Carry
  Add2 => NUM-nil-nil-nil-CFIELD-####0#   (21)

  NUM-nil-nil-nil-CFIELD-######
  NUM-nil-nil-nil-AFIELD-####1#
  NUM-nil-nil-nil-BFIELD-####1#
  Carry
  Add2 => NUM-nil-nil-nil-CFIELD-####1#   (22)
```

```
NUM-nil-nil-nil-CFIELD-######
NUM-nil-nil-nil-AFIELD-####1#
NUM-nil-nil-nil-BFIELD-####1#
Add2 => Carry  (23)
```

(5) Classifiers for the third bit position.

```
  NUM-nil-nil-nil-CFIELD-######
  NUM-nil-nil-nil-AFIELD-###0##
  NUM-nil-nil-nil-BFIELD-###0##
  Carry
  Add3 => NUM-nil-nil-nil-CFIELD-###1##  (24)

  NUM-nil-nil-nil-CFIELD-######
  NUM-nil-nil-nil-AFIELD-###0##
  NUM-nil-nil-nil-BFIELD-###0##
~ Carry
  Add3 => NUM-nil-nil-nil-CFIELD-###0##  (25)

  NUM-nil-nil-nil-CFIELD-######
  NUM-nil-nil-nil-AFIELD-###0##
  NUM-nil-nil-nil-BFIELD-###1##
~ Carry
  Add3 => NUM-nil-nil-nil-CFIELD-###1##  (26)

  NUM-nil-nil-nil-CFIELD-######
  NUM-nil-nil-nil-AFIELD-###0##
  NUM-nil-nil-nil-BFIELD-###1##
  Carry
  Add3 => NUM-nil-nil-nil-CFIELD-###0##  (27)

  NUM-nil-nil-nil-CFIELD-######
  NUM-nil-nil-nil-AFIELD-###0##
  NUM-nil-nil-nil-BFIELD-###1##
  Carry
  Add3 => Carry  (28)

  NUM-nil-nil-nil-CFIELD-######
  NUM-nil-nil-nil-AFIELD-###1##
  NUM-nil-nil-nil-BFIELD-###0##
~ Carry
  Add3 => NUM-nil-nil-nil-CFIELD-###1##  (29)

  NUM-nil-nil-nil-CFIELD-######
  NUM-nil-nil-nil-AFIELD-###1##
  NUM-nil-nil-nil-BFIELD-###0##
  Carry
  Add3 => NUM-nil-nil-nil-CFIELD-###0##  (30)

  NUM-nil-nil-nil-CFIELD-######
  NUM-nil-nil-nil-AFIELD-###1##
  NUM-nil-nil-nil-BFIELD-###0##
  Carry
  Add3 => Carry  (31)

  NUM-nil-nil-nil-CFIELD-######
  NUM-nil-nil-nil-AFIELD-###1##
  NUM-nil-nil-nil-BFIELD-###1##
~ Carry
  Add3 => NUM-nil-nil-nil-CFIELD-###0##  (32)
```

```
NUM-nil-nil-nil-CFIELD-######
NUM-nil-nil-nil-AFIELD-###1##
NUM-nil-nil-nil-BFIELD-###1##
Carry
Add3 => NUM-nil-nil-nil-CFIELD-###1##   (33)

NUM-nil-nil-nil-CFIELD-######
NUM-nil-nil-nil-AFIELD-###1##
NUM-nil-nil-nil-BFIELD-###1##
Add3 => Carry  (34)
```

(6) Classifiers for the fourth bit position.

```
  NUM-nil-nil-nil-CFIELD-######
  NUM-nil-nil-nil-AFIELD-##0###
  NUM-nil-nil-nil-BFIELD-##0###
  Carry
  Add4 => NUM-nil-nil-nil-CFIELD-##1###   (35)

  NUM-nil-nil-nil-CFIELD-######
  NUM-nil-nil-nil-AFIELD-##0###
  NUM-nil-nil-nil-BFIELD-##0###
~ Carry
  Add4 => NUM-nil-nil-nil-CFIELD-##0###   (36)

  NUM-nil-nil-nil-CFIELD-######
  NUM-nil-nil-nil-AFIELD-##0###
  NUM-nil-nil-nil-BFIELD-##1###
~ Carry
  Add4 => NUM-nil-nil-nil-CFIELD-##1###   (37)

  NUM-nil-nil-nil-CFIELD-######
  NUM-nil-nil-nil-AFIELD-##0###
  NUM-nil-nil-nil-BFIELD-##1###
  Carry
  Add4 => NUM-nil-nil-nil-CFIELD-##0###   (38)

  NUM-nil-nil-nil-CFIELD-######
  NUM-nil-nil-nil-AFIELD-##0###
  NUM-nil-nil-nil-BFIELD-##1###
  Carry
  Add4 => Carry  (39)

  NUM-nil-nil-nil-CFIELD-######
  NUM-nil-nil-nil-AFIELD-##1###
  NUM-nil-nil-nil-BFIELD-##0###
~ Carry
  Add4 => NUM-nil-nil-nil-CFIELD-##1###   (40)

  NUM-nil-nil-nil-CFIELD-######
  NUM-nil-nil-nil-AFIELD-##1###
  NUM-nil-nil-nil-BFIELD-##0###
  Carry
  Add4 => NUM-nil-nil-nil-CFIELD-##0###   (41)

  NUM-nil-nil-nil-CFIELD-######
  NUM-nil-nil-nil-AFIELD-##1###
  NUM-nil-nil-nil-BFIELD-##0###
  Carry
  Add4 => Carry  (42)
```

```
  NUM-nil-nil-nil-CFIELD-######
  NUM-nil-nil-nil-AFIELD-##1###
  NUM-nil-nil-nil-BFIELD-##1###
~ Carry
  Add4 => NUM-nil-nil-nil-CFIELD-##0###   (43)

  NUM-nil-nil-nil-CFIELD-######
  NUM-nil-nil-nil-AFIELD-##1###
  NUM-nil-nil-nil-BFIELD-##1###
  Carry
  Add4 => NUM-nil-nil-nil-CFIELD-##1###   (44)

  NUM-nil-nil-nil-CFIELD-######
  NUM-nil-nil-nil-AFIELD-##1###
  NUM-nil-nil-nil-BFIELD-##1###
  Add4 => Carry  (45)
```

(7) Classifiers for the fifth bit position.

```
  NUM-nil-nil-nil-CFIELD-######
  NUM-nil-nil-nil-AFIELD-#0####
  NUM-nil-nil-nil-BFIELD-#0####
  Carry
  Add5 => NUM-nil-nil-nil-CFIELD-#1####   (46)

  NUM-nil-nil-nil-CFIELD-######
  NUM-nil-nil-nil-AFIELD-#0####
  NUM-nil-nil-nil-BFIELD-#0####
~ Carry
  Add5 => NUM-nil-nil-nil-CFIELD-#0####   (47)

  NUM-nil-nil-nil-CFIELD-######
  NUM-nil-nil-nil-AFIELD-#0####
  NUM-nil-nil-nil-BFIELD-#1####
~ Carry
  Add5 => NUM-nil-nil-nil-CFIELD-#1####   (48)

  NUM-nil-nil-nil-CFIELD-######
  NUM-nil-nil-nil-AFIELD-#0####
  NUM-nil-nil-nil-BFIELD-#1####
  Carry
  Add5 => NUM-nil-nil-nil-CFIELD-#0####   (49)

  NUM-nil-nil-nil-CFIELD-######
  NUM-nil-nil-nil-AFIELD-#0####
  NUM-nil-nil-nil-BFIELD-#1####
  Carry
  Add5 => Carry  (50)

  NUM-nil-nil-nil-CFIELD-######
  NUM-nil-nil-nil-AFIELD-#1####
  NUM-nil-nil-nil-BFIELD-#0####
~ Carry
  Add5 => NUM-nil-nil-nil-CFIELD-#1####   (51)

  NUM-nil-nil-nil-CFIELD-######
  NUM-nil-nil-nil-AFIELD-#1####
  NUM-nil-nil-nil-BFIELD-#0####
  Carry
  Add5 => NUM-nil-nil-nil-CFIELD-#0####   (52)
```

```
NUM-nil-nil-nil-CFIELD-######
NUM-nil-nil-nil-AFIELD-#1####
NUM-nil-nil-nil-BFIELD-#0####
Carry
Add5 => Carry  (53)

  NUM-nil-nil-nil-CFIELD-######
  NUM-nil-nil-nil-AFIELD-#1####
  NUM-nil-nil-nil-BFIELD-#1####
~ Carry
  Add5 => NUM-nil-nil-nil-CFIELD-#0####  (54)

NUM-nil-nil-nil-CFIELD-######
NUM-nil-nil-nil-AFIELD-#1####
NUM-nil-nil-nil-BFIELD-#1####
Carry
Add5 => NUM-nil-nil-nil-CFIELD-#1####  (55)

NUM-nil-nil-nil-CFIELD-######
NUM-nil-nil-nil-AFIELD-#1####
NUM-nil-nil-nil-BFIELD-#1####
Add5 => Carry  (56)
```

(8) Classifiers for the sixth bit position.

```
  NUM-nil-nil-nil-CFIELD-######
  NUM-nil-nil-nil-AFIELD-0#####
  NUM-nil-nil-nil-BFIELD-0#####
  Carry
  Add6 => NUM-nil-nil-nil-CFIELD-1#####  (57)

  NUM-nil-nil-nil-CFIELD-######
  NUM-nil-nil-nil-AFIELD-0#####
  NUM-nil-nil-nil-BFIELD-0#####
~ Carry
  Add6 => NUM-nil-nil-nil-CFIELD-0#####  (58)

  NUM-nil-nil-nil-CFIELD-######
  NUM-nil-nil-nil-AFIELD-0#####
  NUM-nil-nil-nil-BFIELD-1#####
~ Carry
  Add6 => NUM-nil-nil-nil-CFIELD-1#####  (59)

  NUM-nil-nil-nil-CFIELD-######
  NUM-nil-nil-nil-AFIELD-0#####
  NUM-nil-nil-nil-BFIELD-1#####
  Carry
  Add6 => NUM-nil-nil-nil-CFIELD-0#####  (60)

  NUM-nil-nil-nil-CFIELD-######
  NUM-nil-nil-nil-AFIELD-0#####
  NUM-nil-nil-nil-BFIELD-1#####
  Carry
  Add6 => OverFlow  (61)

  NUM-nil-nil-nil-CFIELD-######
  NUM-nil-nil-nil-AFIELD-1#####
  NUM-nil-nil-nil-BFIELD-0#####
~ Carry
  Add6 => NUM-nil-nil-nil-CFIELD-1#####  (62)
```

```
  NUM-nil-nil-nil-CFIELD-######
  NUM-nil-nil-nil-AFIELD-1#####
  NUM-nil-nil-nil-BFIELD-0#####
  Carry
  Add6 => NUM-nil-nil-nil-CFIELD-0#####  (63)

  NUM-nil-nil-nil-CFIELD-######
  NUM-nil-nil-nil-AFIELD-1#####
  NUM-nil-nil-nil-BFIELD-0#####
  Carry
  Add6 => OverFlow  (64)

  NUM-nil-nil-nil-CFIELD-######
  NUM-nil-nil-nil-AFIELD-1#####
  NUM-nil-nil-nil-BFIELD-1#####
~ Carry
  Add6 => NUM-nil-nil-nil-CFIELD-0#####  (65)

  NUM-nil-nil-nil-CFIELD-######
  NUM-nil-nil-nil-AFIELD-1#####
  NUM-nil-nil-nil-BFIELD-1#####
  Carry
  Add6 => NUM-nil-nil-nil-CFIELD-1#####  66)

  NUM-nil-nil-nil-CFIELD-######
  NUM-nil-nil-nil-AFIELD-1#####
  NUM-nil-nil-nil-BFIELD-1#####
  Add6 => OverFlow  (67).
```

Two examples of addition using these classifiers are shown below. The messages themselves were generated by the Classifier System program[4] using the classifiers shown above. I have added the time step labels and the column indicating which classifiers activated the messages for clarity.

[4]I have also made slight modifications to the classifiers and messages. These include case changes where I felt they helped readability and changing the representation of (1,0,#) from (l,o,d) in the program output back to (1,0,#). This is a result of the legal characters allowed for LISP atoms.

Time Step	Message List	Activating Classifier
T0:	→ Add1	
	→ NUM–nil–nil–nil–AFIELD–000111	
	→ NUM–nil–nil–nil–BFIELD–100011	
T1:	Add2	1
	NUM–nil–nil–nil–AFIELD–000111	6
	NUM–nil–nil–nil–BFIELD–100011	7
	NUM–nil–nil–nil–CFIELD–000110	8
	Carry	12
T2:	Add3	2
	NUM–nil–nil–nil–AFIELD–000111	6
	NUM–nil–nil–nil–BFIELD–100011	7
	NUM–nil–nil–nil–CFIELD–000110	22
	Carry	23
T3:	Add4	3
	NUM–nil–nil–nil–AFIELD–000111	6
	NUM–nil–nil–nil–BFIELD–100011	7
	NUM–nil–nil–nil–CFIELD–000010	30
	Carry	31
T4:	Add5	4
	NUM–nil–nil–nil–AFIELD–000111	6
	NUM–nil–nil–nil–BFIELD–100011	7
	NUM–nil–nil–nil–CFIELD–001010	35
T6:	Add6	5
	NUM–nil–nil–nil–AFIELD–000111	6
	NUM–nil–nil–nil–BFIELD–100011	7
	NUM–nil–nil–nil–CFIELD–001010	47
T7:	NUM–nil–nil–nil–CFIELD-101010	59

This example shows an overflow. The two NUMbers to be Added are 1 and 111111 (base 2).

Time Step	Message List	Activating Classifier
T0:	→ Add1	
	→ NUM–nil–nil–nil–AFIELD–000001	
	→ NUM–nil–nil–nil–BFIELD–111111	
T1:	Add2	1
	NUM–nil–nil–nil–AFIELD–000001	6
	NUM–nil–nil–nil–BFIELD–111111	7
	NUM–nil–nil–nil–CFIELD–000000	11
	Carry	12
T2:	Add3	2
	NUM–nil–nil–nil–AFIELD–000001	6
	NUM–nil–nil–nil–BFIELD–111111	7
	NUM–nil–nil–nil–CFIELD–000000	16
	Carry	17
T3:	Add4	3
	NUM–nil–nil–nil–AFIELD–000001	6
	NUM–nil–nil–nil–BFIELD–111111	7
	NUM–nil–nil–nil–CFIELD–000000	27
	Carry	28
T4:	Add5	4
	NUM–nil–nil–nil–AFIELD–000001	6
	NUM–nil–nil–nil–BFIELD–111111	7
	NUM–nil–nil–nil–CFIELD–000000	38
	Carry	39
T5:	Add6	5
	NUM–nil–nil–nil–AFIELD–000001	6
	NUM–nil–nil–nil–BFIELD–111111	7
	NUM–nil–nil–nil–CFIELD–000000	49
	Carry	50
T6:	NUM–nil–nil–nil–CFIELD–000000	60
	OverFlow	61

APPENDIX F. Description of Mapping from KL-ONE to the Classifier System

The precise mapping from KL-ONE to classifiers is shown below. For each production of the input grammar, the corresponding classifiers are shown. The notation (val <atom>) represents the bit pattern that corresponds to the terminal string represented by the non-terminal <atom>. This correspondence is maintained in the symbol table. Thus, the value of (val <atom>) is determined by a lookup in the symbol table. In the Lisp implementation, the transformations described here are contained in the file CKLONEGEN.L.

```
<expr-specification> ::= |
    <concept-specification> |
    <role-specification>
```

Action: none.

```
<concept-specification> ::= ( CONCEPTSPEC <atom> <list-of-spec-forms> )
```

Action:

(1) If <atom> has not been added to the universe (check INU field in symbol table), then the following two classifiers are constructed:

```
  NORM-(val <atom>)-nil-nil-nil
  ON-(val <atom>)-nil-nil-nil
  And => HOLD-nil-nil-nil-nil

  NORM-(val <atom>)-nil-nil-nil
~ ON-(val <atom>)-nil-nil-nil
  SetDiff => HOLD-nil-nil-nil-nil.
```

(2) The INU field is set to T.

(3) If there are no explicit SPECIALIZES statements in the definition, then by default the concept <atom> specializes the top element in the lattice (Thing). In this case, SuperC links are constructed between <atom> and Thing (see below for details).

```
<list-of-spec-forms> ::=
    <spec-form> <list-of-spec-forms> |
    NIL
```

Action: none.

```
<spec-form> ::= ( SPECIALIZES <concept-name-or-spec-list> ) |
```

Action:

(1) Find the symbols for concepts in <concept-name-or-spec-list> and construct two classifiers for each concept, sym(i), in the list:

```
NORM-(val sym(i))-SUPERC-DOWN-(prim conceptentry) =>
NORM-(val conceptentry)-SUPERC-DOWN-(prim conceptentry)

NORM-(val conceptentry)-SUPERC-UP-(prim conceptentry) =>
NORM-(val sym(i))-SUPERC-UP-(prim sym(i)).
```

In the direction DOWN the input message must satisfy the primitiveness requirements for the lower (more specific) concept. Therefore, (prim conceptentry) appears in the condition of the down classifier, rather than (prim sym(i)). This restricts the search through the lattice to concepts that are similar in the dimension of primitiveness to the concept under consideration (conceptentry).

```
<spec-form> ::= ( ROLE <atom> <role-spec-list> )
```

Action:

(1) If <atom> is not in universe (check INU field in symbol table), then generate two classifiers as described for <concept-specification>.
(2) If there are no explicit DIFFERENTIATES statements in the definition, then by default the concept <atom> specializes the top element in the role lattice (PART). In this case, DIFF links are constructed between <atom> and (PART) (see below for details).
(3) Construct the following classifier:

```
nil-(val conceptentry)-nil-nil-nil
PRE-RoleMessage => nil-(val <atom>)-DIFF-nil-nil.
```

```
<spec-form> ::= PRIMITIVE
```

Action: none.

```
<spec-form> ::= <role-constraint-form>
```

Action: none.

```
<concept-name-or-spec-list> ::= |
    <concept-name-or-spec> <concept-name-or-spec-list> |
    NIL
```

Action: none.

```
<concept-name-or-spec> ::=
    <concept-specification> |
    <atom>
```

Action: none.

```
<role-spec-list> ::=
    <role-spec> <role-spec-list> [|
    NIL
```

Action: none.

```
<role-spec> ::= ( DIFFERENTIATES <name-form-list> )
```

Action:

(1) Get list of roles (from <name-form-list>) that roleentry differentiates.
(2) Construct two classifiers for every sym(i) on this list:

```
NORM-(val sym(i))-DIFF-UP-(prim sym(i)) =>
NORM-(val roleentry)-DIFF-UP-(prim sym(i))

NORM-(val roleentry)-DIFF-DOWN-(prim sym(i)) =>
NORM-(val sym(i))-DIFF-DOWN-(prim sym(i))
```

```
<role-spec> ::= ( VRCONCEPT <concept-name-or-spec> )
```

Action:

(1) Extract the proper symbol from <concept-name-or-spec>. Call this VRname. Construct the following classifier:

```
nil-(val conceptentry)-nil-nil-nil
nil-(val roleentry)-nil-nil-nil
PRE-VR =>
nil-(val VRname)-SUPERC-nil-(prim VRname).
```

```
<role-spec> ::= ( NUMBER <integer> )
```

Action:

(1) Since this production is syntactically equivalent to (MAX <integer>) (MIN <integer>), two classifiers are constructed as detailed in the next two productions.

```
<role-spec> ::= ( MAX <integer> )
```

Action:

(1) Transform <integer> to its binary representation.
(2) Construct the following classifier:

```
nil-(val roleentry)-nil-nil-nil
nil-(val conceptentry)-nil-nil-nil
PRE-Max => NUM-nil-MAX-nil-nil-<integer>.
```

```
<role-spec> ::= ( MIN <integer> )
```

Action:

(1) Transform <integer> to its binary representation.
(2) Construct the following classifier:

```
nil-(val roleentry)-nil-nil-nil
nil-(val conceptentry)-nil-nil-nil
PRE-Min => NUM-nil-MAX-nil-nil-<integer>.
```

```
<role-constraint-form> ::= |
    ( <role-constraint-type> <role-chain> <role-chain> )

<role-constraint-type> ::= =
```

Action:

(1) This is represented as two Role Value Maps, one using < and one using >. This has several advantages which are discussed in Chapter 5. Two sets of classifiers are constructed as detailed in the next two productions.

```
<role-constraint-type> ::= >
```

Action:

(1) Rearrange the order of the role chains and construct the same classifier detailed in the next production

```
<role-constraint-type> ::= <
```

Action:

(1) Assign the Role Value Map a unique number between 0 and 63. Call this RVMID.
(2) Construct the following classifier:

```
nil-(val conceptentry)-nil-nil-nil
PRE-RVMCheck =>
RVM-(val conceptentry)-nil-nil-RVMID
```

```
<role-chain> ::= |
    <role-name> <role-chain> |
    <role-name>
```

Action:

(1) Every role chain has a direction (LEFT or RIGHT) associated with it. The first role chain in a role constraint is considered to be the left one and the second role chain is considered to be the right one. For the first role in the left role chain the following classifiers are constructed to link the parent concept to the role chain:

```
RVM-(val conceptentry)-LEFT-nil-BFIELD-RVMID
PRE-LeftUndelay =>
NORM-<role-name>-DIFF-UP-BFIELD-RVMID

RVM-(val conceptentry)-LEFT-nil-BFIELD-RVMID
PRE-LeftUndelay =>
RVM-<role-name>-LEFT-nil-RVMID

RVM-(val conceptentry)-LEFT-nil-AFIELD-RVMID
PRE-LeftUndelay =>
RVM-<role-entry>-LEFT-nil-AFIELD-RVMID.
```

If the direction of the role chain is right, classifiers are generated similarly to those for the first link.

(2) If <role-name> has never appeared in a role chain before (check the INRC field of symbol table), then construct the following two classifiers:

```
RVM-<role-name>-LEFT-nil-AFIELD-nil
nil-<role-name>-DIFF-UP-BFIELD-nil
PRE-LeftUndelay => PRE-LeftUndelay

RVM-<role-name>-RIGHT-nil-AFIELD-nil
nil-<role-name>-DIFF-UP-BFIELD-nil
PRE-RightUndelay => PRE-RightUndelay
```

(3) If <role-name> is not the first role in the role chain, then classifiers are constructed that link the previous role in the role chain (call this <prev-role-name>) with the current role (<role-name>).

```
RVM-<prev-role-name>-LEFT-nil-BFIELD-RVMID
PRE-LeftUndelay =>
NORM-<role-name>-DIFF-UP-BFIELD-RVMID

RVM-<prev-role-name>-LEFT-nil-BFIELD-RVMID
PRE-LeftUndelay =>
RVM-<role-name>-LEFT-nil-BFIELD-RVMID
```

```
RVM-<prev-role-name>-LEFT-nil-AFIELD-RVMSYM
PRE-LeftUndelay =>
RVM-<role-name>-LEFT-AFIELD-RVMID
```

```
<role-name> ::= <atom>
```

Action: none.

```
<role-specification> ::= ( ROLESPEC <role-name> <role-form-list> )
```

Action: same as ROLE case of <gen-spec-form> production.

```
<role-form-list> ::= |
   <role-form> <role-form-list> | NIL
```

Action: none.

```
<role-form> ::=
   ( DIFFERENTIATES <role-name-list> ) |
   PRIMITIVE

<role-name-list> ::= |
   <role-name> <role-name-list> |
   NIL
```

APPENDIX G. Overhead Classifiers for Role Value Maps

(1) These classifiers manage the True and False messages.

```
RVMCheck2
False => False

RVMCheck2
True => True
```

(2) These classifiers manage the delay and undelay messages.

```
  RightDelay
~ RightUnDelay
~ QuiescentRVM => RightDelay

  RightUnDelay
~ RightDelay => RightDelay

  RightUnDelay
  RightDelay => RightUnDelay

  LeftDelay
~ LeftUnDelay
~ QuiescentRVM => LeftDelay

  LeftUnDelay
~ LeftDelay => LeftDelay

  LeftUnDelay
  LeftDelay => LeftUnDelay
```

(3) This classifier controls the control message.

```
  RVMCheck2
~ QuiescentRVM => RVMCheck2
```

(4) These classifiers ensure that the role chains are the same length. Four classifiers are required because there is no way to guarantee that both conditions are either left or right (no pass through between conditions).

```
  RVM-nil-LEFT-nil-AFIELD-######
~ RVM-nil-LEFT-nil-BFIELD-######
  LeftDelay => False

~ RVM-nil-LEFT-nil-AFIELD-######
  RVM-nil-LEFT-nil-BFIELD-######
  LeftDelay => False

  RVM-nil-RIGHT-nil-AFIELD-######
~ RVM-nil-RIGHT-nil-BFIELD-######
  RightDelay => False

~ RVM-nil-RIGHT-nil-AFIELD-######
  RVM-nil-RIGHT-nil-BFIELD-######
  RightDelay => False
```

(5) These classifiers confirm the successful completion of a Role Chain check.

```
~ RVM-nil-RIGHT-nil-AFIELD-######
~ RVM-nil-RIGHT-nil-BFIELD-######
  RightDelay
~ QuiescentRVM => RightOK

~ RVM-nil-LEFT-nil-AFIELD-######
~ RVM-nil-LEFT-nil-BFIELD-######
  LeftDelay
~ QuiescentRVM => LeftOK
```

(6) Both Role Chain checks are over and the subsumption test has been successfully completed.

```
  LeftOK
  RightOK => True
```

(7) These classifiers are activated when the DIFFERENTIATES relation between roles of different chains is not confirmed. In this case the propagation continues to the top role Part, indicating a failure, and the False message is emitted.

```
  NORM-Part-nil-nil-nil
  RightDelay => False

  NORM-Part-nil-nil-nil
  LeftDelay => False
```

(8) These classifiers keep the current role (the one that is delayed in the propagation) on the message list while the differentiation test is completed.

```
RVM-nil-RIGHT-nil-nil-nil
RightDelay => RVM-nil-RIGHT-nil-nil-nil

RVM-nil-LEFT-nil-nil-nil
LeftDelay => RVM-nil-LEFT-nil-nil-nil
```

APPENDIX H. Classifier List for Role Value Map Example

This list includes the classifiers that would be activated in the course of the subsumption test described in the text.

```
NORM-GodFather-DIFF-UP-nil =>
NORM-Part-DIFF-UP-nil

NORM-Relative-DIFF-UP-nil =>
NORM-Part-DIFF-UP-nil

NORM-Cousin-DIFF-UP-nil =>
NORM-Relative-DIFF-UP-nil

NORM-GoodFriend-DIFF-UP-nil =>
NORM-Part-DIFF-UP-nil

NORM-BestFriend-DIFF-UP-nil =>
NORM-GoodFriend-DIFF-UP-nil

nil-PersonA-nil-nil-nil
RVMCheck => RVM-PersonA-nil-nil-nil-1

RVM-Cousin-LEFT-nil-AFIELD-nil
nil-Cousin-DIFF-UP-BFIELD-nil
LeftDelay => LeftUnDelay

RVM-Cousin-RIGHT-nil-AFIELD-nil
nil-Cousin-DIFF-UP-BFIELD-nil
RightDelay => RightUnDelay

RVM-GodFather-LEFT-nil-AFIELD-nil
nil-GodFather-DIFF-UP-BFIELD-nil
LeftDelay => LeftUnDelay

RVM-GodFather-RIGHT-nil-AFIELD-nil
nil-GodFather-DIFF-UP-BFIELD-nil
RightDelay => RightUnDelay

RVM-PersonA-LEFT-nil-BFIELD-1
LeftUnDelay => NORM-Cousin-DIFF-UP-BFIELD-1

RVM-PersonA-LEFT-nil-BFIELD-1
LeftUnDelay => RVM-Cousin-LEFT-nil-BFIELD-1

RVM-PersonA-LEFT-nil-AFIELD-1
LeftUnDelay => RVM-Cousin-LEFT-nil-AFIELD-1

RVM-Cousin-LEFT-nil-BFIELD-1
LeftUnDelay => NORM-GodFather-DIFF-UP-BFIELD-1

RVM-Cousin-LEFT-nil-BFIELD-1
LeftUnDelay => RVM-GodFather-LEFT-nil-BFIELD-1

RVM-Cousin-LEFT-nil-AFIELD-1
LeftUnDelay => RVM-GodFather-LEFT-nil-AFIELD-1
```

```
RVM-GoodFriend-LEFT-nil-AFIELD-nil
nil-GoodFriend-DIFF-UP-BFIELD-nil
LeftDelay => LeftUnDelay

RVM-GoodFriend-RIGHT-nil-AFIELD-nil
nil-GoodFriend-DIFF-UP-BFIELD-nil
RightDelay => RightUnDelay

RVM-PersonA-RIGHT-nil-BFIELD-1
RightUnDelay => NORM-GoodFriend-DIFF-UP-BFIELD-1

RVM-PersonA-RIGHT-nil-BFIELD-1
RightUnDelay => RVM-GoodFriend-RIGHT-nil-BFIELD-1

RVM-PersonA-RIGHT-nil-AFIELD-1
RightUnDelay => RVM-GoodFriend-RIGHT-nil-AFIELD-1

nil-PersonD-nil-nil-nil
RVMCheck => RVM-PersonD-nil-nil-nil-2

RVM-Relative-LEFT-nil-AFIELD-nil
nil-Relative-DIFF-UP-BFIELD-nil
LeftDelay => LeftUnDelay

RVM-Relative-RIGHT-nil-AFIELD-nil
nil-Relative-DIFF-UP-BFIELD-nil
RightDelay => RightUnDelay

RVM-GodFather-LEFT-nil-AFIELD-nil
nil-GodFather-DIFF-UP-BFIELD-nil
LeftDelay => LeftUnDelay

RVM-GodFather-RIGHT-nil-AFIELD-nil
nil-GodFather-DIFF-UP-BFIELD-nil
RightDelay => RightUnDelay

RVM-PersonD-LEFT-nil-BFIELD-2
LeftUnDelay => NORM-Relative-DIFF-UP-BFIELD-2

RVM-PersonD-LEFT-nil-BFIELD-2
LeftUnDelay => RVM-Relative-LEFT-nil-BFIELD-2

RVM-PersonD-LEFT-nil-AFIELD-2
LeftUnDelay => RVM-Relative-LEFT-nil-AFIELD-2

RVM-Relative-LEFT-nil-BFIELD-2
LeftUnDelay => NORM-GodFather-DIFF-UP-BFIELD-2

RVM-Relative-LEFT-nil-BFIELD-2
LeftUnDelay => RVM-GodFather-LEFT-nil-BFIELD-2

RVM-Relative-LEFT-nil-AFIELD-2
LeftUnDelay => RVM-GodFather-LEFT-nil-AFIELD-2

RVM-BestFriend-LEFT-nil-AFIELD-nil
nil-BestFriend-DIFF-UP-BFIELD-nil
LeftDelay => LeftUnDelay

RVM-BestFriend-RIGHT-nil-AFIELD-nil
nil-BestFriend-DIFF-UP-BFIELD-nil
RightDelay => RightUnDelay

RVM-PersonD-RIGHT-nil-BFIELD-2
RightUnDelay => NORM-BestFriend-DIFF-UP-BFIELD-2
```

```
RVM-PersonD-RIGHT-nil-BFIELD-2
RightUnDelay => RVM-BestFriend-RIGHT-nil-BFIELD-2

RVM-PersonD-RIGHT-nil-AFIELD-2
RightUnDelay => RVM-BestFriend-RIGHT-nil-AFIELD-2
```

APPENDIX I. Classifiers for The MSS Example

```
NORM-Thing-nil-nil-###########
ON-Thing-nil-nil-###########
And => HOLD-nil-nil-nil-###########

HOLD-Thing-nil-nil-###########
NORM-Thing-nil-nil-###########
SetDiff => HOLD-nil-nil-nil-###########

NORM-Part-nil-nil-###########
ON-Part-nil-nil-###########
And => HOLD-nil-nil-nil-###########

HOLD-Part-nil-nil-###########
NORM-Part-nil-nil-###########
SetDiff => HOLD-nil-nil-nil-###########

NORM-Person-SUPERC-UP-1########## =>
NORM-Thing-SUPERC-UP-###########

NORM-Thing-SUPERC-DOWN-1########## =>
NORM-Person-SUPERC-DOWN-1##########

NORM-Limb-nil-nil-###########
ON-Limb-nil-nil-###########
And => HOLD-nil-nil-nil-###########

HOLD-Limb-nil-nil-###########
NORM-Limb-nil-nil-###########
SetDiff => HOLD-nil-nil-nil-###########

NORM-Limb-DIFF-UP-########### =>
NORM-Part-DIFF-UP-###########
NORM-Part-DIFF-DOWN-########### =>
NORM-Limb-DIFF-DOWN-###########

nil-Person-nil-nil-###########
nil-Limb-nil-nil-###########
VR => nil-Legs-SUPERC-nil-#1#########

nil-Person-nil-nil-###########
rolemess => nil-Limb-DIFF-nil-###########

NORM-Sex-nil-nil-###########
ON-Sex-nil-nil-###########
And => HOLD-nil-nil-nil-###########

HOLD-Sex-nil-nil-###########
NORM-Sex-nil-nil-###########
SetDiff => HOLD-nil-nil-nil-###########

NORM-Sex-DIFF-UP-########### =>
NORM-Part-DIFF-UP-###########
```

```
NORM-Part-DIFF-DOWN-########### =>
NORM-Sex-DIFF-DOWN-###########

nil-Person-nil-nil-###########
nil-Sex-nil-nil-###########
VR => nil-Gender-SUPERC-nil-##1########

nil-Person-nil-nil-###########
rolemess => nil-Sex-DIFF-nil-###########

NORM-Person-nil-nil-###########
ON-Person-nil-nil-###########
And => HOLD-nil-nil-nil-###########

HOLD-Person-nil-nil-###########
NORM-Person-nil-nil-###########
SetDiff => HOLD-nil-nil-nil-###########

NORM-Legs-SUPERC-UP-#1######### =>
NORM-Thing-SUPERC-UP-###########

NORM-Thing-SUPERC-DOWN-#1######### =>
NORM-Legs-SUPERC-DOWN-#1#########

NORM-Legs-nil-nil-###########
ON-Legs-nil-nil-###########
And => HOLD-nil-nil-nil-###########

HOLD-Legs-nil-nil-###########
NORM-Legs-nil-nil-###########
SetDiff => HOLD-nil-nil-nil-###########

NORM-Gender-SUPERC-UP-##1######## =>
NORM-Thing-SUPERC-UP-###########

NORM-Thing-SUPERC-DOWN-##1######## =>
NORM-Gender-SUPERC-DOWN-##1########

NORM-Gender-nil-nil-###########
ON-Gender-nil-nil-###########
And => HOLD-nil-nil-nil-###########

HOLD-Gender-nil-nil-###########
NORM-Gender-nil-nil-###########
SetDiff => HOLD-nil-nil-nil-###########

NORM-Male-SUPERC-UP-##11####### =>
NORM-Gender-SUPERC-UP-##1########

NORM-Gender-SUPERC-DOWN-##11####### =>
NORM-Male-SUPERC-DOWN-##11#######

NORM-Male-nil-nil-###########
ON-Male-nil-nil-###########
And => HOLD-nil-nil-nil-###########

HOLD-Male-nil-nil-###########
NORM-Male-nil-nil-###########
SetDiff => HOLD-nil-nil-nil-###########

NORM-Female-SUPERC-UP-##1#1###### =>
NORM-Gender-SUPERC-UP-##1########

NORM-Gender-SUPERC-DOWN-##1#1###### =>
NORM-Female-SUPERC-DOWN-##1#1######
```

```
NORM-Female-nil-nil-###########
ON-Female-nil-nil-###########
And => HOLD-nil-nil-nil-###########

HOLD-Female-nil-nil-###########
NORM-Female-nil-nil-###########
SetDiff => HOLD-nil-nil-nil-###########

NORM-Man-SUPERC-UP-1########## =>
NORM-Person-SUPERC-UP-1##########

NORM-Person-SUPERC-DOWN-1########## =>
NORM-Man-SUPERC-DOWN-1##########

nil-Man-nil-nil-###########
nil-Sex-nil-nil-###########
VR => nil-Male-SUPERC-nil-##11#######

nil-Man-nil-nil-###########
rolemess => nil-Sex-DIFF-nil-###########

NORM-Man-nil-nil-###########
ON-Man-nil-nil-###########
And => HOLD-nil-nil-nil-###########

HOLD-Man-nil-nil-###########
NORM-Man-nil-nil-###########
SetDiff => HOLD-nil-nil-nil-###########

NORM-Woman-SUPERC-UP-1########## =>
NORM-Person-SUPERC-UP-1##########

NORM-Person-SUPERC-DOWN-1########## =>
NORM-Woman-SUPERC-DOWN-1##########

nil-Woman-nil-nil-###########
nil-Sex-nil-nil-###########
VR => nil-Female-SUPERC-nil-##1#1######

nil-Woman-nil-nil-###########
rolemess => nil-Sex-DIFF-nil-###########

NORM-Woman-nil-nil-###########
ON-Woman-nil-nil-###########
And => HOLD-nil-nil-nil-###########

HOLD-Woman-nil-nil-###########
NORM-Woman-nil-nil-###########
SetDiff => HOLD-nil-nil-nil-###########

NORM-Young-SUPERC-UP-#####1##### =>
NORM-Thing-SUPERC-UP-###########

NORM-Thing-SUPERC-DOWN-#####1##### =>
NORM-Young-SUPERC-DOWN-#####1#####

NORM-Young-nil-nil-###########
ON-Young-nil-nil-###########
And => HOLD-nil-nil-nil-###########

HOLD-Young-nil-nil-###########
NORM-Young-nil-nil-###########
SetDiff => HOLD-nil-nil-nil-###########

NORM-YoungMan-SUPERC-UP-1########## =>
NORM-Person-SUPERC-UP-1##########
```

```
NORM-Person-SUPERC-DOWN-1########## =>
NORM-YoungMan-SUPERC-DOWN-1##########

nil-YoungMan-nil-nil-###########
nil-Sex-nil-nil-###########
VR => nil-Male-SUPERC-nil-##11#######

nil-YoungMan-nil-nil-###########
rolemess => nil-Sex-DIFF-nil-###########

NORM-Age-nil-nil-###########
ON-Age-nil-nil-###########
And => HOLD-nil-nil-nil-###########

HOLD-Age-nil-nil-###########
NORM-Age-nil-nil-###########
SetDiff => HOLD-nil-nil-nil-###########

NORM-Age-DIFF-UP-########### =>
NORM-Part-DIFF-UP-###########

NORM-Part-DIFF-DOWN-########### =>
NORM-Age-DIFF-DOWN-###########

nil-YoungMan-nil-nil-###########
nil-Age-nil-nil-###########
VR => nil-Young-SUPERC-nil-#####1#####

nil-YoungMan-nil-nil-###########
rolemess => nil-Age-DIFF-nil-###########

NORM-YoungMan-nil-nil-###########
ON-YoungMan-nil-nil-###########
And => HOLD-nil-nil-nil-###########

HOLD-YoungMan-nil-nil-###########
NORM-YoungMan-nil-nil-###########
SetDiff => HOLD-nil-nil-nil-###########

NORM-HighRiskDriver-SUPERC-UP-1########## =>
NORM-Person-SUPERC-UP-1##########

NORM-Person-SUPERC-DOWN-1########## =>
NORM-HighRiskDriver-SUPERC-DOWN-1##########

nil-HighRiskDriver-nil-nil-###########
nil-Sex-nil-nil-###########
VR => nil-Male-SUPERC-nil-##11#######

nil-HighRiskDriver-nil-nil-###########
rolemess => nil-Sex-DIFF-nil-###########

nil-HighRiskDriver-nil-nil-###########
nil-Age-nil-nil-###########
VR => nil-Young-SUPERC-nil-#####1#####

nil-HighRiskDriver-nil-nil-###########
rolemess => nil-Age-DIFF-nil-###########

NORM-HighRiskDriver-nil-nil-###########
ON-HighRiskDriver-nil-nil-###########
And => HOLD-nil-nil-nil-###########
```

```
HOLD-HighRiskDriver-nil-nil-###########
NORM-HighRiskDriver-nil-nil-###########
SetDiff => HOLD-nil-nil-nil-###########
```

APPENDIX J. Extended MSS Example

This example shows how all the parts of the MSS algorithm work together. Consider the network described below and shown pictorially in Figure A.2:

```
(CONCEPTSPEC Person PRIMITIVE (SPECIALIZES Thing)
   (ROLE Limb (VRCONCEPT Legs))
   (ROLE Sex (VRCONCEPT Gender))))

(CONCEPTSPEC Legs PRIMITIVE
   (SPECIALIZES Thing))

(CONCEPTSPEC Gender PRIMITIVE (SPECIALIZES Thing))

(CONCEPTSPEC Male PRIMITIVE (SPECIALIZES Gender))

(CONCEPTSPEC Female PRIMITIVE (SPECIALIZES Gender))

(CONCEPTSPEC Man (SPECIALIZES Person)
   (ROLE Sex (VRCONCEPT Male)))

(CONCEPTSPEC Woman (SPECIALIZES Person)
   (ROLE Sex (VRCONCEPT Female))

(CONCEPTSPEC Young PRIMITIVE (SPECIALIZES Thing))

(CONCEPTSPEC VeryYoung PRIMITIVE (SPECIALIZES Young))

(CONCEPTSPEC YoungMan (SPECIALIZES Person)
   (ROLE Sex (VRCONCEPT Male))
   (ROLE Age (VRCONCEPT Young)))

(CONCEPTSPEC HighRiskDriver (SPECIALIZES Person)
   (ROLE Sex (VRCONCEPT Male)))
   (ROLE Age (VRCONCEPT Young)))

(CONCEPTSPEC Child (SPECIALIZES Person)
   (ROLE Age (VRCONCEPT VeryYoung))
   (ROLE Sibling (VRCONCEPT Child)))

(CONCEPTSPEC ChildWithTwin (SPECIALIZES Child)
   (ROLE Twin (DIFFERENTIATES Sibling) (NUMBER 1))
   (= Age (Twin Age)))

(CONCEPTSPEC ChildWithSiblings (SPECIALIZES Child)
   (ROLE Sibling (MIN 1)))

(CONCEPTSPEC ChildWithTwoSisters (SPECIALIZES Child)
   (ROLE Sibling (VRCONCEPT Female) (NUMBER 2))).
```

The queries to find the set of Most Specific Subsumers for the concept ChildWithTwoSisters is shown following Figure A.2.

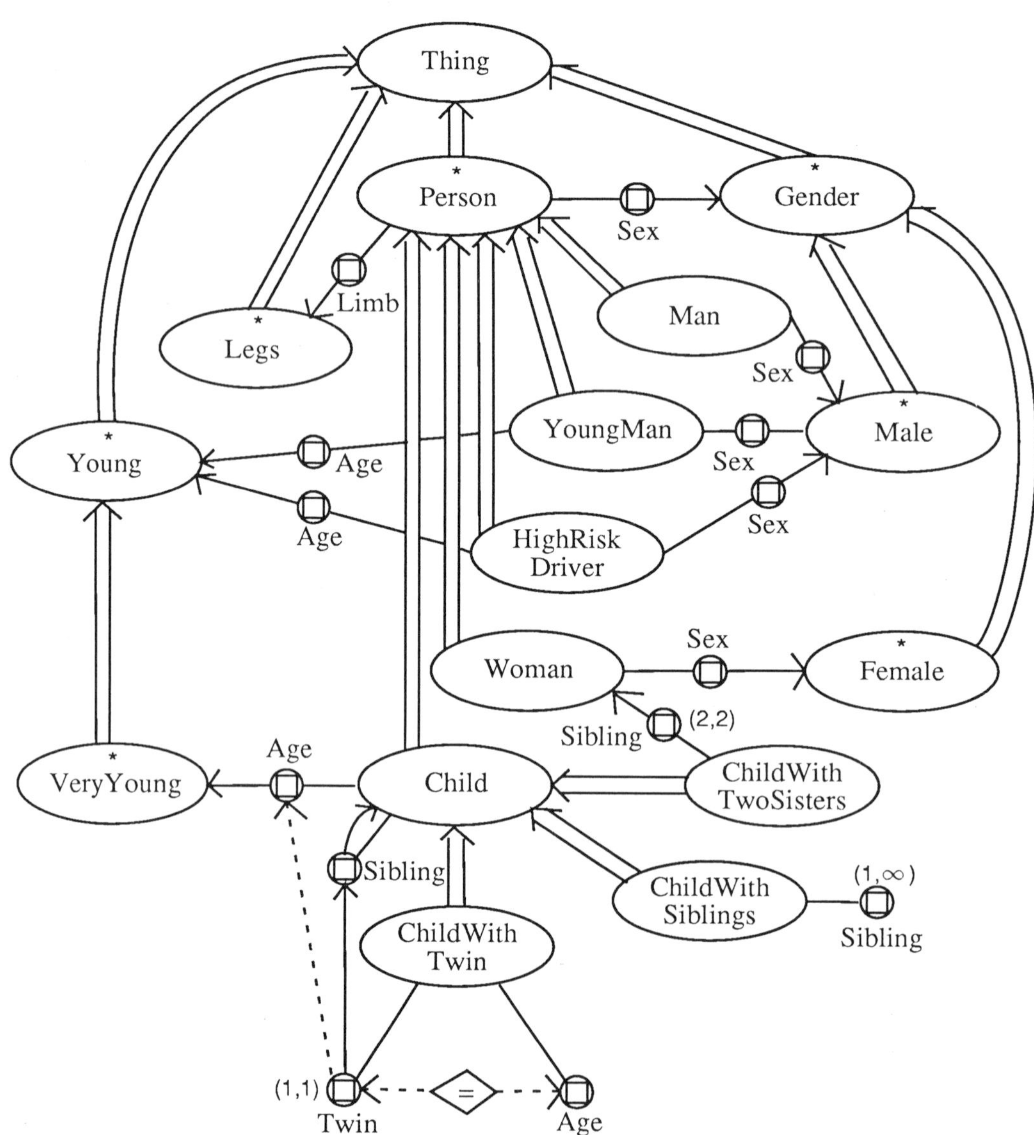

FIGURE A.1 Extended MSS Example

Time Step		Message List
T1:		NORM–Person–SUPERC–DOWN–10000000000
		NORM–ChildWithTwoSisters–SUPERC–DOWN–10000000000
T2:	→	NORM–Person–SUPERC–UP–10000000000
	→	And
T3:		NORM–Thing–SUPERC–UP–10000000000
	→	Quiescent
T4:		Reset
		Save
T5:	→	Or
	→	NORM–Person–SUPERC–UP–10000000000
T6:		NORM–Thing–SUPERC–UP–10000000000
		ON–Person–SUPERC–UP–10000000000
		Or
T7:		ON–Person–SUPERC–UP–10000000000
		ON–Thing–SUPERC–UP–10000000000
		Or
T8:		ON–Person–SUPERC–UP–10000000000
		ON–Thing–SUPERC–UP–10000000000
		Or
	→	Quiescent
T9:		ON–Person–SUPERC–UP–10000000000
		ON–Thing–SUPERC–UP–10000000000
	→	SetHold
	→	Reset
T10:		HOLD–Person–SUPERC–UP–10000000000
		HOLD–Thing–SUPERC–UP–10000000000
		HOLD–Person–SUPERC–UP–10000000000
		HOLD–Thing–SUPERC–UP–10000000000
	→	SetDiff
	→	NORM–ChildWithTwoSisters–SUPERC–UP–10000000000

Time Step		Message List
T11:		HOLD–Thing–SUPERC–UP–10000000000 HOLD–Person–SUPERC–UP–10000000000 NORM–Child–SUPERC–UP–10000000000 SetDiff NORM–Thing–SUPERC–UP–10000000000 NORM–Thing–SUPERC–UP–10000000000
T12:		HOLD–Person–SUPERC–UP–10000000000 NORM–Person–SUPERC–UP–10000000000 SetDiff
T13:	 →	NORM–Thing–SUPERC–UP–10000000000 SetDiff Quiescent
T14:		Save Reset
T15:		
T16:	→ →	Reset rolemess
T17:		(GetSubsumers ChildWithTwoSisters)
T18:	→ →	Or NORM–ChildWithTwoSisters–SUPERC–UP–10000000000
T19:		NORM–Child–SUPERC–UP–10000000000 ON–ChildWithTwoSisters–SUPERC–UP–10000000000 Or NORM–Thing–SUPERC–UP–10000000000 NORM–Thing–SUPERC–UP–10000000000
T20:		NORM–Person–SUPERC–UP–10000000000 ON–ChildWithTwoSisters–SUPERC–UP–10000000000 ON–Child–SUPERC–UP–10000000000 ON–Thing–SUPERC–UP–10000000000 Or

Time Step		Message List
T21:		NORM–Thing–SUPERC–UP–10000000000
		ON–ChildWithTwoSisters–SUPERC–UP–10000000000
		ON–Child–SUPERC–UP–10000000000
		ON–Thing–SUPERC–UP–10000000000
		ON–Person–SUPERC–UP–10000000000
		Or
	→	Quiescent
T22:		ON–ChildWithTwoSisters–SUPERC–UP–10000000000
		ON–Child–SUPERC–UP–10000000000
		ON–Thing–SUPERC–UP–10000000000
		ON–Person–SUPERC–UP–10000000000
		ON–Thing–SUPERC–UP–10000000000
		(FindAllRoles1)
T23:	→	ON–ChildWithTwoSisters–SUPERC–UP–10000000000
	→	ON–Child–SUPERC–UP–10000000000
	→	ON–Thing–SUPERC–UP–10000000000
	→	ON–Person–SUPERC–UP–10000000000
	→	ON–Thing–SUPERC–UP–10000000000
	→	Reset
	→	rolemess
T24:		ON–Limbs–DIFF–UP–10000000000
		ON–Sex–DIFF–UP–10000000000
		ON–Age–DIFF–UP–10000000000
		ON–Sibling–DIFF–UP–10000000000
		ON–Sibling–DIFF–UP–10000000000
		ON–Limbs–DIFF–UP–10000000000
		ON–Sex–DIFF–UP–10000000000
		ON–Age–DIFF–UP–10000000000
		ON–Sibling–DIFF–UP–10000000000
	→	RVMCheck
	→	Reset
T25:		
		(ImmediateSuperCs1)
T26:	→	NORM–Person–SUPERC–UP–10000000000
T27:		NORM–Thing–SUPERC–UP–10000000000
	→	HOLD–Thing–SUPERC–UP–00000000000
	→	SetDiff

Time Step		Message List
T28:		SetDiff
	→	Quiescent
T29:		Save
		Reset
T30:		
		(ImmediateSubCs1)
T31:	→	NORM–Person–SUPERC–DOWN–10000000000
T32:		NORM–Man–SUPERC–DOWN–10000000000
		NORM–Woman–SUPERC–DOWN–10000000000
		NORM–YoungMan–SUPERC–DOWN–10000000000
		NORM–HighRiskDriver–SUPERC–DOWN–10000000000
		NORM–Child–SUPERC–DOWN–10000000000
T33:	→	NORM–Man–SUPERC–UP–10000000000
	→	And
T34:		NORM–Person–SUPERC–UP–10000000000
T35:		NORM–Thing–SUPERC–UP–10000000000
	→	Quiescent
T36:		Reset
		Save
T37:		
		(SubsumesP)
T38:	→	Or
	→	NORM–Man–SUPERC–UP–10000000000
T39:		NORM–Person–SUPERC–UP–10000000000
		ON–Man–SUPERC–UP–10000000000
		Or

Time Step	Message List
T40:	NORM–Thing–SUPERC–UP–10000000000
	ON–Man–SUPERC–UP–10000000000
	ON–Person–SUPERC–UP–10000000000
	Or
T41:	ON–Man–SUPERC–UP–10000000000
	ON–Person–SUPERC–UP–10000000000
	ON–Thing–SUPERC–UP–10000000000
	Or
	→ Quiescent
T42:	ON–Man–SUPERC–UP–10000000000
	ON–Person–SUPERC–UP–10000000000
	ON–Thing–SUPERC–UP–10000000000
	→ SetHold
	→ Reset
T43:	HOLD–Man–SUPERC–UP–10000000000
	HOLD–Person–SUPERC–UP–10000000000
	HOLD–Thing–SUPERC–UP–10000000000
T44:	HOLD–Man–SUPERC–UP–10000000000
	HOLD–Person–SUPERC–UP–10000000000
	HOLD–Thing–SUPERC–UP–10000000000
	→ SetDiff
	→ NORM–ChildWithTwoSisters–SUPERC–UP–10000000000
T45:	HOLD–Thing–SUPERC–UP–10000000000
	HOLD–Person–SUPERC–UP–10000000000
	HOLD–Man–SUPERC–UP–10000000000
	NORM–Child–SUPERC–UP–10000000000
	SetDiff
	NORM–Thing–SUPERC–UP–10000000000
	NORM–Person–SUPERC–UP–10000000000

Time Step		Message List
T46:		NORM–Thing–SUPERC–UP–10000000000
		HOLD–Man–SUPERC–UP–10000000000
		NORM–Person–SUPERC–UP–10000000000
		SetDiff
T47:		NORM–Thing–SUPERC–UP–10000000000
		HOLD–Man–SUPERC–UP–10000000000
		SetDiff
	→	Quiescent
T48:		HOLD–Man–SUPERC–UP–10000000000
		Save
		Reset
T49:		ON–Man–SUPERC–UP–10000000000
		ON–Man–SUPERC–UP–10000000000
	→	Reset
	→	rolemess
T50:		ON–Sex–DIFF–UP–10000000000
		(GetSubsumers)
T51:	→	Or
	→	NORM–ChildWithTwoSisters–SUPERC–UP–10000000000
T52:		NORM–Child–SUPERC–UP–10000000000
		ON–ChildWithTwoSisters–SUPERC–UP–10000000000
		Or
		NORM–Thing–SUPERC–UP–10000000000
		NORM–Person–SUPERC–UP–10000000000
T53:		NORM–Thing–SUPERC–UP–10000000000
		NORM–Person–SUPERC–UP–10000000000
		ON–ChildWithTwoSisters–SUPERC–UP–10000000000
		ON–Child–SUPERC–UP–10000000000
		ON–Thing–SUPERC–UP–10000000000
		ON–Person–SUPERC–UP–10000000000
		Or

Time Step		Message List
T54:		NORM–Thing–SUPERC–UP–10000000000
		ON–ChildWithTwoSisters–SUPERC–UP–10000000000
		ON–Child–SUPERC–UP–10000000000
		ON–Thing–SUPERC–UP–10000000000
		ON–Person–SUPERC–UP–10000000000
		ON–Thing–SUPERC–UP–10000000000
		ON–Person–SUPERC–UP–10000000000
		Or
	→	Quiescent
T55:		ON–ChildWithTwoSisters–SUPERC–UP–10000000000
		ON–Child–SUPERC–UP–10000000000
		ON–Thing–SUPERC–UP–10000000000
		ON–Person–SUPERC–UP–10000000000
		ON–Thing–SUPERC–UP–10000000000
		FindAllRoles1
T56:	→	ON–ChildWithTwoSisters–SUPERC–UP–10000000000
	→	ON–Child–SUPERC–UP–10000000000
	→	ON–Thing–SUPERC–UP–10000000000
	→	ON–Person–SUPERC–UP–10000000000
	→	ON–Thing–SUPERC–UP–10000000000
	→	Reset
	→	rolemess
T57:		ON–Limbs–DIFF–UP–10000000000
		ON–Sex–DIFF–UP–10000000000
		ON–Age–DIFF–UP–10000000000
		ON–Sibling–DIFF–UP–10000000000
		ON–Sibling–DIFF–UP–10000000000
		ON–Limbs–DIFF–UP–10000000000
		ON–Sex–DIFF–UP–10000000000
		ON–Age–DIFF–UP–10000000000
		ON–Sibling–DIFF–UP–10000000000
		(RoleSubsumesP1)
		(FindVR1)

Time Step		Message List
T58:	→	ON–ChildWithTwoSisters–SUPERC–UP–10000000000
	→	ON–Child–SUPERC–UP–10000000000
	→	ON–Thing–SUPERC–UP–10000000000
	→	ON–Person–SUPERC–UP–10000000000
	→	ON–Thing–SUPERC–UP–10000000000
	→	NORM–Sex–DIFF–UP–00000000000
	→	VR
	→	Reset
T59:		NORM–Part–DIFF–UP–00000000000
		ON–Gender–SUPERC–UP–10100000000
	→	ResetNorm
	→	SetHold
	→	Reset
T60:		NORM–Gender–SUPERC–UP–10100000000
		HOLD–Gender–SUPERC–UP–10100000000
T61:		NORM–Thing–SUPERC–UP–10100000000
		HOLD–Gender–SUPERC–UP–10100000000
	→	SetDiff
T62:		HOLD–Gender–SUPERC–UP–10100000000
		SetDiff
T63:		HOLD–Gender–SUPERC–UP–10100000000
		SetDiff
T64:		HOLD–Gender–SUPERC–UP–10100000000
		SetDiff
	→	Quiescent
T65:		HOLD–Gender–SUPERC–UP–10100000000
		Save
		Reset
T66:		ON–Gender–SUPERC–UP–10100000000
T67:		ON–Gender–SUPERC–UP–10100000000
		FindVR1

Time Step		Message List
T68:	→	ON–Man–SUPERC–UP–10000000000
	→	NORM–Sex–DIFF–UP–00000000000
	→	VR
	→	Reset
T69:		NORM–Part–DIFF–UP–00000000000
		ON–Male–SUPERC–UP–10110000000
	→	ResetNorm
	→	SetHold
	→	Reset
T70:		NORM–Male–SUPERC–UP–10110000000
		HOLD–Male–SUPERC–UP–10110000000
T71:		NORM–Gender–SUPERC–UP–10110000000
		HOLD–Male–SUPERC–UP–10110000000
	→	SetDiff
T72:		NORM–Thing–SUPERC–UP–10110000000
		HOLD–Male–SUPERC–UP–10110000000
		SetDiff
T73:		HOLD–Male–SUPERC–UP–10110000000
		SetDiff
T74:		HOLD–Male–SUPERC–UP–10110000000
		SetDiff
	→	Quiescent
T75:		HOLD–Male–SUPERC–UP–10110000000
		Save
		Reset
T76:		ON–Male–SUPERC–UP–10110000000
		(NewSuperCListP)
T77:	→	ON–Male–SUPERC–UP–10110000000
	→	SetHold
	→	Reset

Time Step		Message List
T78:		HOLD–Male–SUPERC–UP–10110000000
	→	ON–Gender–SUPERC–UP–10100000000
	→	ResetNorm
T79:		ON–Gender–SUPERC–UP–10100000000
		HOLD–Male–SUPERC–UP–10110000000
		NORM–Gender–SUPERC–UP–10100000000
	→	SetDiff
T80:		NORM–Thing–SUPERC–UP–10100000000
		HOLD–Male–SUPERC–UP–10110000000
		ON–Gender–SUPERC–UP–10100000000
		SetDiff
T81:		HOLD–Male–SUPERC–UP–10110000000
		ON–Gender–SUPERC–UP–10100000000
		SetDiff
T82:		HOLD–Male–SUPERC–UP–10110000000
		ON–Gender–SUPERC–UP–10100000000
		SetDiff
	→	Quiescent
T83:		HOLD–Male–SUPERC–UP–10110000000
		ON–Gender–SUPERC–UP–10100000000
		Save
		Reset
T84:		ON–Male–SUPERC–UP–10110000000
T85:		ON–Male–SUPERC–UP–10110000000
T86:	→	ON–Man–SUPERC–UP–10000000000
	→	NORM–Woman–SUPERC–UP–10000000000
	→	And
T87:		NORM–Person–SUPERC–UP–10000000000
		ON–Man–SUPERC–UP–10000000000
T88:		NORM–Thing–SUPERC–UP–10000000000
		ON–Man–SUPERC–UP–10000000000
		Quiescent

Time Step		Message List
T89:		ON–Man–SUPERC–UP–10000000000
		Reset
		Save
		(SubsumesP)
T90:	→	Or
	→	NORM–Woman–SUPERC–UP–10000000000
T91:		NORM–Person–SUPERC–UP–10000000000
		ON–Woman–SUPERC–UP–10000000000
		Or
T92:		NORM–Thing–SUPERC–UP–10000000000
		ON–Woman–SUPERC–UP–10000000000
		ON–Person–SUPERC–UP–10000000000
		Or
T93:		ON–Woman–SUPERC–UP–10000000000
		ON–Person–SUPERC–UP–10000000000
		ON–Thing–SUPERC–UP–10000000000
		Or
	→	Quiescent
T94:		ON–Woman–SUPERC–UP–10000000000
		ON–Person–SUPERC–UP–10000000000
		ON–Thing–SUPERC–UP–10000000000
	→	SetHold
	→	Reset
T95:		HOLD–Woman–SUPERC–UP–10000000000
		HOLD–Person–SUPERC–UP–10000000000
		HOLD–Thing–SUPERC–UP–10000000000
		HOLD–Woman–SUPERC–UP–10000000000
		HOLD–Person–SUPERC–UP–10000000000
		HOLD–Thing–SUPERC–UP–10000000000
	→	SetDiff
	→	NORM–ChildWithTwoSisters–SUPERC–UP–10000000000

Time Step	Message List
T96:	HOLD–Thing–SUPERC–UP–10000000000 HOLD–Person–SUPERC–UP–10000000000 HOLD–Woman–SUPERC–UP–10000000000 NORM–Child–SUPERC–UP–10000000000 SetDiff NORM–Thing–SUPERC–UP–10000000000 NORM–Person–SUPERC–UP–10000000000
T97:	NORM–Thing–SUPERC–UP–10000000000 HOLD–Woman–SUPERC–UP–10000000000 NORM–Person–SUPERC–UP–10000000000 SetDiff
T98:	NORM–Thing–SUPERC–UP–10000000000 HOLD–Woman–SUPERC–UP–10000000000 SetDiff → Quiescent
T99:	HOLD–Woman–SUPERC–UP–10000000000 Save Reset
T100:	ON–Woman–SUPERC–UP–10000000000
T101:	ON–Woman–SUPERC–UP–10000000000 → Reset → rolemess
T102:	ON–Sex–DIFF–UP–10000000000
	(GetSubsumers)
T103:	→ Or → NORM–ChildWithTwoSisters–SUPERC–UP–10000000000
T104:	NORM–Child–SUPERC–UP–10000000000 ON–ChildWithTwoSisters–SUPERC–UP–10000000000 Or NORM–Thing–SUPERC–UP–10000000000 NORM–Person–SUPERC–UP–10000000000

Time Step		Message List
T105:		NORM–Thing–SUPERC–UP–10000000000
		NORM–Person–SUPERC–UP–10000000000
		ON–ChildWithTwoSisters–SUPERC–UP–10000000000
		ON–Child–SUPERC–UP–10000000000
		ON–Thing–SUPERC–UP–10000000000
		ON–Person–SUPERC–UP–10000000000
		Or
T106:		NORM–Thing–SUPERC–UP–10000000000
		ON–ChildWithTwoSisters–SUPERC–UP–10000000000
		ON–Child–SUPERC–UP–10000000000
		ON–Thing–SUPERC–UP–10000000000
		ON–Person–SUPERC–UP–10000000000
		ON–Thing–SUPERC–UP–10000000000
		ON–Person–SUPERC–UP–10000000000
		Or
	→	Quiescent
T107:		ON–ChildWithTwoSisters–SUPERC–UP–10000000000
		ON–Child–SUPERC–UP–10000000000
		ON–Thing–SUPERC–UP–10000000000
		ON–Person–SUPERC–UP–10000000000
		ON–Thing–SUPERC–UP–10000000000
		(FindAllRoles1)
T108:	→	ON–ChildWithTwoSisters–SUPERC–UP–10000000000
	→	ON–Child–SUPERC–UP–10000000000
	→	ON–Thing–SUPERC–UP–10000000000
	→	ON–Person–SUPERC–UP–10000000000
	→	ON–Thing–SUPERC–UP–10000000000
	→	Reset
	→	rolemess
T109:		ON–Limbs–DIFF–UP–10000000000
		ON–Sex–DIFF–UP–10000000000
		ON–Age–DIFF–UP–10000000000
		ON–Sibling–DIFF–UP–10000000000
		ON–Sibling–DIFF–UP–10000000000

Time Step		Message List
T110:		ON–Limbs–DIFF–UP–10000000000
		ON–Sex–DIFF–UP–10000000000
		ON–Age–DIFF–UP–10000000000
		ON–Sibling–DIFF–UP–10000000000
		(RoleSubsumesP1)
		(FindVR1)
T111:	→	ON–ChildWithTwoSisters–SUPERC–UP–10000000000
	→	ON–Child–SUPERC–UP–10000000000
	→	ON–Thing–SUPERC–UP–10000000000
	→	ON–Person–SUPERC–UP–10000000000
	→	ON–Thing–SUPERC–UP–10000000000
	→	NORM–Sex–DIFF–UP–00000000000
	→	VR
	→	Reset
T112:		NORM–Part–DIFF–UP–00000000000
		ON–Gender–SUPERC–UP–10100000000
	→	ResetNorm
	→	SetHold
	→	Reset
T113:		NORM–Gender–SUPERC–UP–10100000000
		HOLD–Gender–SUPERC–UP–10100000000
T114:		NORM–Thing–SUPERC–UP–10100000000
		HOLD–Gender–SUPERC–UP–10100000000
	→	SetDiff
T115:		HOLD–Gender–SUPERC–UP–10100000000
		SetDiff
T116:		HOLD–Gender–SUPERC–UP–10100000000
		SetDiff
T117:		HOLD–Gender–SUPERC–UP–10100000000
		SetDiff
	→	Quiescent

Time Step	Message List
T118:	HOLD–Gender–SUPERC–UP–10100000000 Save Reset
T119:	ON–Gender–SUPERC–UP–10100000000 ON–Gender–SUPERC–UP–10100000000
	(FindVR1)
T120:	→ ON–Woman–SUPERC–UP–10000000000 → NORM–Sex–DIFF–UP–00000000000 → VR → Reset
T121:	NORM–Part–DIFF–UP–00000000000 ON–Female–SUPERC–UP–10101000000 → ResetNorm → SetHold → Reset
T122:	NORM–Female–SUPERC–UP–10101000000 HOLD–Female–SUPERC–UP–10101000000
T123:	NORM–Gender–SUPERC–UP–10101000000 HOLD–Female–SUPERC–UP–10101000000 → SetDiff
T124:	NORM–Thing–SUPERC–UP–10101000000 HOLD–Female–SUPERC–UP–10101000000 SetDiff
T125:	HOLD–Female–SUPERC–UP–10101000000 SetDiff
T126:	HOLD–Female–SUPERC–UP–10101000000 SetDiff → Quiescent
T127:	HOLD–Female–SUPERC–UP–10101000000 Save Reset
T128:	ON–Female–SUPERC–UP–10101000000

Time Step		Message List
T129:		ON–Female–SUPERC–UP–10101000000
		(NewSuperCListP)
T130:	→	ON–Female–SUPERC–UP–10101000000
	→	SetHold
	→	Reset
T131:		HOLD–Female–SUPERC–UP–10101000000
	→	ON–Gender–SUPERC–UP–10100000000
	→	ResetNorm
T132:		ON–Gender–SUPERC–UP–10100000000
		HOLD–Female–SUPERC–UP–10101000000
		NORM–Gender–SUPERC–UP–10100000000
	→	SetDiff
T133:		NORM–Thing–SUPERC–UP–10100000000
		HOLD–Female–SUPERC–UP–10101000000
		ON–Gender–SUPERC–UP–10100000000
		SetDiff
T134:		HOLD–Female–SUPERC–UP–10101000000
		ON–Gender–SUPERC–UP–10100000000
		SetDiff
T135:		HOLD–Female–SUPERC–UP–10101000000
		ON–Gender–SUPERC–UP–10100000000
		SetDiff
	→	Quiescent
T136:		HOLD–Female–SUPERC–UP–10101000000
		ON–Gender–SUPERC–UP–10100000000
		Save
		Reset
T137:		ON–Female–SUPERC–UP–10101000000
T138:		ON–Female–SUPERC–UP–10101000000

Time Step		Message List
T139:	→	ON–Man–SUPERC–UP–10000000000
	→	ON–Woman–SUPERC–UP–10000000000
	→	NORM–YoungMan–SUPERC–UP–10000000000
	→	And
T140:		NORM–Person–SUPERC–UP–10000000000
		ON–Man–SUPERC–UP–10000000000
		ON–Woman–SUPERC–UP–10000000000
T141:		NORM–Thing–SUPERC–UP–10000000000
		ON–Man–SUPERC–UP–10000000000
		ON–Woman–SUPERC–UP–10000000000
	→	Quiescent
T142:		ON–Man–SUPERC–UP–10000000000
		ON–Woman–SUPERC–UP–10000000000
		Reset
		Save
		(SubsumesP)
T143:	→	Or
	→	NORM–YoungMan–SUPERC–UP–10000000000
T144:		NORM–Person–SUPERC–UP–10000000000
		ON–YoungMan–SUPERC–UP–10000000000
		Or
T145:		NORM–Thing–SUPERC–UP–10000000000
		ON–YoungMan–SUPERC–UP–10000000000
		ON–Person–SUPERC–UP–10000000000
		Or
T146:		ON–YoungMan–SUPERC–UP–10000000000
		ON–Person–SUPERC–UP–10000000000
		ON–Thing–SUPERC–UP–10000000000
		Or
	→	Quiescent

Time Step		Message List
T147:		ON–YoungMan–SUPERC–UP–10000000000
		ON–Person–SUPERC–UP–10000000000
		ON–Thing–SUPERC–UP–10000000000
	→	SetHold
	→	Reset
T148:		HOLD–YoungMan–SUPERC–UP–10000000000
		HOLD–Person–SUPERC–UP–10000000000
		HOLD–Thing–SUPERC–UP–10000000000
T149:		HOLD–YoungMan–SUPERC–UP–10000000000
		HOLD–Person–SUPERC–UP–10000000000
		HOLD–Thing–SUPERC–UP–10000000000
	→	SetDiff
	→	NORM–ChildWithTwoSisters–SUPERC–UP–10000000000
T150:		HOLD–Thing–SUPERC–UP–10000000000
		HOLD–Person–SUPERC–UP–10000000000
		HOLD–YoungMan–SUPERC–UP–10000000000
		NORM–Child–SUPERC–UP–10000000000
		SetDiff
		NORM–Thing–SUPERC–UP–10000000000
		NORM–Person–SUPERC–UP–10000000000
T151:		NORM–Thing–SUPERC–UP–10000000000
		HOLD–YoungMan–SUPERC–UP–10000000000
		NORM–Person–SUPERC–UP–10000000000
		SetDiff
T152:		NORM–Thing–SUPERC–UP–10000000000
		HOLD–YoungMan–SUPERC–UP–10000000000
		SetDiff
	→	Quiescent
T153:		HOLD–YoungMan–SUPERC–UP–10000000000
		Save
		Reset
T154:		ON–YoungMan–SUPERC–UP–10000000000

Time Step	Message List
T155:	ON–YoungMan–SUPERC–UP–10000000000 → Reset → rolemess
T156:	ON–Sex–DIFF–UP–10000000000 ON–Age–DIFF–UP–10000000000 (GetSubsumers)
T157:	→ Or → NORM–ChildWithTwoSisters–SUPERC–UP–10000000000
T158:	NORM–Child–SUPERC–UP–10000000000 ON–ChildWithTwoSisters–SUPERC–UP–10000000000 Or NORM–Thing–SUPERC–UP–10000000000 NORM–Person–SUPERC–UP–10000000000
T159:	NORM–Thing–SUPERC–UP–10000000000 NORM–Person–SUPERC–UP–10000000000 ON–ChildWithTwoSisters–SUPERC–UP–10000000000 ON–Child–SUPERC–UP–10000000000 ON–Thing–SUPERC–UP–10000000000 ON–Person–SUPERC–UP–10000000000 Or
T160:	NORM–Thing–SUPERC–UP–10000000000 ON–ChildWithTwoSisters–SUPERC–UP–10000000000 ON–Child–SUPERC–UP–10000000000 ON–Thing–SUPERC–UP–10000000000 ON–Person–SUPERC–UP–10000000000 ON–Thing–SUPERC–UP–10000000000 ON–Person–SUPERC–UP–10000000000 Or → Quiescent

Time Step	Message List
T161:	ON–ChildWithTwoSisters–SUPERC–UP–10000000000 ON–Child–SUPERC–UP–10000000000 ON–Thing–SUPERC–UP–10000000000 ON–Person–SUPERC–UP–10000000000 ON–Thing–SUPERC–UP–10000000000
	(FindAllRoles1)
T162:	→ ON–ChildWithTwoSisters–SUPERC–UP–10000000000 → ON–Child–SUPERC–UP–10000000000 → ON–Thing–SUPERC–UP–10000000000 → ON–Person–SUPERC–UP–10000000000 → ON–Thing–SUPERC–UP–10000000000 → Reset → rolemess
T163:	ON–Limbs–DIFF–UP–10000000000 ON–Sex–DIFF–UP–10000000000 ON–Age–DIFF–UP–10000000000 ON–Sibling–DIFF–UP–10000000000 ON–Sibling–DIFF–UP–10000000000
T164:	ON–Limbs–DIFF–UP–10000000000 ON–Sex–DIFF–UP–10000000000 ON–Age–DIFF–UP–10000000000 ON–Sibling–DIFF–UP–10000000000
	(RoleSubsumesP1)
	(FindVR1)
T165:	→ ON–ChildWithTwoSisters–SUPERC–UP–10000000000 → ON–Child–SUPERC–UP–10000000000 → ON–Thing–SUPERC–UP–10000000000 → ON–Person–SUPERC–UP–10000000000 → ON–Thing–SUPERC–UP–10000000000 → NORM–Sex–DIFF–UP–00000000000 → VR → Reset

Time Step	Message List
T166:	NORM–Part–DIFF–UP–00000000000
	ON–Gender–SUPERC–UP–10100000000
	→ ResetNorm
	→ SetHold
	→ Reset
T167:	NORM–Gender–SUPERC–UP–10100000000
	HOLD–Gender–SUPERC–UP–10100000000
T168:	NORM–Thing–SUPERC–UP–10100000000
	HOLD–Gender–SUPERC–UP–10100000000
	→ SetDiff
T169:	HOLD–Gender–SUPERC–UP–10100000000
	SetDiff
T170:	HOLD–Gender–SUPERC–UP–10100000000
	SetDiff
T171:	HOLD–Gender–SUPERC–UP–10100000000
	SetDiff
	→ Quiescent
T172:	HOLD–Gender–SUPERC–UP–10100000000
	Save
	Reset
T173:	ON–Gender–SUPERC–UP–10100000000
T174:	ON–Gender–SUPERC–UP–10100000000
	(FindVR1)
T175:	→ ON–YoungMan–SUPERC–UP–10000000000
	→ NORM–Sex–DIFF–UP–00000000000
	→ VR
	→ Reset

Time Step		Message List
T176:		NORM–Part–DIFF–UP–00000000000
		ON–Male–SUPERC–UP–10110000000
	→	ResetNorm
	→	SetHold
	→	Reset
T177:		NORM–Male–SUPERC–UP–10110000000
		HOLD–Male–SUPERC–UP–10110000000
		NORM–Gender–SUPERC–UP–10110000000
		HOLD–Male–SUPERC–UP–10110000000
	→	SetDiff
T178:		NORM–Thing–SUPERC–UP–10110000000
		HOLD–Male–SUPERC–UP–10110000000
		SetDiff
T179:		HOLD–Male–SUPERC–UP–10110000000
		SetDiff
T180:		HOLD–Male–SUPERC–UP–10110000000
		SetDiff
	→	Quiescent
T181:		HOLD–Male–SUPERC–UP–10110000000
		Save
		Reset
T182:		ON–Male–SUPERC–UP–10110000000
T183:		ON–Male–SUPERC–UP–10110000000
		(NewSuperCListP)
T184:	→	ON–Male–SUPERC–UP–10110000000
	→	SetHold
	→	Reset
T185::		HOLD–Male–SUPERC–UP–10110000000
	→	ON–Gender–SUPERC–UP–10100000000
	→	ResetNorm

Time Step		Message List
T186:		ON–Gender–SUPERC–UP–10100000000
		HOLD–Male–SUPERC–UP–10110000000
		NORM–Gender–SUPERC–UP–10100000000
	→	SetDiff
T187:		NORM–Thing–SUPERC–UP–10100000000
		HOLD–Male–SUPERC–UP–10110000000
		ON–Gender–SUPERC–UP–10100000000
		SetDiff
T188:		HOLD–Male–SUPERC–UP–10110000000
		ON–Gender–SUPERC–UP–10100000000
		SetDiff
T189:		HOLD–Male–SUPERC–UP–10110000000
		ON–Gender–SUPERC–UP–10100000000
		SetDiff
	→	Quiescent
T190:		HOLD–Male–SUPERC–UP–10110000000
		ON–Gender–SUPERC–UP–10100000000
		Save
		Reset
T191:		ON–Male–SUPERC–UP–10110000000
T192:		ON–Male–SUPERC–UP–10110000000
T193:	→	ON–Man–SUPERC–UP–10000000000
	→	ON–Woman–SUPERC–UP–10000000000
	→	ON–YoungMan–SUPERC–UP–10000000000
	→	NORM–HighRiskDriver–SUPERC–UP–10000000000
	→	And
T194:		NORM–Person–SUPERC–UP–10000000000
		ON–Man–SUPERC–UP–10000000000
		ON–Woman–SUPERC–UP–10000000000
		ON–YoungMan–SUPERC–UP–10000000000

Time Step		Message List
T195:		NORM–Thing–SUPERC–UP–10000000000
		ON–Man–SUPERC–UP–10000000000
		ON–Woman–SUPERC–UP–10000000000
		ON–YoungMan–SUPERC–UP–10000000000
	→	Quiescent
T196:		ON–Man–SUPERC–UP–10000000000
		ON–Woman–SUPERC–UP–10000000000
		ON–YoungMan–SUPERC–UP–10000000000
		Reset
		Save
		(SubsumesP)
T197:	→	Or
	→	NORM–HighRiskDriver–SUPERC–UP–10000000000
T198:		NORM–Person–SUPERC–UP–10000000000
		ON–HighRiskDriver–SUPERC–UP–10000000000
		Or
T199:		NORM–Thing–SUPERC–UP–10000000000
		ON–HighRiskDriver–SUPERC–UP–10000000000
		ON–Person–SUPERC–UP–10000000000
		Or
T200:		ON–HighRiskDriver–SUPERC–UP–10000000000
		ON–Person–SUPERC–UP–10000000000
		ON–Thing–SUPERC–UP–10000000000
		Or
	→	Quiescent
T201:		ON–HighRiskDriver–SUPERC–UP–10000000000
		ON–Person–SUPERC–UP–10000000000
		ON–Thing–SUPERC–UP–10000000000
	→	SetHold
	→	Reset
T202:		HOLD–HighRiskDriver–SUPERC–UP–10000000000
		HOLD–Person–SUPERC–UP–10000000000
		HOLD–Thing–SUPERC–UP–10000000000

Time Step	Message List
T203:	HOLD–HighRiskDriver–SUPERC–UP–10000000000
	HOLD–Person–SUPERC–UP–10000000000
	HOLD–Thing–SUPERC–UP–10000000000
	→ SetDiff
	→ NORM–ChildWithTwoSisters–SUPERC–UP–10000000000
T204:	HOLD–Thing–SUPERC–UP–10000000000
	HOLD–Person–SUPERC–UP–10000000000
	HOLD–HighRiskDriver–SUPERC–UP–10000000000
	NORM–Child–SUPERC–UP–10000000000
	SetDiff
	NORM–Thing–SUPERC–UP–10000000000
	NORM–Person–SUPERC–UP–10000000000
T205:	NORM–Thing–SUPERC–UP–10000000000
	HOLD–HighRiskDriver–SUPERC–UP–10000000000
	NORM–Person–SUPERC–UP–10000000000
	SetDiff
T206:	NORM–Thing–SUPERC–UP–10000000000
	HOLD–HighRiskDriver–SUPERC–UP–10000000000
	SetDiff
	→ Quiescent
T207:	HOLD–HighRiskDriver–SUPERC–UP–10000000000
	Save
	Reset
	ON–HighRiskDriver–SUPERC–UP–10000000000
T208:	ON–HighRiskDriver–SUPERC–UP–10000000000
	→ Reset
	→ rolemess
T209:	ON–Sex–DIFF–UP–10000000000
	ON–Age–DIFF–UP–10000000000
	(GetSubsumers)
T210:	→ Or
	→ NORM–ChildWithTwoSisters–SUPERC–UP–10000000000

Time Step	Message List
T211:	NORM–Child–SUPERC–UP–10000000000
	ON–ChildWithTwoSisters–SUPERC–UP–10000000000
	Or
	NORM–Thing–SUPERC–UP–10000000000
	NORM–Person–SUPERC–UP–10000000000
T212:	NORM–Thing–SUPERC–UP–10000000000
	NORM–Person–SUPERC–UP–10000000000
	ON–ChildWithTwoSisters–SUPERC–UP–10000000000
	ON–Child–SUPERC–UP–10000000000
	ON–Thing–SUPERC–UP–10000000000
	ON–Person–SUPERC–UP–10000000000
	Or
T213:	NORM–Thing–SUPERC–UP–10000000000
	ON–ChildWithTwoSisters–SUPERC–UP–10000000000
	ON–Child–SUPERC–UP–10000000000
	ON–Thing–SUPERC–UP–10000000000
	ON–Person–SUPERC–UP–10000000000
	ON–Thing–SUPERC–UP–10000000000
	ON–Person–SUPERC–UP–10000000000
	Or
	→ Quiescent
T214:	ON–ChildWithTwoSisters–SUPERC–UP–10000000000
	ON–Child–SUPERC–UP–10000000000
	ON–Thing–SUPERC–UP–10000000000
	ON–Person–SUPERC–UP–10000000000
	ON–Thing–SUPERC–UP–10000000000
	(FindAllRoles1)
T215:	→ ON–ChildWithTwoSisters–SUPERC–UP–10000000000
	→ ON–Child–SUPERC–UP–10000000000
	→ ON–Thing–SUPERC–UP–10000000000
	→ ON–Person–SUPERC–UP–10000000000
	→ ON–Thing–SUPERC–UP–10000000000
	→ Reset
	→ rolemess

Time Step	Message List
T216:	ON–Limbs–DIFF–UP–10000000000 ON–Sex–DIFF–UP–10000000000 ON–Age–DIFF–UP–10000000000 ON–Sibling–DIFF–UP–10000000000 ON–Sibling–DIFF–UP–10000000000
T217:	ON–Limbs–DIFF–UP–10000000000 ON–Sex–DIFF–UP–10000000000 ON–Age–DIFF–UP–10000000000 ON–Sibling–DIFF–UP–10000000000 (RoleSubsumesP1) (FindVR1)
T218:	→ ON–ChildWithTwoSisters–SUPERC–UP–10000000000 → ON–Child–SUPERC–UP–10000000000 → ON–Thing–SUPERC–UP–10000000000 → ON–Person–SUPERC–UP–10000000000 → ON–Thing–SUPERC–UP–10000000000 → NORM–Sex–DIFF–UP–00000000000 → VR → Reset
T219:	NORM–Part–DIFF–UP–00000000000 ON–Gender–SUPERC–UP–10100000000 → ResetNorm → SetHold → Reset
T220:	NORM–Gender–SUPERC–UP–10100000000 HOLD–Gender–SUPERC–UP–10100000000
T221:	NORM–Thing–SUPERC–UP–10100000000 HOLD–Gender–SUPERC–UP–10100000000 → SetDiff
T222:	HOLD–Gender–SUPERC–UP–10100000000 SetDiff
T223:	HOLD–Gender–SUPERC–UP–10100000000 SetDiff

Time Step		Message List
T224:		HOLD–Gender–SUPERC–UP–10100000000
		SetDiff
	→	Quiescent
T225		HOLD–Gender–SUPERC–UP–10100000000
		Save
		Reset
T226:		ON–Gender–SUPERC–UP–10100000000
T227:		ON–Gender–SUPERC–UP–10100000000
		(FindVR1)
T228:	→	ON–HighRiskDriver–SUPERC–UP–10000000000
	→	NORM–Sex–DIFF–UP–00000000000
	→	VR
	→	Reset
T229:		NORM–Part–DIFF–UP–00000000000
		ON–Male–SUPERC–UP–10110000000
	→	ResetNorm
	→	SetHold
	→	Reset
T230:		NORM–Male–SUPERC–UP–10110000000
		HOLD–Male–SUPERC–UP–10110000000
T231:		NORM–Gender–SUPERC–UP–10110000000
		HOLD–Male–SUPERC–UP–10110000000
	→	SetDiff
T232:		NORM–Thing–SUPERC–UP–10110000000
		HOLD–Male–SUPERC–UP–10110000000
		SetDiff
T233:		HOLD–Male–SUPERC–UP–10110000000
		SetDiff
T234:		HOLD–Male–SUPERC–UP–10110000000
		SetDiff
	→	Quiescent

Time Step	Message List
T235:	HOLD–Male–SUPERC–UP–10110000000
	Save
	Reset
T236:	ON–Male–SUPERC–UP–10110000000
T237:	ON–Male–SUPERC–UP–10110000000
	(NewSuperCListP)
T238:	→ ON–Male–SUPERC–UP–10110000000
	→ SetHold
	→ Reset
T239:	HOLD–Male–SUPERC–UP–10110000000
	→ ON–Gender–SUPERC–UP–10100000000
	→ ResetNorm
T240:	ON–Gender–SUPERC–UP–10100000000
	HOLD–Male–SUPERC–UP–10110000000
	NORM–Gender–SUPERC–UP–10100000000
	→ SetDiff
T241:	NORM–Thing–SUPERC–UP–10100000000
	HOLD–Male–SUPERC–UP–10110000000
	ON–Gender–SUPERC–UP–10100000000
	SetDiff
T242:	HOLD–Male–SUPERC–UP–10110000000
	ON–Gender–SUPERC–UP–10100000000
	SetDiff
T243:	HOLD–Male–SUPERC–UP–10110000000
	ON–Gender–SUPERC–UP–10100000000
	SetDiff
	→ Quiescent
T244:	HOLD–Male–SUPERC–UP–10110000000
	ON–Gender–SUPERC–UP–10100000000
	Save
	Reset
T245:	ON–Male–SUPERC–UP–10110000000

Time Step		Message List
T246:		ON–Male–SUPERC–UP–10110000000
T247:	→	ON–Man–SUPERC–UP–10000000000
	→	ON–Woman–SUPERC–UP–10000000000
	→	ON–YoungMan–SUPERC–UP–10000000000
	→	ON–HighRiskDriver–SUPERC–UP–10000000000
	→	NORM–Child–SUPERC–UP–10000000000
	→	And
T248:		NORM–Person–SUPERC–UP–10000000000
		ON–Man–SUPERC–UP–10000000000
		ON–Woman–SUPERC–UP–10000000000
		ON–YoungMan–SUPERC–UP–10000000000
		ON–HighRiskDriver–SUPERC–UP–10000000000
T249:		NORM–Thing–SUPERC–UP–10000000000
		ON–Man–SUPERC–UP–10000000000
		ON–Woman–SUPERC–UP–10000000000
		ON–YoungMan–SUPERC–UP–10000000000
		ON–HighRiskDriver–SUPERC–UP–10000000000
	→	Quiescent
T250:		ON–Man–SUPERC–UP–10000000000
		ON–Woman–SUPERC–UP–10000000000
		ON–YoungMan–SUPERC–UP–10000000000
		ON–HighRiskDriver–SUPERC–UP–10000000000
		Reset
		Save
		(SubsumesP)
T251:	→	Or
	→	NORM–Child–SUPERC–UP–10000000000
T252:		NORM–Person–SUPERC–UP–10000000000
		ON–Child–SUPERC–UP–10000000000
		Or
T253:		NORM–Thing–SUPERC–UP–10000000000
		ON–Child–SUPERC–UP–10000000000
		ON–Person–SUPERC–UP–10000000000
		Or

Time Step	Message List
T254:	ON–Child–SUPERC–UP–10000000000
	ON–Person–SUPERC–UP–10000000000
	ON–Thing–SUPERC–UP–10000000000
	Or
	→ Quiescent
T255:	ON–Child–SUPERC–UP–10000000000
	ON–Person–SUPERC–UP–10000000000
	ON–Thing–SUPERC–UP–10000000000
	→ SetHold
	→ Reset
T256:	HOLD–Child–SUPERC–UP–10000000000
	HOLD–Person–SUPERC–UP–10000000000
	HOLD–Thing–SUPERC–UP–10000000000
	HOLD–Child–SUPERC–UP–10000000000
	HOLD–Person–SUPERC–UP–10000000000
	HOLD–Thing–SUPERC–UP–10000000000
	→ SetDiff
	→ NORM–ChildWithTwoSisters–SUPERC–UP–10000000000
T257:	HOLD–Thing–SUPERC–UP–10000000000
	HOLD–Person–SUPERC–UP–10000000000
	HOLD–Child–SUPERC–UP–10000000000
	NORM–Child–SUPERC–UP–10000000000
	SetDiff
	NORM–Thing–SUPERC–UP–10000000000
	NORM–Person–SUPERC–UP–10000000000
	NORM–Thing–SUPERC–UP–10000000000
	NORM–Person–SUPERC–UP–10000000000
	SetDiff
	NORM–Thing–SUPERC–UP–10000000000
	SetDiff
	→ Quiescent
T258:	Save
	Reset
	→ Reset
	→ rolemess

(GetSubsumers)

Time Step		Message List
T259:	→	Or
	→	NORM–ChildWithTwoSisters–SUPERC–UP–10000000000
T260:		NORM–Child–SUPERC–UP–10000000000
		ON–ChildWithTwoSisters–SUPERC–UP–10000000000
		Or
		NORM–Thing–SUPERC–UP–10000000000
		NORM–Person–SUPERC–UP–10000000000
T261:		NORM–Thing–SUPERC–UP–10000000000
		NORM–Person–SUPERC–UP–10000000000
		ON–ChildWithTwoSisters–SUPERC–UP–10000000000
		ON–Child–SUPERC–UP–10000000000
		ON–Thing–SUPERC–UP–10000000000
		ON–Person–SUPERC–UP–10000000000
		Or
T262:		NORM–Thing–SUPERC–UP–10000000000
		ON–ChildWithTwoSisters–SUPERC–UP–10000000000
		ON–Child–SUPERC–UP–10000000000
		ON–Thing–SUPERC–UP–10000000000
		ON–Person–SUPERC–UP–10000000000
		ON–Thing–SUPERC–UP–10000000000
		ON–Person–SUPERC–UP–10000000000
		Or
	→	Quiescent
T263:		ON–ChildWithTwoSisters–SUPERC–UP–10000000000
		ON–Child–SUPERC–UP–10000000000
		ON–Thing–SUPERC–UP–10000000000
		ON–Person–SUPERC–UP–10000000000
		ON–Thing–SUPERC–UP–10000000000
		(FindAllRoles1)
T264:	→	ON–ChildWithTwoSisters–SUPERC–UP–10000000000
	→	ON–Child–SUPERC–UP–10000000000
	→	ON–Thing–SUPERC–UP–10000000000
	→	ON–Person–SUPERC–UP–10000000000
	→	ON–Thing–SUPERC–UP–10000000000
	→	Reset
	→	rolemess

Time Step		Message List
T265:		ON–Limbs–DIFF–UP–10000000000
		ON–Sex–DIFF–UP–10000000000
		ON–Age–DIFF–UP–10000000000
		ON–Sibling–DIFF–UP–10000000000
		ON–Sibling–DIFF–UP–10000000000
T266:		ON–Limbs–DIFF–UP–10000000000
		ON–Sex–DIFF–UP–10000000000
		ON–Age–DIFF–UP–10000000000
		ON–Sibling–DIFF–UP–10000000000
	→	RVMCheck
	→	Reset
		(ImmediateSuperCs1)
T267:	→	NORM–Child–SUPERC–UP–10000000000
T268:		NORM–Person–SUPERC–UP–10000000000
	→	HOLD–Person–SUPERC–UP–10000000000
	→	SetDiff
T269:		NORM–Thing–SUPERC–UP–10000000000
		SetDiff
	→	Quiescent
T270:		Save
		Reset
		(ImmediateSubCs1)
T271:	→	NORM–Child–SUPERC–DOWN–10000000000
T272:		NORM–ChildWithTwin–SUPERC–DOWN–10000000000
		NORM–ChildWithSiblings–SUPERC–DOWN–10000000000
		NORM–ChildWithTwoSisters–SUPERC–DOWN–10000000000
T273:	→	ON–Man–SUPERC–UP–10000000000
	→	ON–Woman–SUPERC–UP–10000000000
	→	ON–YoungMan–SUPERC–UP–10000000000
	→	ON–HighRiskDriver–SUPERC–UP–10000000000
	→	NORM–ChildWithTwin–SUPERC–UP–10000000000
	→	And

Time Step		Message List
T274:		NORM–Child–SUPERC–UP–10000000000
		ON–Man–SUPERC–UP–10000000000
		ON–Woman–SUPERC–UP–10000000000
		ON–YoungMan–SUPERC–UP–10000000000
		ON–HighRiskDriver–SUPERC–UP–10000000000
T275:		NORM–Person–SUPERC–UP–10000000000
		ON–Man–SUPERC–UP–10000000000
		ON–Woman–SUPERC–UP–10000000000
		ON–YoungMan–SUPERC–UP–10000000000
		ON–HighRiskDriver–SUPERC–UP–10000000000
T276:		NORM–Thing–SUPERC–UP–10000000000
		ON–Man–SUPERC–UP–10000000000
		ON–Woman–SUPERC–UP–10000000000
		ON–YoungMan–SUPERC–UP–10000000000
		ON–HighRiskDriver–SUPERC–UP–10000000000
	→	Quiescent
T275:		ON–Man–SUPERC–UP–10000000000
		ON–Woman–SUPERC–UP–10000000000
		ON–YoungMan–SUPERC–UP–10000000000
		ON–HighRiskDriver–SUPERC–UP–10000000000
		Reset
		Save
		(SubsumesP)
T278:	→	Or
	→	NORM–ChildWithTwin–SUPERC–UP–10000000000
T279:		NORM–Child–SUPERC–UP–10000000000
		ON–ChildWithTwin–SUPERC–UP–10000000000
		Or
T280:		NORM–Person–SUPERC–UP–10000000000
		ON–ChildWithTwin–SUPERC–UP–10000000000
		ON–Child–SUPERC–UP–10000000000
		Or

Time Step		Message List
T281:		NORM–Thing–SUPERC–UP–10000000000
		ON–ChildWithTwin–SUPERC–UP–10000000000
		ON–Child–SUPERC–UP–10000000000
		ON–Person–SUPERC–UP–10000000000
		Or
	→	Quiescent
T282:		ON–ChildWithTwin–SUPERC–UP–10000000000
		ON–Child–SUPERC–UP–10000000000
		ON–Person–SUPERC–UP–10000000000
		ON–Thing–SUPERC–UP–10000000000
	→	SetHold
	→	Reset
T283:		HOLD–ChildWithTwin–SUPERC–UP–10000000000
		HOLD–Child–SUPERC–UP–10000000000
		HOLD–Person–SUPERC–UP–10000000000
		HOLD–Thing–SUPERC–UP–10000000000
T284:		HOLD–ChildWithTwin–SUPERC–UP–10000000000
		HOLD–Child–SUPERC–UP–10000000000
		HOLD–Person–SUPERC–UP–10000000000
		HOLD–Thing–SUPERC–UP–10000000000
	→	SetDiff
	→	NORM–ChildWithTwoSisters–SUPERC–UP–10000000000
T285:		HOLD–Thing–SUPERC–UP–10000000000
		HOLD–Person–SUPERC–UP–10000000000
		HOLD–Child–SUPERC–UP–10000000000
		HOLD–ChildWithTwin–SUPERC–UP–10000000000
		NORM–Child–SUPERC–UP–10000000000
		SetDiff
T286:		NORM–Thing–SUPERC–UP–10000000000
		NORM–Child–SUPERC–UP–10000000000
		HOLD–Person–SUPERC–UP–10000000000
		NORM–Person–SUPERC–UP–10000000000
		HOLD–ChildWithTwin–SUPERC–UP–10000000000
		SetDiff

Time Step		Message List
T287:		NORM–Thing–SUPERC–UP–10000000000
		HOLD–ChildWithTwin–SUPERC–UP–10000000000
		SetDiff
	→	Quiescent
T288:		HOLD–ChildWithTwin–SUPERC–UP–10000000000
		Save
		Reset
T289:		ON–ChildWithTwin–SUPERC–UP–10000000000
		ON–ChildWithTwin–SUPERC–UP–10000000000
	→	Reset
	→	rolemess
T290:		ON–Twin–DIFF–UP–10000000000
		(GetSubsumers)
T291:	→	Or
	→	NORM–ChildWithTwoSisters–SUPERC–UP–10000000000
T292:		NORM–Child–SUPERC–UP–10000000000
		ON–ChildWithTwoSisters–SUPERC–UP–10000000000
		Or
T293:		NORM–Thing–SUPERC–UP–10000000000
		NORM–Child–SUPERC–UP–10000000000
		NORM–Person–SUPERC–UP–10000000000
		ON–ChildWithTwoSisters–SUPERC–UP–10000000000
		ON–Thing–SUPERC–UP–10000000000
		ON–Child–SUPERC–UP–10000000000
		Or
T294:		NORM–Thing–SUPERC–UP–10000000000
		ON–ChildWithTwoSisters–SUPERC–UP–10000000000
		ON–Thing–SUPERC–UP–10000000000
		ON–Child–SUPERC–UP–10000000000
		ON–Person–SUPERC–UP–10000000000
		Or
	→	Quiescent

Time Step	Message List
T295:	ON–ChildWithTwoSisters–SUPERC–UP–10000000000 ON–Thing–SUPERC–UP–10000000000 ON–Child–SUPERC–UP–10000000000 ON–Person–SUPERC–UP–10000000000 ON–Thing–SUPERC–UP–10000000000 (FindAllRoles1)
T296:	→ ON–ChildWithTwoSisters–SUPERC–UP–10000000000 → ON–Thing–SUPERC–UP–10000000000 → ON–Child–SUPERC–UP–10000000000 → ON–Person–SUPERC–UP–10000000000 → ON–Thing–SUPERC–UP–10000000000 → Reset → rolemess
T297:	ON–Limbs–DIFF–UP–10000000000 ON–Sex–DIFF–UP–10000000000 ON–Age–DIFF–UP–10000000000 ON–Sibling–DIFF–UP–10000000000 ON–Sibling–DIFF–UP–10000000000
T298:	ON–Limbs–DIFF–UP–10000000000 ON–Sex–DIFF–UP–10000000000 ON–Age–DIFF–UP–10000000000 ON–Sibling–DIFF–UP–10000000000 (RoleSubsumesP1)
T299:	→ ON–Man–SUPERC–UP–10000000000 → ON–Woman–SUPERC–UP–10000000000 → ON–YoungMan–SUPERC–UP–10000000000 → ON–HighRiskDriver–SUPERC–UP–10000000000 → ON–ChildWithTwin–SUPERC–UP–10000000000 → NORM–ChildWithSiblings–SUPERC–UP–10000000000 → And
T300:	NORM–Child–SUPERC–UP–10000000000 ON–Man–SUPERC–UP–10000000000 ON–Woman–SUPERC–UP–10000000000 ON–YoungMan–SUPERC–UP–10000000000 ON–HighRiskDriver–SUPERC–UP–10000000000 ON–ChildWithTwin–SUPERC–UP–10000000000

Time Step	Message List
T301:	NORM–Person–SUPERC–UP–10000000000
	ON–Man–SUPERC–UP–10000000000
	ON–Woman–SUPERC–UP–10000000000
	ON–YoungMan–SUPERC–UP–10000000000
	ON–HighRiskDriver–SUPERC–UP–10000000000
	ON–ChildWithTwin–SUPERC–UP–10000000000
T302:	NORM–Thing–SUPERC–UP–10000000000
	ON–Man–SUPERC–UP–10000000000
	ON–Woman–SUPERC–UP–10000000000
	ON–YoungMan–SUPERC–UP–10000000000
	ON–HighRiskDriver–SUPERC–UP–10000000000
	ON–ChildWithTwin–SUPERC–UP–10000000000
	→ Quiescent
T303:	ON–Man–SUPERC–UP–10000000000
	ON–Woman–SUPERC–UP–10000000000
	ON–YoungMan–SUPERC–UP–10000000000
	ON–HighRiskDriver–SUPERC–UP–10000000000
	ON–ChildWithTwin–SUPERC–UP–10000000000
	Reset
	Save
	(SubsumesP)
T304:	→ Or
	→ NORM–ChildWithSiblings–SUPERC–UP–10000000000
T305:	NORM–Child–SUPERC–UP–10000000000
	ON–ChildWithSiblings–SUPERC–UP–10000000000
	Or
T306:	NORM–Person–SUPERC–UP–10000000000
	ON–ChildWithSiblings–SUPERC–UP–10000000000
	ON–Child–SUPERC–UP–10000000000
	Or
T307:	NORM–Thing–SUPERC–UP–10000000000
	ON–ChildWithSiblings–SUPERC–UP–10000000000
	ON–Child–SUPERC–UP–10000000000
	ON–Person–SUPERC–UP–10000000000
	Or
	→ Quiescent

Time Step	Message List
T308:	ON–ChildWithSiblings–SUPERC–UP–10000000000 ON–Child–SUPERC–UP–10000000000 ON–Person–SUPERC–UP–10000000000 ON–Thing–SUPERC–UP–10000000000 → SetHold → Reset
T309:	HOLD–ChildWithSiblings–SUPERC–UP–10000000000 HOLD–Child–SUPERC–UP–10000000000 HOLD–Person–SUPERC–UP–10000000000 HOLD–Thing–SUPERC–UP–10000000000
T310:	HOLD–ChildWithSiblings–SUPERC–UP–10000000000 HOLD–Child–SUPERC–UP–10000000000 HOLD–Person–SUPERC–UP–10000000000 HOLD–Thing–SUPERC–UP–10000000000 → SetDiff → NORM–ChildWithTwoSisters–SUPERC–UP–10000000000
T311:	HOLD–Thing–SUPERC–UP–10000000000 HOLD–Person–SUPERC–UP–10000000000 HOLD–Child–SUPERC–UP–10000000000 HOLD–ChildWithSiblings–SUPERC–UP–10000000000 NORM–Child–SUPERC–UP–10000000000 SetDiff
T312:	NORM–Thing–SUPERC–UP–10000000000 NORM–Child–SUPERC–UP–10000000000 HOLD–Person–SUPERC–UP–10000000000 NORM–Person–SUPERC–UP–10000000000 HOLD–ChildWithSiblings–SUPERC–UP–10000000000 SetDiff
T313:	NORM–Thing–SUPERC–UP–10000000000 HOLD–ChildWithSiblings–SUPERC–UP–10000000000 SetDiff → Quiescent
T314:	HOLD–ChildWithSiblings–SUPERC–UP–10000000000 Save Reset

Time Step		Message List
T315:		ON–ChildWithSiblings–SUPERC–UP–10000000000
		ON–ChildWithSiblings–SUPERC–UP–10000000000
	→	Reset
	→	rolemess
T316:		ON–Sibling–DIFF–UP–10000000000
		(GetSubsumers)
T317:	→	Or
	→	NORM–ChildWithTwoSisters–SUPERC–UP–10000000000
T318:		NORM–Child–SUPERC–UP–10000000000
		ON–ChildWithTwoSisters–SUPERC–UP–10000000000
		Or
T319:		NORM–Thing–SUPERC–UP–10000000000
		NORM–Child–SUPERC–UP–10000000000
		NORM–Person–SUPERC–UP–10000000000
		ON–ChildWithTwoSisters–SUPERC–UP–10000000000
		ON–Thing–SUPERC–UP–10000000000
		ON–Child–SUPERC–UP–10000000000
		Or
T320:		NORM–Thing–SUPERC–UP–10000000000
		ON–ChildWithTwoSisters–SUPERC–UP–10000000000
		ON–Thing–SUPERC–UP–10000000000
		ON–Child–SUPERC–UP–10000000000
		ON–Person–SUPERC–UP–10000000000
		Or
	→	Quiescent
T321:		ON–ChildWithTwoSisters–SUPERC–UP–10000000000
		ON–Thing–SUPERC–UP–10000000000
		ON–Child–SUPERC–UP–10000000000
		ON–Person–SUPERC–UP–10000000000
		ON–Thing–SUPERC–UP–10000000000
		(FindAllRoles1)

Time Step		Message List
T322:	→	ON–ChildWithTwoSisters–SUPERC–UP–10000000000
	→	ON–Thing–SUPERC–UP–10000000000
	→	ON–Child–SUPERC–UP–10000000000
	→	ON–Person–SUPERC–UP–10000000000
	→	ON–Thing–SUPERC–UP–10000000000
	→	Reset
	→	rolemess
T323:		ON–Limbs–DIFF–UP–10000000000
		ON–Sex–DIFF–UP–10000000000
		ON–Age–DIFF–UP–10000000000
		ON–Sibling–DIFF–UP–10000000000
		ON–Sibling–DIFF–UP–10000000000
T324:		ON–Limbs–DIFF–UP–10000000000
		ON–Sex–DIFF–UP–10000000000
		ON–Age–DIFF–UP–10000000000
		ON–Sibling–DIFF–UP–10000000000
		(RoleSubsumesP1)
		(FindVR1)
T325:	→	ON–ChildWithTwoSisters–SUPERC–UP–10000000000
	→	ON–Thing–SUPERC–UP–10000000000
	→	ON–Child–SUPERC–UP–10000000000
	→	ON–Person–SUPERC–UP–10000000000
	→	ON–Thing–SUPERC–UP–10000000000
	→	NORM–Sibling–DIFF–UP–00000000000
	→	VR
	→	Reset

Time Step		Message List
T326:		NORM–Part–DIFF–UP–00000000000
		ON–Child–SUPERC–UP–10000000000
		ON–Female–SUPERC–UP–10101000000
	→	ResetNorm
	→	SetHold
	→	Reset
T327:		NORM–Child–SUPERC–UP–10000000000
		NORM–Female–SUPERC–UP–10101000000
		HOLD–Child–SUPERC–UP–10000000000
		HOLD–Female–SUPERC–UP–10101000000
		NORM–Gender–SUPERC–UP–10101000000
		NORM–Person–SUPERC–UP–10000000000
		HOLD–Child–SUPERC–UP–10000000000
		HOLD–Female–SUPERC–UP–10101000000
	→	SetDiff
T328:		NORM–Thing–SUPERC–UP–10000000000
		NORM–Thing–SUPERC–UP–10101000000
		HOLD–Female–SUPERC–UP–10101000000
		HOLD–Child–SUPERC–UP–10000000000
		SetDiff
T329:		HOLD–Female–SUPERC–UP–10101000000
		HOLD–Child–SUPERC–UP–10000000000
		SetDiff
T330:		HOLD–Female–SUPERC–UP–10101000000
		HOLD–Child–SUPERC–UP–10000000000
		SetDiff
	→	Quiescent
T331:		HOLD–Female–SUPERC–UP–10101000000
		HOLD–Child–SUPERC–UP–10000000000
		Save
		Reset
T332:		ON–Female–SUPERC–UP–10101000000
		ON–Child–SUPERC–UP–10000000000
		ON–Female–SUPERC–UP–10101000000
		ON–Child–SUPERC–UP–10000000000

Time Step		Message List
T333:		FindVR1
T334:	→	ON–ChildWithSiblings–SUPERC–UP–10000000000
	→	NORM–Sibling–DIFF–UP–00000000000
	→	VR
	→	Reset
T335:		NORM–Part–DIFF–UP–00000000000
	→	ResetNorm
	→	SetHold
	→	Reset
	→	SetDiff
T336:		SetDiff
T337:		SetDiff
T338:		SetDiff
	→	Quiescent
T339:		Save
		Reset
		(NewSuperCListP)
T340:	→	SetHold
	→	Reset
	→	ON–Female–SUPERC–UP–10101000000
	→	ON–Child–SUPERC–UP–10000000000
	→	ResetNorm
T341:		ON–Female–SUPERC–UP–10101000000
		ON–Child–SUPERC–UP–10000000000
		NORM–Female–SUPERC–UP–10101000000
		NORM–Child–SUPERC–UP–10000000000
	→	SetDiff

Time Step	Message List
T342:	NORM–Gender–SUPERC–UP–10101000000 NORM–Person–SUPERC–UP–10000000000 ON–Female–SUPERC–UP–10101000000 ON–Child–SUPERC–UP–10000000000 SetDiff
T343:	NORM–Thing–SUPERC–UP–10000000000 NORM–Thing–SUPERC–UP–10101000000 ON–Female–SUPERC–UP–10101000000 ON–Child–SUPERC–UP–10000000000 SetDiff
T344:	ON–Female–SUPERC–UP–10101000000 ON–Child–SUPERC–UP–10000000000 SetDiff → Quiescent
T345:	ON–Female–SUPERC–UP–10101000000 ON–Child–SUPERC–UP–10000000000 Save Reset (NRSubsumesP) (FindMinRestriction)
T346:	→ Or → NORM–ChildWithSiblings–SUPERC–UP–10000000000 → NORM–Sibling–DIFF–UP–00000000000
T347:	NORM–Part–DIFF–UP–00000000000 NORM–Child–SUPERC–UP–10000000000 ON–ChildWithSiblings–SUPERC–UP–10000000000 ON–Sibling–DIFF–UP–00000000000 Or
T348:	NORM–Person–SUPERC–UP–10000000000 ON–ChildWithSiblings–SUPERC–UP–10000000000 ON–Sibling–DIFF–UP–00000000000 ON–Part–DIFF–UP–00000000000 ON–Child–SUPERC–UP–10000000000 Or

Time Step	Message List
T349:	NORM–Thing–SUPERC–UP–10000000000
	ON–ChildWithSiblings–SUPERC–UP–10000000000
	ON–Sibling–DIFF–UP–00000000000
	ON–Part–DIFF–UP–00000000000
	ON–Child–SUPERC–UP–10000000000
	ON–Person–SUPERC–UP–10000000000
	Or
	→ Quiescent
T350:	ON–ChildWithSiblings–SUPERC–UP–10000000000
	ON–Sibling–DIFF–UP–00000000000
	ON–Part–DIFF–UP–00000000000
	ON–Child–SUPERC–UP–10000000000
	ON–Person–SUPERC–UP–10000000000
	ON–Thing–SUPERC–UP–10000000000
	→ Min
	→ Reset
T351:	→ MaxSort1
T352:	MaxSort2
T353:	MaxSort3
T354:	MaxSort4
T355:	MaxSort5
T356:	MaxSort6
	(FindMaxRestriction)
T357:	→ Or
	→ NORM–ChildWithSiblings–SUPERC–UP–10000000000
	→ NORM–Sibling–DIFF–UP–00000000000
T358:	NORM–Part–DIFF–UP–00000000000
	NORM–Child–SUPERC–UP–10000000000
	ON–ChildWithSiblings–SUPERC–UP–10000000000
	ON–Sibling–DIFF–UP–00000000000
	Or

Time Step		Message List
T359:		NORM–Person–SUPERC–UP–10000000000
		ON–ChildWithSiblings–SUPERC–UP–10000000000
		ON–Sibling–DIFF–UP–00000000000
		ON–Part–DIFF–UP–00000000000
		ON–Child–SUPERC–UP–10000000000
		Or
T360:		NORM–Thing–SUPERC–UP–10000000000
		ON–ChildWithSiblings–SUPERC–UP–10000000000
		ON–Sibling–DIFF–UP–00000000000
		ON–Part–DIFF–UP–00000000000
		ON–Child–SUPERC–UP–10000000000
		ON–Person–SUPERC–UP–10000000000
		Or
	→	Quiescent
T361:		ON–ChildWithSiblings–SUPERC–UP–10000000000
		ON–Sibling–DIFF–UP–00000000000
		ON–Part–DIFF–UP–00000000000
		ON–Child–SUPERC–UP–10000000000
		ON–Person–SUPERC–UP–10000000000
		ON–Thing–SUPERC–UP–10000000000
	→	Max
	→	Reset
T362:	→	MinSort1
T363:		MinSort2
T364:		MinSort3
T365:		MinSort4
T366:		MinSort5
T367:		MinSort6
T368:	→	ON–ChildWithSiblings–SUPERC–UP–10000000000
	→	RVMCheck
	→	Reset

(ImmediateSuperCs1)

Time Step		Message List
T369:	→	NORM–ChildWithSiblings–SUPERC–UP–10000000000
T370:		NORM–Child–SUPERC–UP–10000000000
	→	HOLD–Child–SUPERC–UP–10000000000
	→	SetDiff
T371:		NORM–Person–SUPERC–UP–10000000000
		SetDiff
	→	Quiescent
T372:		NORM–Thing–SUPERC–UP–10000000000
		Save
		Reset
		(ImmediateSubCs1)
T373:	→	NORM–ChildWithSiblings–SUPERC–DOWN–10000000000
		(ImmediateSuperCs1)
T374:	→	HOLD–ChildWithSiblings–SUPERC–UP–10000000000
	→	SetDiff
T375:		HOLD–ChildWithSiblings–SUPERC–UP–10000000000
		SetDiff
	→	Quiescent
T376:		HOLD–ChildWithSiblings–SUPERC–UP–10000000000
		Save
		Reset
T377:		ON–ChildWithSiblings–SUPERC–UP–10000000000
T378:		ON–ChildWithSiblings–SUPERC–UP–10000000000

Bibliography

[1] Allard, J. R. & Kaemmerer, W. F. (1987) The goal/subgoal knowledge representation for real-time process monitoring. *The Proceedings of the National Conference on Artificial Intelligence.* AAAI, Los Altos, CA.

[2] Arthur, B. (1989) On classifer systems and models of learning. Unpublished manuscript.

[3] Arvind, K., Gostelow, P. & Plouffe, W. (1978) An asynchronous programming language and computing machine. *TR-11a.* Department of Information and Computer Science, The University of California, Irvine, CA.

[4] Axelrod, R. (1986) An evolutionary approach to norms. *The American Political Science Review*, **80**.

[5] Barnes, G., Brown, R., Kato, M., Kuck, D., Slotnick, D. & Stokes, R. (1968) The Illiac IV computer. *IEEE Transactions on Computers*, **C-17(8)**, 746–757.

[6] Batcher, K. E. (1980) Design of a massively parallel processor. *Transactions on Computers*, **C-29(9)**, 836–840.

[7] Belew, R. K. & Forrest, S. (1988) Learning and programming in classifier systems. *Machine Learning*, **3**, 192–223.

[8] Belew, R. K. & Gherrity, M. (1989) Back propagation for the classifier system. *Proceedings of the Third International Conference on Genetic Algorithms.* Morgan Kaufmann, San Mateo, CA, 275–281.

[9] Berkling, K. J. (1975) Reduction languages for reduction machines. *Second Annual Symposium on Computer Architecture.* IEEE, Houston, 133–140.

[10] Booker, L. (1982) Intelligent behavior as an adaptation to the task environment. *PhD Thesis, The University of Michigan, Ann Arbor, Michigan.*

[11] Booker, L. B., Goldberg, D. E. & Holland, J. H. (1989) Classifier systems and genetic algorithms. *Artificial Intelligence*, **40**, 235–282.

[12] Booker, L. B. Using classifier systems to implement distributed representations. *Advances in Neural Information Processing Systems II.* Morgan Kaufmann, San Mateo, CA, in press.

[13] Borgida, A., Brachman, R. J., McGuinness, D. L. & Resnick, L. A. (1989) CLASSIC: a structural data model for objects. *Proceedings of the ACM SIGMOD International Conference on Management of Data.*

[14] Brachman, R. J. (1978) A structural paradigm for representing knowledge. *Technical Report 3605.* Bolt Beranek and Newman Inc., Cambridge, MA.

[15] Brachman, R. J. (1983) What IS-A is and isn't: an analysis of taxonomic links in semantic networks. *Computer*, **6(10)**, 67–74.

[16] Brachman, R. J., Fikes, R. E., & Levesque, H. L. (1983) Krypton: a functional approach to knowledge representation. *Computer*, **16(10)**, 67–74.

[17] Brachman, R. J. & Levesque, H. L. (1984) The tractability of subsumption in frame-based description languages. *The Proceedings of the National Conference on Artificial Intelligence.* AAAI, Los Altos, CA.

[18] Brachman, R. J. & Levesque, H. L. (editors). (1985) *Readings in Knowledge Representation.* Morgan Kaufmann, San Mateo, CA.

[19] Brachman, R. J. & Schmolze, J. G. (1985) An overview of the KL-ONE knowledge representation system. *Cognitive Science*, **9(2)**.

[20] Brachman, R. J., McGuinnes, D. L., Patel-Schneider, P. & Resnick, L. A. Living with CLASSIC: when and how to use a KL-ONE-like language. *Principles of Semantic Networks* (ed. J. Sowa). Morgan Kaufmann, San Mateo, CA, to appear.

[21] Buchanan, B. G. & Shortliffe, E. H. (1984) *Rule-Based Expert Systems.* Addison-Wesley, Reading, MA.

[22] Burks, A. W. (1970) *Essays on Cellular Automata.* University of Illinois Press, Urbana, IL.

[23] Carbonell, Jaime G. (1983) Derivational analogy in problem solving and knowledge acquisition. *The Proceedings of the International Machine Learning Workshop.* Monticello, IL.

[24] Clancy, W. J. (1984) Classification problem solving. *The Proceedings of the National Conference on Artificial Intelligence.* AAAI, Los Altos, CA.

[25] Codd, E. F. (1968) *Cellular Automata.* Academic Press, New York.

[26] Crutchfield, J. P., Farmer, J. D., Packard, N. H., & Shaw, R. S. (1986) Chaos. *Scientific American*, **255(6)**, 46–57.

[27] D'Ambrosio, B., Fehling, M. & Forrest, S. (1987) Real-time process management for materials composition in chemical manufacturing. *IEEE Expert*, **2(2)**, 80–93.

[28] Davis, L. D. (1987) *Genetic Algorithms and Simulated Annealing.* Research Notes in Artificial Intelligence. Morgan Kaufmann, Los Altos, CA.

[29] Davis, R. & King, J. (1977) An overview of production systems. *Machine Intelligence*, **8**, 300–331.

[30] Davis, R. & Buchanan, B. G. (1984) Meta-level knowledge. *Rule-Based Expert Systems* (eds. B. G. Buchanan & E. H. Shortliffe). Addison-Wesley, Reading, MA, chapt. 28, 507–530.

[31] Dennis, J. B. (1976) First version of a data flow procedure language. *Technical Report TM-61.* Massachusetts Institute of Technology, Laboratory for Computer Science.

[32] Derthick, M. A. (1987) A connectionist architecture for representing and reasoning about structured knowledge. *Proceedings of the Ninth Annual Conference of the Cognitive Science Society.* Lawrence Erlbaum, Hillsdale, NJ, 131–142.

[33] Dickinson, A. (1990) Cytoarchitectures: machines in genes. *Technical Report.* AT&T Bell Laboratories, Homdel, NJ, unpublished.

[34] Erman, L. D., Hayes-Roth, F., Lesser, V., & Reddy, R. (1980) The HEARSAY-II speech-understanding system: integrating knowledge to resolve uncertainty. *Computing Surveys*, **12(2)**, 213–253.

[35] Erman, L. D., London, P. E. & Scott, A. C. (1984) Separating and integrating control in a rule-based tool. *Proceedings of the IEEE Workshop on Principles of Knowledge-Based Systems.* IEEE, Denver, CO, 37–43.

[36] Fahlman, S. E. (1979) *NETL: A System for Representing and Using Real-World Knowledge.* The MIT Press,Cambridge, MA.

[37] Fahlman, S. E. (1981) Cancellation in a parallel semantic network. *Proceedings of the Seventh International Joint Conference on Artificial Intelligence.* Menlo Park, CA.

[38] Fahlman, S. E., Hinton, G. E., & Sejnowski, T. (1983) Massively parallel architectures for AI: NETL, Thistle, and Boltzmann machines. *Proceedings of The Third Annual National Conference on Artificial Intelligence.* Menlo Park, CA.

[39] Farmer, J. D. Connectionism: a rosetta stone for adaptive dynamics. *Physica D,* to appear.

[40] Fikes, R. (1981) STRIPS. *The Handbook of Artificial Intelligence* (eds. A. Barr & E. Feigenbaum). William Kaufmann, Inc., vol. 1, 128–134.

[41] Fjellheim, R. and Pettersen T. (1987) Knowledge-based steam plant operation. *Technical Report CX-TN-87-4.* Computas Expert SystemsVeritasveien 1, Postbox 410, 1322 Hovik, Norway. Also presented at Applications of Artificial Intelligence in Engineering, Cambridge, MA, August, 1987.

[42] Forgy, C., Gupta, A., Newell, A. & Wedig, R. (1984) Initial assessment of architectures for production systems. *Proceedings of the National Conference on Artificial Intelligence.* AAAI, Los Altos, CA.

[43] Forrest, S. (1982) KL-ONE, CUE, and process scripts. *Consul Note #14.* USC/ Information Sciences Institute, Marina del Rey, CA.

[44] Forrest, S. (1982) A parallel algorithm for classification in KL-ONE networks. *Consul Note #15.* USC/Information Sciences Institute, Marina del Rey, CA.

[45] Forrest, S. (1985) Implementing semantic network structures using the classifier system. *Proceedings of An International Conference on Genetic Algorithms and Their Applications* (ed. John J. Grefenstette). NCARAI and Texas Instruments.

[46] Forrest, S. (1985) A study of parallelism in the classifier system and its application to classification in KL-ONE semantic networks. *PhD Thesis, The University of Michigan, Ann Arbor, Michigan.*

[47] Forrest, S. (1990) *Emergent Computation: Self-Organizing, Collective, and Cooperative Phenomena in Natural and Artificial Computing Networks.* MIT Press, Cambridge, MA. To appear. Also published as a special issue of *Physica D.*

[48] Forrest, S. (1990) Introduction to the proceedings of the Ninth Annual CNLS Conference. *Physica D,* to appear.

[49] Forrest, S. & Miller, J. H. (1990) Emergent behaviors of classifier systems. *Physica D,* to appear.

[50] Goldberg, D. E. (1983) Computer-aided gas pipeline operation using genetic algorithms and rule learning. *PhD Thesis, The University of Michigan, Ann Arbor, MI.*

[51] Goldberg, D. E. (1988) Probability matching, the magnitude of reinforcement, and classifier system bidding. *TCGA Report 88002.* The University of Alabama, Department of Engineering Mechanics, Tuscaloosa, AL.

[52] Goldberg, D. E. (1989) *Genetic Algorithms in Search, Optimization, and Machine Learning.* Addison-Wesley, Reading, MA.

[53] Grefenstette, J. J. (1985) *Proceedings of An International Conference on Genetic Algorithms and Their Applications.* NCARAI and Texas Instruments.

[54] Grefenstette, J. J. (1987) *Proceedings of the Second International Conference on Genetic Algorithms.* Lawrence Erlbaum, Hillsdale, NJ.

[55] Grefenstette, J. J. (1989) *Proceedings of the Third International Conference on Genetic Algorithms.* Morgan Kaufmann, San Mateo, CA.

[56] Griesmer, J., Hong, S., Karnaugh, M., Kastner J. & Schor, M. (1984) YES/MVS: a continuous real time expert system. *The Proceedings of the National Conference on Artificial Intelligence.* William Kaufmann, Los Altos, CA.

[57] Gupta, G. (1986) Parallelism in production systems. *PhD Thesis, Carnegie-Mellon University, Pittsburgh, PA.*

[58] Hamilton, E. & Huntington, C., eds. (1961) *The Dialogues of Plato.* Princeton University Press, Princeton, NJ, 353–384.

[59] Haynes, L. S., Lau, R. L., Siewiorek, D. P. & Mizell, D. W. (1982) A survey of highly parallel computing. *Computer*, 7–24.

[60] Hewitt, C. (1977) Viewing control structures as patterns of passing messages. *Artificial Intelligence*, **8**, 323–364.

[61] Hillis, W. D. (1981) The Connection Machine. *A.I. Memo No. 646.* MIT Artificial Intelligence.

[62] Hillis, W. D. (1985) *The Connection Machine.* MIT Press, Cambridge, MA.

[63] Hinton, G. E. & Sejnowski, T. J. (1983) Analyzing cooperative computation. *Proceedings of the Fifth Annual Conference of the Cognitive Science Society.* Rochester, NY.

[64] Hinton, G. E., Sejnowski, T. J. & Ackley, D. H. (1984) Boltzmann machines: constraint satisfaction networks that learn. *Technical Report CMU-CS-84-119.* Carnegie-Mellon University.

[65] Hoare, C. A. R. (1978) Communicating sequential processes. *Communications of the ACM*, **21**, 666–677.

[66] Hofstadter, D. R. (1982) Artificial intelligence: subcognition as computation. *Technical Report 132.* Indiana University.

[67] Holland, J. H. (1975) *Adaptation in Natural and Artificial Systems.* The University of Michigan Press, Ann Arbor, MI.

[68] Holland, J. H. & Reitman, J. S. (1978) Cognitive systems based on adaptive algorithms. *Pattern-Directed Inference Systems* (ed. D. A. Waterman and F. Hayes-Roth). Academic Press, New York, 313–329.

[69] Holland, J. H. (1980) Adaptive algorithms for discovering and using general patterns in growing knowledge bases. *International Journal of Policy Analysis*, **4(3)**.

[70] Holland, J. H. (1983) Genetic algorithms and adaptation. *Proceedings NATO Advanced Research Institute on Adaptive Approaches to Ill-Defined Problems.*

[71] Holland, J. H. (1985) Properties of the bucket brigade. *Proceedings of An International Conference on Genetic Algorithms and Their Applications* (ed. J. J. Grefenstette). Texas Instruments, Inc. and NCARAI, 1–7.

[72] Holland, J. H. (1986) Escaping brittleness: the possibilities of general-purpose learning algorithms applied to parallel rule-based systems. *Machine Learning*

(eds. R. S. Michalski, J. G. Carbonell & T. M. Mitchell). Morgan Kaufmann, Los Altos, CA, chapt. 20, 593–623.

[73] Holland, J. H., Holyoak, K. J., Nisbett, R. E. & Thagard, P. (1986) *Induction: Processes of Inference, Learning, and Discovery.* MIT Press.

[74] Huberman, B. The performance of cooperative processes. *Physica D*, to appear.

[75] Ichbiah, J., et al. (1980) *Reference Manual for the Ada Programming Language.* U.S. Department of Defense.

[76] Jones, A. K., Segall, G., Seitz, C. & Wilson, A. (1983) *Workshop on Multiprocessors for High Performance Parallel Computation.* Champion, PA.

[77] Kaczmarek, T., Bates, R. & Robbins, G. (1986) Recent developments in NIKL. *Proceedings of the AAAI-86.* Morgan Kaufmann, Los Altos, CA, 275–281.

[78] Kanerva, P. (1988) *Sparse Distributed Memory.* MIT Press, Cambridge, MA.

[79] Kephart, J., Hogg, T. & Huberman, B. Collective behavior of predictive agents. *Physica D*, to appear.

[80] Kung, H. T. (1982) Why systolic architectures? *Computer*, January, 37–46.

[81] Langton, C. (1985) Personal communication.

[82] Langton, C. (1989) Artificial life. *Artificial Life: The Proceedings of an Interdisciplinary Workshop on the Synthesis and Simulation of Living Systems* (edited by C. Langton). Santa Fe Institute Studies in the Sciences of Complexity, proceedings volume VI. Addison-Wesley, Redwood City, CA, 1–48.

[83] Lenat, D. B. & Brown, J. S. (1984) Why AM and EURISKO appear to work. *Artificial Intelligence*, **23(3)**, 269–298.

[84] Levesque, H. J. & Brachman, R. J. (1987) Expressiveness and tractability in knowledge representation and reasoning. *Comput. Intelligence*, **3(2)**, 78–93.

[85] Lipkis, Thomas. (1981) A KL-ONE classifier. *Consul Note #5.* University of Southern California, Information Sciences Institute.

[86] Mac Gregor, R. M. & Bates, R. (1987) The loom knowledge representation language. *Technical Report RS-87-188.* USC/Information Sciences Institute, Marina del Rey, CA.

[87] Mac Gregor, R. M. (1988) A deductive pattern matcher. *Proceedings of the AAAI-88.* Morgan Kaufmann, Los Altos, CA.

[88] Mark, W. (1981) The consul realizer. *Consul Note #12.* University of Southern California, Information Sciences Institute.

[89] Metcalf, R. M. & Boggs, D. R. (1976) Ethernet: distributed packet switching for local computer networks. *CACM*, July, **19**, 395–403.

[90] Nebel, B. & von Luck, K. (1988) Hybrid reasoning in BACK. *Methodologies for Intelligent Systems* (eds. Z. W. Ras & L. Saitta). North Holland, New York, 260–269.

[91] Newell, A. (1973) Production systems: models of control structures. *Visual Information Processing* (ed. W. G. Chase). Academic Press, New York.

[92] Newell, A. (1980) Physical symbol systems. *Cognitive Science*, **4**, 135–183.

[93] Patel-Schneider, P. F. (1984) Small can be beautiful in knowledge representation. *Proceedings of the IEEE Workshop on Principles of Knowledge-Based Systems.* IEEE, Denver, CO. Also published as FLAIR Tech. Rept. No. 37, Schlumberger Palo Alto Researc 1.

[94] Patel-Schneider, P. F. (1989) Undecidability of subsumption in NIKL. *Artificial Intelligence*, **39**, 263–272.

[95] Pinker, S. & Mehler, J. (1988) *Connections and Symbols.* MIT Press, Cambridge, MA.

[96] Pinker, S. & Prince, A. (1990) On language and connectionism: analysis of a parallel distributed processing model of language acquisition. In press.

[97] Potter, J. L. (1983) Image processing on the massively parallel processor. *Computer IEEE*, January, 62–67.

[98] Preston, K., Jr. (1981) Real-time/parallel computing. *Languages for Parallel Processing of Images* (ed. Morio Onoe). Plenum Press, New York.

[99] Riolo, R. L. (1987) Bucket brigade performance: I. long sequences of classifiers. *Genetic Algorithms and Their Applications: Proceedings of the Second International Conference on Genetic Algorithms.* Lawrence Erlbaum, Hillsdale, NJ, 1987, 184–195.

[100] Riolo, R. L. (1987) Bucket brigade performance: II. default Hierarchies. *Genetic Algorithms and Their Applications: Proceedings of the Second International Conference on Genetic Algorithms* Lawrence Erlbaum, Hillsdale, NJ, 1987, 196-201.

[101] Riolo, R. L. (1988) CFS-C: a package of domain independent aubroutines for implementing classifier systems in arbitrary user-defined environments. *Technical Report.* Logic of Computers Group, EECS Dept, University of Michigan, Ann Arbor, MI.

[102] Robertson, G. (1987) Parallel implementation of genetic algorithms in a classifier system. *Genetic Algorithms and Simulated Annealing.* Pitman Publishing, London, 129–140.

[103] Robins, G. (1986) The NIKL manual. *Technical Report.* University of Southern California, Information Sciences Institute.

[104] Rumelhard, D. E., McClelland, J. L., & the PDP Research Group. (1986) *Parallel Distributed Processing: Explorations in the Microstructure of Cognition.* MIT Press, Cambridge, MA.

[105] Schmolze, J. G. & Brachman, R. J. (1982) Proceedings of the 1981 KL-ONE Workshop. *Technical Report No. 4842.* Bolt Beranek and Newman Inc., Cambridge, MA.

[106] Schmolze, J. G. & Israel, D. (1983) KL-ONE: semantics and classification. *Technical Report 5421.* Bolt Beranek and Newman Inc., Cambridge, MA.

[107] Schriber, Thomas J. (1974) *Simulation Using GPSS.* John Wiley & Sons, New York, NY.

[108] Seitz, Charles L. (1984) Concurrent VLSI architectures. *IEEE Transactions on Computers*, December, **C-33**.

[109] Shastri, L. (1985) A massively parallel encoding of semantic networks. *Proceedings of the Distributed Artificial Intelligence Workshop.* AAAI, Los Altos, CA, 277–286.

[110] Simon, C. (1989) Personal communication.

[111] Simon, Herbert A. (1969) *The Sciences of the Artificial.* MIT Press, Cambridge MA.

[112] Skolnick, M., Kim, S. & O'Bara, R. (1988) Morphological algorithms for computing non-planar point neighborhoods on cellular automata. *Proceedings of the Second International Conference on Computer Vision.* IEEE Computer Society Press, Washington, DC.

[113] Smith, S. (1980) A learning system based on genetic algorithms. *PhD Thesis, The University of Pittsburg, Pittsburg, PA.*

[114] Smolensky, P. On the proper treatment of connectionism. *Behavioral and Brain Sciences*, in press.

[115] Touretzky, D. & Hinton, G. E. (1985) Symbols among the neurons: details of a connectionist inference architecture. *Proceedings of the Ninth International Joint Conference on Artificial Intelligence* (eds. Touretzky and Hinton).

[116] Touretzky, D. & Geva, S. (1987) A distributed connectionist representation for concept structures. *Proceedings of the Ninth Annual Conference of the Cognitive Science Society.* Lawrence Erlbaum, Hillsdale, NJ, 155–164.

[117] Treleaven, Philip C., Brownbridge, D. R., & Hopkins, R. P. (1982) Data-driven and demand-driven computer architecture. *Computer Surveys*, **14(1)**, 93–142.

[118] Tung, Y-W., Matthiessen, C. & Sondheimer, N. (1987) On parallelism and the penman natural language generation system. *Technical Report.* U.S.C. Information Sciences Institute, Marina del Rey, CA.

[119] Vilain, M. & McAllester, D. (1983) Assertions in NIKL. *Technical Report #5421.* Bolt Beranek and Newman, Inc., Cambridge, MA.

[120] Vilain, M. (1985) The restricted language architecture of a hybrid representation system. *Proceedings of the Ninth International Join Conference on Artificial Intelligence, Los Angeles, CA.* 547–551.

[121] Waldrop, M. M. (1984) Artificial intelligence in parallel. *Science*, **225**, 608–610.

[122] Wilson, S. (1982) Adaptive "cortical" pattern recognition. *Internal Report.* Research Laboratories, Polaroid Corporation, Cambridge, MA.

[123] Wolfram, S. (1984) Universality and complexity in cellular automata. *Physica*, **10D**.

[124] Woods, William A. (1979) Parallel algorithms for real time knowledge based systems. *Technical Report 4181.* Bolt Beranek and Newman Inc., Cambridge, MA.